This book is due for return by the last date shown
above. To avoid paying fines please
renew or return promptly.

www.portsmouth.gov.uk

Portsmouth
CITY COUNCIL
Library Service

D1338257

ORIGINS

ORIGINS

Amin Maalouf

Translated from the French by
Catherine Temerson

PICADOR

Published 2008 by Farrar, Straus and Giroux, New York

First published in Great Britain 2008 by Picador
an imprint of Pan Macmillan Ltd
Pan Macmillan, 20 New Wharf Road, London N1 9RR
Basingstoke and Oxford
Associated companies throughout the world
www.panmacmillan.com

ISBN 978-0-330-44248-0

Originally published 2004 as *Origines* by Grasset, France

Cet ouvrage, publié dans le cadre d'un programme d'aide à la publication,
bénéficie du soutien financier du ministère des Affaires étrangères et du
Service culturel de l'ambassade de France aux États-Unis.

This work, published as part of a program providing publication assistance,
received financial support from the French Ministry of Foreign Affairs and
the Cultural Services of the French Embassy in the United States.

1 3 5 7 9 8 6 4 2

A CIP catalogue record for this book is available from
the British Library.

Printed and bound in the UK by
CPI Mackays, Chatham ME5 8TD

For Téta Nazeera

For Kamal and Charles Abou-Chaar

And in memory of
Laurice Sader Abou-Chdid

Contents

Someone other than I might have used the word "roots." It is not part of my vocabulary. I don't like the word, and I like even less the image it conveys. Roots burrow into the ground, twist in the mud, and thrive in darkness; they hold trees in captivity from their inception and nourish them at the price of blackmail: "Free yourself and you'll die!"

Trees are forced into resignation; they need their roots. Men do not. We breathe light and covet the heavens. When we sink into the ground, we decompose. The sap from our native soil does not flow upward from our feet to our heads; we use our feet only to walk. What matters to us are roads. Roads convey us from poverty to wealth or back to poverty, from bondage to freedom or to a violent death. Roads hold out promises, bear our weight, urge us on, and then abandon us. And we die, just as we were born, at the edge of a road not of our choosing.

· · ·

Roads, unlike trees, do not sprout from the ground wherever the seeds happen to fall. Like us, they have origins—illusory origins, since roads don't have real starting points. Before the first curve, just behind us, there was a prior curve, and another one behind that one. The origin of every road is elusive because at every crossroad other roads have merged, with other origins. If we were to take into account all these tributaries, the earth would be en-circled a hundred times.

In my family, these tributaries must be taken into account. I come from a clan that has been nomadic from time immemorial in a desert as wide as the world. Our countries are oases that we leave when the spring goes dry; our houses are tents clad in stone, our nationalities a matter of dates and ships. The only thing connecting us to one another, beyond the generations, the seas, and the Babel of languages, is the soft sound of a name.

Is a family name a homeland? Yes, that's the way it is. And instead of religious faith, an old-fashioned faithfulness.

I've never had a true religious affiliation. If anything, I've had several incompatible ones. Nor have I ever felt an overriding loyalty to one nation. It is true, I don't have just one country. On the other hand, I willingly identify with the history of my large family—with its history and its legends. Like the ancient Greeks, I ground my identity in a mythology; I know it is fictitious, but I revere it as though it reveals truth.

How strange, actually, that up until now I have devoted no more than a few paragraphs to the lives of my relatives. Yet this silence is also part of my heritage.

Preliminary Gropings

oNε

My research began with a false start: an experience I had at age thirty, an experience I should never have had. In fact, none of the protagonists should have had it. In the past, whenever I wanted to bring it up, I managed to persuade myself it was still too soon.

Of course it is not too soon now. It is almost too late.

It was a Sunday, a Sunday in the summer, in a village in the Mountains. My father had died shortly before dawn, and I had been given the most painful task imaginable—to go to my grandmother's and hold her hand when she was told she had just lost a son.

My father was her second child, and we had agreed that my uncle, her eldest son, would phone her to give her the news. Told this way, things have a semblance of normality. But in my family, normality is always an illusion. For instance, before that summer I had seen this uncle, who had just turned sixty-seven, only once before in my life.

So I had come in the morning, and my grandmother had clasped me in her arms for a long time, as she always did. Then, inevitably, she asked the question I dreaded most: "How is your father doing this morning?"

I had prepared an answer, coaching myself on my way over.

"I've come directly from the house. I didn't stop by the hospital . . ."

This was both the absolute truth and the most horrid lie.

A few minutes later the telephone rang. Normally I would have hurried to answer it so my grandmother would be spared the effort of getting up. On that day, I just asked if she wanted me to answer for her.

"If you could just bring the phone closer to me . . ."

I moved it closer, picked up the receiver, and handed it to her.

I couldn't hear what was being said on the other end, but I'll never forget my grandmother's response.

"Yes, I'm sitting down."

My uncle was afraid that she might be standing and might fall to the ground after hearing what he was going to tell her.

I also remember the look in her eyes as she said, "Yes, I'm sitting down." It was the look of someone condemned to death who has just seen the gallows looming in the distance. Later, when I thought about it, I realized it was probably she who had advised her children to make sure a person is sitting down before announcing devastating news. As soon as her son asked the question, she knew to expect the worst.

We cried, she and I, sitting side by side, holding hands, for a long time.

Then she said to me, "I still expected to hear that your father had regained consciousness."

"No. From the minute he collapsed, it was over."

· · ·

My father had fallen in the street, near his car, ten days earlier. The person who was with him had heard him exclaim only a surprised "ah!" before he collapsed, unconscious. A few hours later my telephone rang in Paris. A cousin told me the news, leaving very little room for hope: "He's in a bad state, a very bad state."

I returned to my native country on the next flight and found my father in a coma. He seemed to be sleeping peacefully; he was breathing and sometimes moved a hand. It was hard to believe he was no longer alive. I begged the physicians to test his brain once again, then a third time. It was pointless. The encephalogram was flat. He had suffered a massive hemorrhage. We had to resign ourselves.

"I still had hope," my grandmother whispered. No one had dared tell her the truth till now.

We soon lapsed into silence, our sanctuary. In my family, we speak very little and with deliberation; we are always careful to be restrained, polite, and dignified. While this can sometimes be irritating to others, it is a long-ingrained habit, one that will be passed down to future generations.

We were still holding hands. She let go of mine only to remove her glasses and wipe them in the fold of her dress. As she was putting them back on, she gave a start.

"What day is today?"

"August 17."

"Your grandfather also died on August 17!"

She frowned in a way that she sometimes did. Then she seemed to get over her outrage and settle into resignation. She didn't say another word. I took her hand in mine again and held it tight. Though the same loss weighed on our hearts, the images in our minds weren't the same.

My mind wasn't on my grandfather that day, or indeed on the following days. I thought only about my father, his large face, his artist's hands, his serene voice, his Lebanon, his sorrows, and the bed in which he had passed away. For me, and for all those close to him, his death was an emotional cataclysm. The fact that he had had a kind of "rendezvous" with his own father on a predetermined date merely elicited, from those to whom I mentioned it at the time, a brief and banal meditation on the irony of fate and the unfathomable ways of Heaven.

There, that's all, end of episode.

There should have been a sequel, but there wasn't. I should have drawn my grandmother into a long conversation about the person who had been the man in her life, but she died five years later without our broaching the subject again. By then she and I didn't live in the same country. I had settled in France, and she never traveled outside Lebanon again. But I used to come back to see her every so often, and I could have found time to question her. I didn't. To be honest, I simply didn't think of it.

It was strange behavior that can probably be explained in the jargon of specialists who plumb the depths of the psyche, but I shall blame myself for it to my last day. How could I—by nature an inquisitive person capable of getting up from the dinner table five times in the course of a single meal to check the etymology of a word or its exact spelling, or the date of birth of a Czech composer—have exhibited such a woeful lack of curiosity about my own grandfather?

And this even though, ever since childhood, I had been told many stories about him—whose given name was Botros—stories that should have roused me from my indifference.

The following story, for instance. One day, one of his brothers, who lived in Cuba, was in serious trouble and wrote him anxious letters begging him to come to his rescue. On the last letters to reach him, the four corners of the paper were burned, a sign of danger and emergency. So my grandfather quit his work and set sail on the next ship. He learned Spanish on board in forty days. By the time he arrived, he could take the floor in court and get his brother out of trouble.

This is a story I've heard since the day I was born, yet I never tried to find out whether there was anything to it, or if it was just a boastful legend of the kind so many families cultivate. Nor did I try to find out the full story behind my family's Cuban adventure. Only now do I know it.

I was also always told, "Your grandfather was a great poet, a courageous thinker, an inspired orator, and people came from far and wide to listen to him. Alas, all his writings have been lost!" Yet I later found his writings; all I had to do was look for them. My grandfather had assembled and dated them all in a neat, calligraphic handwriting; he had cared about his writings to the end of his life and had always wanted to bring them to public attention. But he died unpublished, as others die intestate, and he remained anonymous.

Another oft-repeated tale: Botros never wanted to baptize his children; he didn't believe in God or the Devil, and he made a point of trumpeting this loudly, causing a permanent scandal in the village. Again, I never really looked into this. And my family was very careful not to discuss it.

Do I have the courage to confess that I spent my entire youth in our village without ever putting flowers on my grandfather's grave, or even knowing where it was located, or having the curiosity to look for it?

I could list a thousand other reasons for crying mea culpa, but I shall refrain from doing so. After all, what is the point? I need say only that I would probably have remained in the same state of ignorance forever had the road of my ancestors not intersected with mine, in Paris, via a detour.

TWO

After this false start, there was the real start, many years later. I don't deserve credit for it, or hardly. Admittedly, after my father's death I made it clear that I wanted to know more about my family's past. I followed up by asking several close relatives seven or eight questions about my grandfather and my other forebears. This in no way resembled the obsessive dedication that takes hold of me regularly when I throw myself into real research. It seemed that where my own origins were concerned, I reverted to a kind of hereditary placidity and the sterile dignity of silence.

Credit is due—all the credit—to my diplomat friend Luis Domingo. One day in the course of conversation he asked me whether I was related to a Cuban official who had the same family name as mine.

I made him repeat the first name—Arnaldo? No, it wasn't familiar to me. But then I told him, casually, that I had had family in Havana a long time ago. The instant

I heard myself say this, I felt as though I were being informed of it for the first time.

I had got to know Luis Domingo in Beirut in the early 1970s. I was a young journalist and he a young diplomat at the Spanish embassy. Since then, we've never lived in the same city, but we've remained close.

Every time he came through Paris, we would meet and take long strolls through the streets, usually talking until daybreak, reminiscing, speculating, and reinventing the world. We reinvented the destiny of Lebanon mainly, but also of Cuba, where Luis Domingo had been posted for many years and whose future worried him. Yet I had never once thought of mentioning my family's Cuban connection.

In fact, I never would have brought it up if he hadn't pressed me so insistently that night. Under his barrage of questions, I made the effort of putting together all the bits and pieces of stories that had filtered down to me through the years. That's how I discovered, not without astonishment, that entire lives were already there, in my memory, in vague outline.

The first thing I described, with pride, was my grandfather's trip to Havana, especially his quick mastery of Spanish and his successful argument in court.

"He was a lawyer?"

"As far as I know, he was a teacher and headmaster, but I guess he also studied law."

To be honest, I didn't really know!

"And his brother?"

"His name was Gebrayel, which is the equivalent of Gabriel for us. He was a businessman. He made a fortune in Cuba and had great political ambitions. But he made enemies and died in mysterious circumstances."

"In what year?"

"Around 1900, or the twenties, I don't know exactly . . ."

"He may have had children or grandchildren who are still living in Cuba . . ."

Once again I had to admit that I was completely in the dark.

· · ·

Later that evening I remembered a family legend; I almost told it to Luis Domingo but refrained from doing so. I was afraid of his incredulity and his contempt if he suspected me of believing it. We were both in the habit of mocking the irrational and its followers, and this incident certainly didn't fit in with our shared convictions.

The legend involves another brother of my grandfather's, a priest in the Melchite Church whose religious name was Theodoros. He kept a personal diary all his life, with painstaking regularity; he made his daily entries just as he read his breviary, at set hours. He wrote the dates and chapter headings in red ink and the body of the text in black ink.

One evening, the story went, he was sitting at his worktable in front of his diary when one of the inkwells suddenly cracked apart and a thin trickle of red ink ran down the table and over the sheet. The priest followed it with his eyes, terrified; his throat tightened, and his limbs no longer obeyed him. After a moment he pulled himself together and took up his pen again to relate the incident. He noted the day and then pulled his watch out of his pocket to jot down the hour. The hands had stopped.

Great-uncle Theodoros lived in a monastery in the Mountains at the time; he came out of his cell, called all the other monks who were present, and asked them to join him in prayer.

Need I add that what happened next is what always happens in stories that begin like this? Namely, that several months after this incident, a letter arrived from Cuba announcing that Gebrayel had died at the precise moment when his brother's red inkwell had cracked apart.

Don't ask me if I believe in this small miracle. I really don't know . . . Probably not . . . The angel of reason is always by my side restraining me. The one thing I can state with certainty, however, is that Theodoros kept telling this story until his dying day, and all those who heard it believed it.

Before we parted that night, Luis Domingo asked me if I wanted to get in touch with Arnaldo, my Havana "cousin," and send him some sort of message. He would make sure it reached him. I went to my bookcase and fetched a book in Castilian about the old country, where there is a brief mention of our family. I inscribed it with a few courteous lines and entrusted the book to my friend with the feeling of throwing not a bottle into the sea, but a stone into a well filled with ghosts.

THREE

The following night, during my regular bout of insomnia, I kept brooding over our conversation. By morning I wanted to know more about this great-uncle who had sailed away and perished in that distant isle.

This didn't call for a serious investigation. I had only to call an eighty-nine-year-old cousin in Beirut, whose memory was still crystal clear, and ask her a few simple questions that I had never formulated or thought of before.

First of all: Did she know the year of Gebrayel's death?

"Not the precise year," Léonore admitted. But she remembered that at the end of the First World War, when the family could once again receive mail, she had learned of the death of a number of relatives who were living in the Americas. One of them was Gebrayel. "Yes, he died a violent death, but unrelated to the war. An accident . . ."

My mother, on the other hand, whom I phoned immediately after talking to Léonore, echoed the other theory, the one that is still most widely believed in our family: "He was assassinated! That's what your father always said. An act of sabotage or something of the sort . . ."

These brief exchanges took place in June. A short time later, my mother left on vacation. For some twenty years she has been spending her winters in France and her summers in Lebanon, just as we used to spend the winter in Beirut and the summer in the village.

When she returned to Paris in September, she told me she had brought back something that would interest me: letters; letters dating from "that period."

"Your grandmother gave them to me, along with other things. She said, 'I know you at least will preserve them!' Since you quizzed me, I spent a bit of time searching through these papers. It wasn't easy. There's a trunkful!"

A trunkful of documents? At home?

"Yes, in the big closet in my bedroom. Letters, photographs, notebooks, newspaper clippings, receipts, notarized deeds . . . Initially I was going to sort them out, but I had to give up. It was too complicated. I left everything as is. But I brought you these letters because they're from Gebrayel."

From Gebrayel!

I had let out a cry, but it was an inward cry, and it didn't show, except for a slight trembling of the lips.

My mother took the letters out of her handbag and handed them to me unceremoniously, as if they were yesterday's mail.

Three letters. All three mailed in Havana in 1912. In the blink of an eye Gebrayel ceased to be a ghostly figure lost in an indeterminate past. I now held in my hands pages that bore his handwriting, his voice, his breathing, his sweat. Pages addressed to my grandfather, who had kept them and left them to his widow—his widow, who had given them to her daughter-in-law, who, by this gesture, was entrusting them to me.

I rested the letters flat on my open palms. I turned them over one by one and took time to feel their weight, delighted to note that they were heavy and plump, but not yet daring to take the sheets out of the envelopes.

It wasn't until the following morning, in the tranquillity of my study, behind closed doors, on a bare wooden table I had carefully cleared of all clutter and carefully dusted, that I felt ready to let these fragile witnesses speak.

I spread them out before me very gently. And before giving them a close reading, I started by lazily running my eyes over them, gleaning a few sentences here and there.

From Havana, April 25, 1912, to my brother Botros, may the Lord preserve him and allow me to see him again in perfect health . . .

May God's Grace inspire us to put an end to the scattering of our family and thereby extinguish the sufferings of absence from our hearts . . .

Last month I was constantly sick, and had to leave Havana for several days to recover my strength. In fact, I decided to go live by the oceanfront for a time, very close to Castillo del Moro, to get away from my work and breathe some pure air . . .

My business worries are weighing too heavily on my mind, which is the mind of an ordinary man, and even slightly below ordinary . . .

Finally I must beg you to excuse my style for being so dull, and all my mistakes, which you certainly noticed in these pages; I must tell you that I've forgotten Arabic, which, by the way, I learned very badly in my youth . . .

My Cuban great-uncle's humility, apparent beyond the polite manners of the period and the use of accepted epistolary phrases, could not but move me. Yet another palpable, omnipresent fact lay right before my eyes: his ardent desire to show off, obvious from the moment you looked at his envelopes. His full name was spread out across the middle in large navy blue characters headed by shaded dropped initials; his name, or at least his initials, appeared in six other places, in smaller type, sometimes legible only with a magnifying glass. Gabriels, G's, and M's were everywhere. In the upper-left-hand corner, the initials were even drawn like vines clasping the terrestrial globe.

I couldn't help but smile at this, but with tenderness. Our ancestors are our children; we peer through a hole in the wall and watch them play in their rooms, and they can't see us.

How could I blame Gebrayel for wanting to show the whole world, particularly his relatives, how successful he had become? In addressing his brother Botros, who was older and obviously more educated than he, he tried hard to make himself small and humble, and he apologized for his ignorance. But then he began to brag again, with a swagger, not always gauging the effect his words might have on those who still lived in the village and struggled to make ends meet, toiling under the weight of debts and taxes. To complain about having too much business! And blithely writing:

> *As far as the customs are concerned, please let my suppliers know they have no reason to worry! They can send me all the merchandise they want without giving it much thought, and they don't have to bother to change the invoices; here they let me pay whatever I agree to pay, and if I don't want to pay anything, I don't pay anything . . .*

There was better, or worse:

> *Soon I plan to buy the house that the government built eight years ago for General Máximo Gómez. It is located at the corner of Prado and Monte avenues. The new government palace is being built across the street, and right behind it will be the new railroad station linking the capital to the rest of the island . . .*

Having no idea who this general was, I looked him up in some books and discovered that in Cuba, Máximo Gómez was—and still is—an important historical figure. A native of Santo Domingo, he had sided with the Cubans in the war of independence, even rising to the rank of commander in chief of their revolutionary armies. When the Spanish were defeated in 1898 and the young Republic was born, Gómez could have played a prominent role, but perhaps because of his foreign descent he felt he should become an ordinary citizen again, so he lived the rest of his life in seclusion, poor, without an official post, though revered by all. In 1904, as a mark of gratitude, the government decided to build a beautiful villa for him in the heart of the capital, but he died the following year before having had time to move into it.

That my great-uncle Gebrayel could covet this very house seemed to substantiate the wildest family legends. Particularly since he wasn't just expressing a vague desire, as can be seen by the telegram written in English and sent from Havana to Beirut on October 25, 1912, to the address of a bookseller friend. I found it inserted in one of the three envelopes:

TELL BOTROS BOUGHT GOMEZ BUILDING SEVENTY THOUSAND ARRANGE COMING CONDITIONS MAIL GEBRAYEL

Indeed, there is also the letter of confirmation:

I sent you a telegram yesterday, at our friend Baddour's address, telling you I had just purchased the building I mentioned in my previous letters; the registration was done this week, and tomorrow, God willing, I'll start the renovation work . . . In that telegram, I also asked you to come to Cuba as soon as possible . . .

FOUR

What facts I had learned so far reassured me: my relatives had not made things up. I almost felt ashamed for thinking they were capable of it. My family isn't in the habit of inventing things. If anything, they are excessively silent, with a tendency—why deny it?—to conceal things. They are usually loath to brag in any way.

So the great-uncle in America had really existed. And he had really become wealthy. But this did not necessarily mean that the story I had been told in my childhood was true. In fact, the opposite seemed to be the case; in his letters, as far as I could tell from a first reading, Gebrayel seemed to have no more difficulties with the courts than with the customs. He seemed radiant, prosperous, self-confident, and I saw no reason why my grandfather would have sailed halfway around the globe to come to his rescue.

I decided to read the correspondence more attentively.

This was no easy matter. Many words were no more than shapeless brown ink spots, the characters hardly distinguishable; in other places, the paper had softened, as though, over time, it had been attacked by a corrosive acid. With patience and luck, I would probably manage to decipher, or at least guess, the essentials, but I was resigned to the idea that some passages would remain impenetrable.

Was it after receiving these letters, and this appeal, that my future grandfather sailed to Cuba?

The first of the three letters, posted in Havana on May 8, 1912, had arrived in Beirut on June 2, according to the postmark on the back. Someone, in all likelihood Botros, had written in lead pencil at the very top of the envelope, in Arabic, *"Tajawab aleih,"* meaning "He has been answered."

The postmarks on the second letter are faded, but it must have been received very soon after the first, because it was written on May 19, 1912. In the stamped circle, where you could still make out the H of Havana but hardly anything else, there is the same sentence penciled in the same handwriting: "He has been answered."

On the third letter, only the dispatch date is still legible: October 28 of the same year. We can assume that Botros received it in late November or early December, but there is no indication that he replied to it.

Was that because he had already left for Cuba in response to his brother's entreaty?

I had a sudden urge to know the answer immediately—an irrepressible urge, the kind I have grown to fear as one might fear certain temptations of the flesh, though these urges are the beginning of all my passions, exhilarations, and excesses.

Only one person could enlighten me: Léonore. But it was probably better to wait until the following day. According to my watch, it was four in the morning; that meant it was either five or six o'clock in

Beirut, I couldn't remember which. In any case it was too early, much too early, even for my octogenarian cousin.

I thought this through rationally, then dialed the phone number. It was as though my rational self had completed its assignment and my other self had taken over.

Léonore picked up after three rings. No "hello," just, "First swear no misfortune has occurred!"

Her voice didn't sound sleepy, which was one good thing. But she was clearly nervous and worried. Obediently, I swore that no misfortune had occurred, and I stopped speaking.

She breathed noisily. "Thank God! Now you can speak. I'm listening. Who is it?"

She hadn't recognized my voice. I identified myself, told her I was calling from Paris, and said I hoped she wasn't angry with me for scaring her.

She sighed. "You've always been incredibly impatient, just like your father."

This wasn't serious criticism, just playful teasing. My father had been her favorite cousin. Thanks to him, she was fond of me too, and I could do no wrong. In fact, we then exchanged all the tender words that were customary between us.

Afterward she said, "But I shouldn't be chattering like this long-distance; calls are expensive. And I'm sure you had something urgent . . ."

I paused momentarily to avoid following up on this last word. Then I asked her if by chance she remembered what year my grandfather had gone to Cuba to visit Gebrayel.

There was silence at the other end and slow breathing, followed by, "This was clearly very urgent."

I stammered a few embarrassed words.

"Don't say anything. Let me think . . . Well, no, I don't have the foggiest idea. I don't think I ever knew. I was told that Botros went to see his brother in Cuba and that on the boat, he learned—"

"Spanish, yes, that I know! And what else?"

"Nothing else! No point in racking my old brain, there's nothing there. No date. Sorry."

So I asked her if she could think of anyone in the family who would know the answer.

She pondered for a while.

"No! Among the living, no one."

Then a bitter laugh reached me from the other end of the phone. I joined in politely before hanging up. I spent the rest of the day blaming myself for having let all my elderly family members pass away one after the other without ever bothering to record their words. And I promised myself that any time I met one in the future, I would make them speak at length.

Remorse having run its course, I said to myself that probably Léonore had unwittingly directed me to the only path still available to me. Since questioning the living didn't serve much purpose, I was going to question the dead. At least those who had left records of their lives. Wasn't there an entire trunk in my mother's closet humming with their voices?

FIVE

Logically, I should have hopped onto the first plane to see the documents that were waiting for me. I had promised myself that I would. I had even announced my intention to my relatives—yet I failed to take the plunge. This kind of decision has never been easy for me. I seldom return to my country of origin, and then only when circumstances compel me to.

Does this mean I don't miss my Mountains? Of course I do—as God is my witness! There are love affairs like this; they thrive on absence and distance. So long as one is elsewhere, one can curse the separation and sincerely believe that one need only get together again to be happy. Once the couple is together, the scales fall from one's eyes. Distance preserves love; abolish distance, and you run the risk of abolishing love.

Because of this, I have cultivated distance for many years, as I might water sad-looking flowers on my windowsill.

Occasionally, however, I do return to my Mountains. The circumstance is almost always the death of a loved one—someone who has died over there, or died in exile but could never conceive of being exiled eternally in a foreign burial place. So I return. I retread the paths of my origins and weep openly, as though I were grieving only for the dead.

That is what happened this time. A close relative had passed away in Paris. She was far too considerate of other people's convenience to demand being buried in her village, but there is no doubt that this is what she would have wished. Arrangements were made for her final trip home so she could rest next to her parents, her sister, who had died young, and her brothers, and not far from the man who had been her husband.

When the days of mourning were over, I felt the need, after so many years of indifference, to go and commune at my grandfather's grave.

There has never been a cemetery in my village. The graves are scattered within range of the houses, sometimes on promontories, sometimes in olive groves (my father's grave, for instance), in terraced vineyards, or under hundred-year-old trees. There are also some ancient tombs hollowed in the rocks that have attracted the attention of archaeologists.

As for my grandfather, I was told that he was buried not far from his house in a field of mulberry trees, and I was given no further details. I went looking for him with two elderly village men who had known him in their childhood and had attended his funeral. They pointed to a row of old tombs, saying one of these was "probably" his. The fact that I wanted to know exactly which one seemed to them praiseworthy, but odd—clearly the quirk of an émigré.

The presence of these two elderly men, instead of making the memory of my grandfather more vivid, brought a cloud of unreality to the pilgrimage. The scene was comical, and in other circumstances I might even have been amused. But on that day, "the émigré" that I was didn't want to be distracted from his belated emotions. As sometimes happens, life lacks tact, displaying its incongruities at a bad moment, when we have no desire to smile.

My guides were brothers, both bachelors. I could easily tell them apart when I lived in the village, but with age, they had grown to look identical. In my recollection they didn't even resemble each other. The brothers had followed widely divergent paths. The elder, who was ninety-four at this meeting, was an educated man and had never done manual work. A former émigré, he had lived in various countries, briefly in Italy, France, and, I think, Argentina, but especially in Egypt, where he had picked up the accent he still had.

The younger brother had never left the village and had been a capable builder all his life. He would certainly have disliked my using the past tense, since he boasted to me of still directing construction sites and of carrying stones, at age ninety-one. He nicknamed himself Chitân, which literally means "Satan" but in our parts has the milder meaning of "Devil." He claims to chat with "the other one," his namesake, every day, and in the village no one makes much of it, except for two or three devout widows who disapprove of jokes on these subjects. Our Chitân likes to say he is immortal, proof being the fact that he is as fit as a fiddle at nearly a hundred, while at twenty he was sickly.

The elder brother has no nickname. Everyone has always called him respectfully *ustaz* Eliya, the customary title for teachers, lawyers, and learned people in general. Dignified, levelheaded, a bit formal, always dressed with studied elegance, a shawl around his shoulders, he speaks slowly and cautiously in a meticulous, literary Arabic, close to the written language. His younger brother, by contrast, continuously shouts provocative, sometimes even filthy words in a village dialect that is so colloquial that it is only distantly related to Arabic.

Having learned that the elder brother had been my grandfather's student, I wished he was alone with me on this pilgrimage, but the two brothers had become inseparable with age, and I had to reconcile myself to the presence of the youthful nonagenarian devil shouting at me in a jovial voice near my grandfather's possible gravesite.

"You've been living abroad for too long. You've forgotten that around here we don't visit the dead. In fact, if I were ever to die, I'd have a supply of stones so I could throw them at anyone who had the nerve to come near my grave!"

His elder brother shot him an admonishing look, and the younger fell silent and let him speak.

"My brother has a point. You've been living in France for too long, where every village has a cemetery and monuments bearing lists of all those who died in the various wars. Here, families have sons buried in Beirut, Egypt, Argentina, Brazil, Mexico, Australia, and the United States. Our fate is to be as scattered in death as we were in life."

"If I'm buried under the ground," the younger one began again, "I'll come back out as a serpent and scare the women!"

His brother took his arm and led him a short distance away, to take shelter from the wind and rain and give me a few minutes alone with my grandfather.

Indeed, the rain, which had started as a drizzle, was coming down harder and harder, and the ground under my feet was becoming muddy. But this didn't compel me to run and take shelter. On the contrary, enduring the bad weather was almost a comfort. I certainly owed him this mild mortification to atone for all those years of oblivion and neglect. Therefore I stood erect, letting raindrops stream down my face, raindrops that could have been tears.

After several long minutes I walked away slowly. In the course of this brief pilgrimage I had made no prayer, but I had made my grandfather a quiet promise . . .

Leaving there drenched, I felt the need to stay in the village and shut myself up in my childhood home, alone. I asked to be dropped off at the front door, and I searched through my key holder to find the key that would open the lock that had been installed since the most recent local war and the most recent lootings. I had to try three or four keys before finding the right one. It was cold on that late afternoon, even windier and rainier than it had been earlier. It was not the kind of weather I remembered from my childhood, but it is true that I seldom went to the village in the winter. I was glad the weather was like this. I would have found it harder to bear if everything resembled the days of my happiness and only my happiness was missing.

six

Having double-locked the door of the family house, I experienced, unexpectedly, a warm sensation of well-being. Night had not yet fallen, and a rosy light shone through the tall bay window. I was reunited with the two old Morris armchairs, the red-cushioned twins I used to love and had since forgotten. I moved one of them so I could sit facing the sea; it was far in the distance below and would have been visible on the horizon had the sky not been overcast.

I sat without moving, impervious to the cold dampness, staring vacantly ahead and closing my eyes intermittently. A long time ago I saw my future as inseparable from this place. I never thought I could bear to live far from this land, this village, or this house. I didn't rule out spending a few months in France or America if I suddenly wanted to, but settling in another country, no thank you.

My large family had had a habit of leaving, but this

was limited to my uncles, cousins, and great-uncles. My direct fore-bears—my father, grandfather, and all their parents—had always re-mained on their native soil. In fact, this is how we had come to own the big house: we deserved it because we had never left. Now it is mine, and very much so; the villagers probably even use my first name to re-fer to it.

But I never come here anymore. In the past twenty years I haven't spent a single night in the house, and I have seldom visited. The last time I was here was seven or eight years ago. I was with a group of people who trooped in with me, looked around, then came back out, me with them. I had felt as though I had scoured each room, trying to find myself, and not succeeded.

For this second visit, I was alone. I was determined not to hurry and not to let anything chase me away—neither the cold nor hunger, nor sadness.

When the light from the sky faded, I suddenly remembered where to find the electrical panel—under the stairway leading to the second floor. I pulled a lever and was almost surprised that the power had not been cut off. Then I went to my parents' bedroom and opened the closet my mother had mentioned. There, against the wall, behind the hanging clothes and rows of pumps, stood a trunk—like two leather shoulders facing mine. It was expecting me!

I pulled the trunk out of its hiding place, dragged it to my parents' bed, strained and hoisted it up, then opened it like a book. I removed my shoes and sat cross-legged in front of it, my back supported by a big pillow wedged against the wall, and I vowed that I wouldn't budge before dawn.

I began by extracting the old papers one by one, timidly holding them up by the corners, my fingers curved like tongs. I read the first twenty or thirty in full and, whenever possible, carefully recorded in my note-book the author, the addressee, the state of preservation, and a sum-mary of the contents. After two hours, seeing the untouched mass of documents that remained, I had to resign myself to skimming the rest, without taking notes, and sorting them summarily. To my left went the ones with my grandfather's handwriting; to my right, those concerning my grandmother; in a pile nearby, those that mentioned Gebrayel or his wife; and on the chest of drawers behind me, next to the bed, those involving other family members—my father, my uncles and aunts, and the priest Theodoros. But the piles were growing higher and higher, even becoming precarious. And strange papers surfaced that I felt should be separated from the rest. And then photos appeared, a whole bunch, almost all without captions, of countless persons mostly unknown, imposing their own separate classification. All this, and still the trunk was three-quarters full.

I gave up. Whether from fatigue or hunger or the days of mourning, I started to cry. I wished I could vanish from the earth that instant without leaving a trace. I felt crushed by an overwhelming burden that had been unloaded into this trunk by one ancestor after the other, a burden I would never have the courage (or cowardice) to dispose of on my own.

Here I was, having begun by searching for the key to my door, and I now saw looming before me a thousand doors and no keys. What was I supposed to do with this mass of old papers? They would never lead to my writing anything about my family! Worse: so long as these relics obstructed my path, I would never be able to write about anything else.

Three days later I was back in Paris, at the airport, in front of the baggage carousel, waiting for the trunk of my ancestors to make its appearance. I had had to resign myself to its traveling in the hold, but given my recent experiences, it was not without apprehension. I had lost a suitcase between Copenhagen and Brussels several months before, another between Addis Ababa and Cairo, and a third had arrived from Milan disemboweled. Yet it still seemed to me the least risky alternative. In any case, I reasoned, if the recent events in my life had any coherence, the script couldn't possibly be interrupted at this stage by a vulgar farce.

When the trunk emerged intact from the tunnel and I had to drag it

and lift it onto my cart, it felt heavier than ever. In a flash, the mild ap-
prehensiveness induced by the trip faded and gave way to the persistent anxiety I felt about the documents themselves and the use I would
make of them.

When I arrived home, I didn't open the trunk right away. My mind
was agitated and confused, thirsting for order. I ran to the neighborhood stationery store to buy a supply of files, both large and small, as
well as folders, albums, and labels. Among them, two dozen document
holders with plastic-coated sleeves in which you can insert sheets and
see both sides. No sooner had I returned home, loaded down with supplies, than I decided to go back out and purchase a photocopying machine, at great expense. For rather than handle these fragile folded
documents often, I thought it would be better to ill-treat copies and
preserve the originals.

It wasn't until I woke up the next morning that I felt sufficiently calm
to tackle the trunk of my ancestors again. I gave myself a week to
empty it out, but then I had to give myself an additional two weeks,
followed by two more. I read, filed, reread, refiled differently, jotted
down a few answers to old questions, then jotted down new questions.
I smiled, or became indignant, or wiped away tears. My old certainties
were constantly challenged; I was shaken, troubled, and distraught.

I felt out of my depth amid all these letters that were vague in
intent and written in illegible handwriting, often undated and un-
signed; all these individuals who had been forgotten by their descendants; and all these lives pulverized into a cloud of words. Fortunately,
some familiar names kept cropping up. First, that of Botros, my grandfather—these archives were clearly his. Most of the letters were
addressed to him, or else they were in his handwriting; and all the
schoolboy's notebooks had been his, as well as the thousands of loose
pages. This trunk contained his life, his entire life, haphazardly deposited inside, with the years all mixed up, in the hope that one day a
descendant would come along and sort it out, reconstruct it, and interpret it—a task I could no longer shirk from. I couldn't possibly foist

the trunk off on the next generation. I was the last stop before oblivion. After me, the chain of souls would be broken; no one would be able to decipher the papers.

In the absence of all his contemporaries, or nearly all, I had to grope in the dark, speculate, and sometimes mix the facts with fiction, legend, and genealogy—a composite I would have preferred to avoid, but how else could I compensate for the silent gaps in the archives? Moreover, I must confess, these ambiguities enabled me to set aside a special territory where I could maintain and protect my filial sense of propriety. Without the freedom to obscure some facts and faces, I didn't feel free to say "I." This is a family atavism. My relatives could never have lived through so many hostile centuries without learning how to hide their souls behind a mask.

Longitudes and Latitudes

seven

I had to grasp one thread in order to untangle the skein of documents. I chose to start, sensibly, with the oldest letter of all—a large sheet of paper with vertical lines, folded, crumpled, torn, and so brown it is hard to believe it was originally white. It bears the date October 11, 1889, and the signature of my grandfather Botros, then age twenty-one.

After gazing at it, rereading it, looking at it carefully under the lamp, and rereading it again, I set about translating it hastily on the corner of my table. I had no idea how I could use it, but I thought that transposing it from one language to another might blunt the stiff, old-fashioned formalities.

Respected Father,

After bowing down over your hand and soliciting your benediction, let me inform you that I am presently at Abey, where I am teaching at the American mission school, and am also learning a number of things. Thank Heaven, I am well.

Today, my brother Semaan came to see me. He set my mind at rest regarding your state of health and told me you were no longer angry with me and were willing to let me continue my studies. If that is true, I would be grateful if you could send me money and a mattress. If you do not wish to do so, I shall put my trust in God, who will find solutions for me, for shouldn't we always put our trust in Him in all matters?

I kiss my respected mother's hands, soliciting her benediction, and request that you greet my brothers and all our loved ones.

Do not be harsh with me and do not forget me in your prayers.

Your son,

Botros

The words are reverential and submissive, but only superficially so. The words between the lines are clear: if you don't help me, I'll manage without you. In any case, the young man's respectfulness is that of a winner, since his father had apparently just given in to his demand and was letting him pursue his studies at the institution of his choice.

Actually the tone had almost gone sour. After "money and a mattress," my grandfather had written "Otherwise," but had crossed out the word and the comma and written, less rudely, "If you do not wish to do so . . ."

I know this detail because the letter in my possession isn't the one that Botros mailed to his father that day—which is probably lost. It is a copy, or rather a first draft, scribbled in pencil. My grandfather was in the habit of keeping a record of his letters—a useful precaution and a valuable gift, particularly for me, the belated reader!

That said, the correction is purely stylistic; it doesn't in any way change what I've learned from the timeworn letter. My grandfather and his father had had a falling-out, and their reconciliation had been to the son's advantage.

In those days such conflicts were far from uncommon in the Mountains. The youth who swore off farmwork and left the village to pursue his education against his parents' will was a familiar figure, nearly as emblematic as that of the émigré who leaves penniless and goes on to earn a fortune. What is more unusual is the fact that my future grandfather went to the American mission school.

But his choice doesn't really surprise me. Though the letter I just quoted is the oldest I found, it actually represents the last act in a drama. There had been "previous episodes," some of which are known to me. I know, for instance, that study was an escape route that had already been mapped out by another father-son conflict a quarter of a century before.

The reason I am going back in time is not just to put Botros's attitude into an intelligible context, but also because these other protagonists are close family members as well, and their dispute weighed—and still weighs heavily to this day—on my relatives' lives.

The earlier crisis occurred in 1862, in the only house in the village that might have seemed safe: the priest's house.

The priest's name was Gerjis—our equivalent of George—and he belonged to the Melchite Church, also called the Greek Catholic Church. Though under the pope's authority, the priests in this denomination are not pledged to celibacy; though they are not allowed to marry after being ordained, they can be ordained after having taken a wife.

Gerjis the priest had several children, but only one outlived him: Khalil. A hardworking, scrupulous boy with a thirst for knowledge, he was compelled by some of his readings to express doubts about the Catholic faith. At first his father tried to reason with him, but he was intellectually inferior to his son, and their discussions became stormier and stormier, less and less restricted to theology. What made matters worse was that Khalil had no qualms about airing his opinions outside the home, putting the unfortunate priest in a very embarrassing position.

And then one day, inevitably, there was a falling-out. I don't know if the father threw the son out of the house or if the young man slammed the door of his own free will. Whatever the case, it caused a great deal of bitterness and resentment.

In the library my father left me, there is an invaluable book that recounts the history of our family from the first centuries to the beginning of the twentieth. Like most old Arabic books, it has a long title with rhyming hemistiches and can be translated roughly as *The Tree Whose Branches Are So Spread Out and So Tall That There Can Be No Hope of Picking All the Fruits*—an allusion to the immense challenge facing the researcher who would attempt to reconstruct the history of such a family. From now on, whenever I quote the book, I shall refer to it as *The Tree.*

This book devotes a paragraph to the biography of the priest Gerjis, where we learn that he died blind in 1878, and two full pages to his son Khalil. Their disagreement is never mentioned explicitly, but it does say that the son left the village in 1862—"for Abey, where the American missionary Cornelius Van Dyck had just founded a school"—and returned home only after his father's death.

In the course of the twenty-odd years he spent away from the village, the priest's son collected diplomas in botany and astronomy. He also studied English and, predictably, theology. Then, after having duly converted to the Protestant faith—the Presbyterian denomination— he became a preacher, a missionary, a teacher, and, at the peak of his career, the administrator of an entire network of Protestant schools throughout the Levant.

His dream, however, was to set up an educational institution in his own village that would one day rival the ones he had known. Linking his own name and the name of his birthplace to a famous school was to be the crowning achievement of his life.

As soon as he returned home, he rented a building and enrolled his first students, among them Botros. The year was 1882; my future grandfather was fourteen years old. He was alert and ambitious, had good powers of concentration, and was obviously a quick learner, though he had learned very little up until then. In those days the village children spent their days in the fields; at most, they dropped into the priest's house from time to time to acquire the rudiments of reading and writing. The only boys to acquire more education were the ones destined for an ecclesiastic career.

Khalil took Botros under his wing. He patiently taught him everything he could teach him. When his young student successfully completed the cycle of studies offered by the new village school, Khalil strongly advised him not to stop there, but to follow the path he himself had taken in his youth by going to Abey and attending the American mission school. Khalil supported his candidacy with a warm recommendation and got him admitted immediately. And since Botros left without his father's consent and didn't have the means to pay for his education or his living expenses, his protector suggested that he be allowed to teach in the lower grades while attending the advanced classes.

My grandfather remained infinitely grateful all his life to the man who had opened the gates of knowledge for him. In his letters he always respectfully called him *"ustazi"*—"my master." A lasting friendship developed between them, which constantly prevented them from seeing just how different they in fact were.

EIGHT

When Khalil founded his new school, Botros's father—whose name was Tannous—enrolled him without a moment's hesitation. Though he wasn't remotely attracted to the Protestant faith, he had great esteem for the preacher, who, in addition, happened to be a cousin and a close neighbor. It was only when his son announced that he planned to leave the village that Tannous objected. He thought that over there, in Abey, associating with Englishmen and Americans, Botros was bound to stray from the faith of his fathers and come back home with a warped mind, causing grief to his mother and everyone else in the family. Indeed, he might not come back at all. This was common wisdom at the time and often repeated: if the child studies a little, he will help his parents; if he studies too much, he won't want to speak to them anymore. This was the litany Botros heard from his father each time he expressed his desire to leave. "You can't study all your life; one day you have to stop and go back to work in the fields. Unless you want to become a priest . . ."

No, Botros didn't want to work in the fields, nor did he want to become a priest. He was tired of arguing. One morning he left without saying goodbye to his family. He walked all the way to Beirut, then all the way to Abey, in the Shuf, at the other end of the Mountains.

Unlike the quarrel that had taken place a quarter of a century before in Gerjis's house and was settled only by the latter's death, the clash between Botros and Tannous was short-lived. In this the 1889 letter is revealing. Since Botros wrote, "I would be grateful if you could send me money and a mattress," he couldn't have been away from home a long time. After all, if he had, he would have managed to find a mattress on which to sleep. Since the letter is dated October 11, we can reasonably assume that the rebel son had left home shortly before the start of the school year. His father had immediately tried to mend fences. He had sent an emissary—in this case, another of his sons—to find Botros, tell him he had forgiven him and was complying with his wishes, and make sure he had everything he needed.

A simple hypothesis, in keeping with the man's personality, for my great-grandfather Tannous seems not to have been a tyrannical or acrimonious person. At least judging by the few stories he is still remembered by.

The one below was told to me by Léonore. I won't swear to its being the pure, unadulterated truth; I even suspect that my cousin added some borrowed embellishments, or dreamed them up. But I can't be fussy. I have only one story about Tannous's youth, and it comes in only one version, so I have no choice but to record it as such.

The story is set during one of the darkest periods in the region's history, the sectarian massacres of 1860, which led to the slaughter of thousands of people under horrifying conditions. The country never recovered from the trauma of this tragedy; the wounds are unhealed and still reopen whenever a new conflict arises.

Our village and the entire surrounding mountainside were spared.

So much so that it became a refuge for all the members of our extended family (extended in the literal sense) who lived in unsafe areas. Among them the elderly notable, originally from our village, who had been living for half a century in Zahlé, the largest city in the Bekáa plain. To escape the massacres, he had tried to reach our village—with his children, brothers, sisters, and their entire families—by taking hidden footpaths, but this was precisely where the killers had lain in wait for them. The younger men tried in vain to fight the assailants. One adolescent was killed then and there; three others were wounded and captured and never seen again. The rest of the convoy took advantage of the fight to take to the road again and flee.

When the "cousins" from Zahlé reached our village, everyone gathered around them to reacquaint themselves, touch them, comfort them, and ask about their plight. Among the survivors was one young woman whose name was Soussène. Tannous noticed her immediately. She noticed that he had noticed her, and she blushed through her tears.

From then on, whenever there was a village gathering, whether festive or funereal, they both spent their time trying to make eye contact, and though besieged by horrific events, they felt happy as soon as they saw each other.

When peace was restored several months later—in large part thanks to Napoleon III's expeditionary corps—and the refugees could return home, Tannous and Soussène were probably among the rare few who didn't rejoice wholeheartedly.

A few days after the inevitable separation, Tannous had to face the facts. Now that the young girl was absent, he found his days completely drab. What was the point of a stroll down the main road if there was no hope of meeting Soussène? What was the point of going to church on Sunday if he couldn't look for her during mass and smile at her as they filed out? What was the point of attending banquets or wakes?

One morning, after a sleepless night, he couldn't bear it any longer and decided to go see her. He picked some figs and a few bunches of grapes so he wouldn't arrive empty-handed, and he set off.

It takes a good six hours, through mountain paths, to get to Zahlé on foot from our village. The most energetic walkers used to cover the distance in one day, the others in two stages. Tannous arrived at

Soussène's parents' house in the middle of the day. Not daring to admit that he had made the entire journey just to see her, he pretended that he had work in Zahlé for a few days. "Then come back to see us tomorrow too," said the young girl's father. Tannous was delighted to accept the invitation. He left his beloved's house and took the same route back. Only now it certainly took much longer, since he had to walk uphill from the plain to the high mountain, with no other light than the moon, on a road where there were wolves, hyenas, and bears, not to mention brigands.

He arrived in the village well after midnight and slept like a log. But at daybreak he was up; he went to pick some fruit and rushed down the mountain again.

According to Léonore, this little game lasted three or four days; by the end of that time, Tannous had carved out a lifelong reputation as a love-struck madman. Everyone in the village was afraid for him, everyone gently poked fun at him, but everyone also envied him such passion.

The epilogue occurred when Soussène's parents, seeing the young man grow paler and thinner from day to day, asked him where he was sleeping in Zahlé. He answered evasively the first and second time they asked. But when they insisted in a peremptory tone, Tannous feared they might think he had a dangerous illness or a dreadful vice, and he made a detailed confession. Yes, he had gone back to the village every evening and come back down the next day, but he took the safest paths! No, he wasn't exhausted; he could swear to it, his legs were stronger than ever. He recited poems to entertain himself as he walked . . .

The father heard him out with knitted brows. The mother covered her face so no one would see that she was laughing. When the walker finished talking, his host said, "Tonight you're sleeping here, next to my sons. When you're rested, you'll go back up to the village. During the day, not at night! You'll return to Zahlé only for your betrothal."

On hearing that last word, *khotbeh*, Tannous almost fainted. His love madness had paid off!

Soussène and he were married several months later. As in the fairy tale, they lived more or less happily ever after—though modestly—and had many children. Ten to be exact; eight lived to adulthood: two girls and six boys. Alas, they all died without my knowing them, including Botros, my grandfather. All except Theodoros, the priest. Nor do I have a personal recollection of him, for he passed away when I was a year old, but I was told that he held me in his arms when I was born, whispering at length into my ear and watching my reactions, as if I could hear him and agree with him.

After writing these last paragraphs, I spread out before me on my desk the oldest photographs from our family archives, to match faces and names. What I am looking for, without much hope, is a picture of Tannous. Evidently there is none. On the other hand, there are at least two photographs of Soussène. In one, she is changing one of her grandchildren's diapers; in the other, she is at a picnic with other members of the family, in a spot called Khanouq, the "stifling room," probably so dubbed because it is sheltered from the wind and it is impossible to breathe there during days of intense heat, but it is very pleasant when the weather is cool, in early spring or September.

My great-grandmother's appearance makes me smile. Her head is tiny, flattened and almost oval, under an overly large hat. She is roaring with laughter, probably because of that hat, which stands out as not being from the village, but which someone must have lent her to shade her from the sun.

I plan to make a duplicate of this photograph, which is more yellowed than sepia, so I can frame it and put it up on the wall in my room. It exudes a mischievous happiness seldom associated with departed ancestors. Our ancestors derived less from life than we do, but they also expected much less and were less intent on controlling the future. We are of the arrogant generations who believe a lasting happiness was promised to us at birth. Promised? By whom?

nine

Before I go on with my narrative, a digression is called for. I shall try to explain why, from the outset, I have adopted the peculiar tendency of saying "my village" or "my family," without naming them, and "my country," "the old country," "the Mountains," with no further details. This should not be interpreted as a fondness for poetic vagueness, but rather as a symptom of what might be called a hazy identity and a way of skirting around a difficulty—not a very praiseworthy tendency, I admit. I shall have to discuss my family and country later, separately, but it is time to say a few words about my village.

As a child, whenever I was quizzed about my place of origin, I used to waver momentarily. This is because I have several villages that are mine. Ordinarily, I end up replying Ain-el-Qabou or, more accurately, in the local pronunciation, Ain-el-Abou, though the name doesn't appear on any of my identity papers. Machrah is listed on these, a village very close to the first, but whose name is hardly ever used anymore, possibly because the only road suitable for cars now turns away from Machrah and crosses the above-mentioned Ain-el-Qabou.

It is also true that this name has the advantage of corresponding to a concrete reality: *ain* is the Arabic word for "spring," and *qabou* means "vaulted room." When you visit the village, you see that there actually exists a gushing spring inside a man-made cavern of sorts with a vaulted roof. On the stone half-moon there is an ancient Greek inscription that was once deciphered by a Norwegian archaeologist: it is a biblical quote starting with "Flow, Jordan, flow on . . ." The source of the Jordan River is about ten kilometers away, but in Byzantine times, these kinds of inscriptions were probably a traditional way of blessing the waters.

Thanks to this monument, the name Ain-el-Qabou has acquired a kind of geographic specificity that Machrah lacks. Machrah is an Aramaic term whose meaning is uncertain, though it calls to mind the exposed, slippery slope of a mountain, or perhaps simply an open area. Machrah is indeed on the side of a mountain, a vertical village with steep paths, where no house lives in the shadow of another.

There is an additional complication, as far as I am concerned: the house I am accustomed to calling my own is located neither in Ain-el-Qabou nor in Machrah, but in yet a third village. This one cannot be found on any road sign or any document in the public records office and is known by its real name only to its own inhabitants and a few initiates: Kfar-Yaqda, or, in the local pronunciation which softens the guttural Semitic *q*, Kfar-Ya'da, which I've sometimes changed to Kfaryabda, thereby hoping to make it easier to pronounce.

I should perhaps add that all these names revered by my kinsmen cover a microscopic reality: the three villages together house about a hundred souls at most. Thus, in Kfar-Yaqda, there is just a small church and four houses, including mine. Yet this hamlet is mentioned in the oldest history books for having once been the capital (yes, the capital!) of a mighty Christian principality.

In the seventh century, this part of the Mountains was the sanctuary of a people called the "brigand princes," valiant men, retrenched in their impregnable villages, who stood up to the most powerful empires of the time. Thus the Umayyad caliphate—though it was enjoying its period of greatest expansion and conquest and had carved out a huge empire extending from India to Andalusia—was so terrified of these mountain devils that it agreed to pay them an annual tribute so it could avoid trouble and peacefully pass through with its caravans.

Mind you, these were Christians who managed to extract a tribute from the caliph of Damascus, whereas everywhere else it was the caliph who imposed a tribute on the "people of the book." Quite an accomplishment, but these reckless warriors—the most famous among them was Youhanna—felt completely safe in their sanctuary. As the rather affectionate name they were given in books indicates, these men were not just brigands but also princes of a people jealous of their independence. A people whose origins are poorly known; they may have come from the shores of the Caspian Sea or from the Taurus region. They were fiercely committed to maintaining their freedom in the midst of the rocky terrain. I wish to emphasize this in passing: these men fought for their freedom, not their land. The Mountains were no more theirs than anyone else's; they settled there late, and it was only a refuge, a setting for their prized dignity. This is why they could shed their blood there one day and leave it without hesitation the next.

In their unequal combat against the Umayyads, Youhanna and his people had initially benefited from the support of Byzantium, a sworn enemy of the caliph. This was before the caliph came up with the idea of offering the Christian emperor a compact: instead of paying a tribute to the "brigand prince," he would pay it directly to the Byzantine emperor. In exchange, the latter would help him get rid of these outlaws. The Byzantine emperor accepted because, for one thing, the offer of gold was enticing; but there were also other reasons, such as his distrust of the Mountain people, who were disrespectful, undaunted, and, though Christian, professed rather unorthodox doctrines. He therefore agreed to lure the rebels by treachery into the Bekáa plain, where they were massacred. Then an expeditionary corps razed their villages and set them all on fire, including the one most renowned, where Youhanna's palace was located—my village, my tiny village, the improbable capital, pretentiously called Sparta by the brigand princes and later, after its fall, tearfully renamed Kfar-Yaqda, "the Torched Village."

Even now, in the fields near my house, one occasionally discovers the capitals of columns formerly belonging to the demolished aristocratic residences.

These strange princes were not my ancestors. If they are at all a part of my origins, it is a heredity based on ancient stones. My own "tribe" arrived much later; in Youhanna's day, they were still leading a nomadic existence in the desert, somewhere between Syria and Arabia.

In fact, for more than a thousand years no one wanted to settle in this mountainous region; it was as if it were cursed territory. It was only in the eighteenth century that one of my ancestors boldly bought land in the area and built a house for his family. The deed, which dates from 1734, says that the acquired property is located "in the Torched Village, in the place known as the Ruins."

It was here that Tannous was born a century later. It was here that he settled with Soussène in 1861. And it was here that their ten children were born.

TEN

Being the head of a large family, my great-grandfather exercised, as might be expected, the authority that his status—and his era—conferred upon him. As might also be expected, he was the obstacle against which his sons sharpened their claws. But the prompt and judicious way in which he put an end to Botros's rebellion suggests that he didn't abuse his prerogatives, and he knew how to avoid irreparable domestic crises of the kind that occurred several decades later among his own descendants. One of his grandchildren would later die because he wanted to do precisely what Botros had done in his youth—keep studying longer than his parents deemed necessary.

In the days when the wise Tannous was head of the family, conflicts did not lead to tragedies, but rather to progress, as can be seen in the following passage, excerpted from a letter Tannous wrote to Botros in late 1895.

As far as your sister Yamna is concerned, I agree with what you said
regarding the need for her to be given an education. So choose the school
that seems suitable to you and we'll send her there.

In other words, this man who had refused to let his son pursue his
education far from the village six years earlier now agreed to let his
daughter follow the same path and even instructed this same rebellious
son to choose a suitable school for her. He had made rapid strides.

. After translating these few lines, I spread my great-grandfather's
letter out on the table in front of me, caressed it with the back of my
hand, smoothed it, unfolded a dog-eared corner, then blew on it to get
rid of some filaments of dust.

I couldn't stop looking at it and skimming it. It is the only letter in
my archives to bear Tannous's signature, and I doubt he wrote many
others. The fact that it exists is virtually a miracle; my uncles and
aunts were all convinced that their grandfather was illiterate. I had to
show them this letter! And particularly point out the lines, at the very
end, where he writes to his son:

That newspaper you subscribed me to—well, sometimes it arrives and
sometimes it doesn't, or it arrives a month late. So warn the director: either
he sends it to us regularly, or we'll stop paying!

I am delighted by this innocent little sentence. All of a sudden, after centuries of darkness, resignation, submission to arbitrary rule, we
see this Ottoman villager, my great-grandfather, reacting like a citizen.
He had paid for his subscription and demanded to receive his newspaper on time.

On rereading his letter, however, I had to temper my enthusiasm.
Though my great-grandfather could write, it is obvious that it wasn't
easy for him; his calligraphy is that of a child, and his style is closer to
the spoken language than the written one. This is confirmed, implic-
itly, in our family reference book, *The Tree*, where he is described as "a
zajjal with an acknowledged intelligence." In the Mountains, *zajjal*
means "dialect poet"—a generally clever person, but one often inca-

pable of setting his own poems down on paper. (Besides, here the very fact of saying "with an acknowledged intelligence" is a coded way of saying "illiterate." This is the way my family members tend to express themselves; when they are loath to divulge a kinsman's shortcomings, they conceal them in suggestive praise.)

Nothing more is said in *The Tree*. This work, which is no less than seven hundred and fifty pages long, devotes only half a line to Tannous and doesn't quote any of his poems. Nor has a single verse been preserved in our archives. I searched and searched, without much conviction. I didn't find anything.

Thus everything my ancestor may have composed, everything he expressed—desire, anxiety, pride, fear, pain, hope, wounds—everything has been lost, destroyed for all eternity without leaving a trace.

It was probably not a major oeuvre; it wasn't Khayyám or Virgil. Maybe there was nothing worth remembering. On the other hand, maybe there was one verse, yes, just one, or an image, or a metaphor that deserved to survive and rescue its author from the limbo of oblivion.

From not having been set down in writing, so many poems and so many narratives, both truthful and imagined, have evaporated in thin air. Indeed, what is left of the past—both the past of our kinsmen and the past of humanity as a whole? What has come down to us of all the things that were said, whispered, and devised for countless generations? Scarcely anything—just a few bits and pieces of stories and that residual morality unduly baptized "popular wisdom," an education in powerlessness and resignation.

Tribute should be paid to the oral tradition, people often say. Personally, I leave this reverential awe to reformed colonials. I revere written work only. And I thank heaven that for more than a century my ancestors recorded, collected, and preserved these thousands of pages, while so many other families threw papers into the fire or left them in the attic to mildew. Or simply neglected to write.

ELEVEN

After this detour through old reminiscences and old resentments, let me pick up my narrative where I left off—namely, at the point where Botros left his parents' house to go to the mission school. He studied and taught for five school years, first in Abey, then in another school, founded by the same American pastors, in Souk-el-Gharb, a town where they had succeeded in converting a large part of the population to the Protestant faith.

From reading the family documents of that period, I discovered that the young man who later became my grandfather did not have as his sole objective the acquiring of diplomas and knowledge. He also entertained another dream—that of leaving one day for distant lands.

This can be gleaned from a revealing text in our archives—a speech he delivered in English at a school ceremony. The use of English must have been very unusual, since Botros felt the need to justify it with childish, slightly irritating enthusiasm.

Respected sirs,

I will speak English with you today, though I know the most part of the crowd cannot understand me, not to show you that I can speak that language, but to prove to you that English is nowadays more necessary for every person than all the other languages which we wish to learn. Besides, English is very easy to learn.

Various arguments follow, aimed at praising the usefulness of English for the businessman, the traveler, the physician, the pharmacist, the engineer, the teacher.

English is necessary for every learned man, because English books contain, no doubt, much useful knowledge, in every science, which is not found in other languages.

Then the speaker adds that for his compatriots particularly,

English is necessary because the poor among them as well as the rich shall leave for America or Australia either at present or in a short time for reasons not unknown by any one of you. And what a difficulty and misery for a man to find himself unable to speak with the people with whom he has to live, and by whom he hopes to profit.

After having candidly stated, without the slightest doubt or stylistic caution, what must have seemed to him—and to a large part of his audience—as an obvious fact requiring no substantiation, my future grandfather explains why English is easy to learn. Then he asks the audience to join him in cheering,

> *Long live the English countries*
> *And long live the English language!*

I try not to smile as I listen to these poignant, incongruous exclamations. Instead, I try to imagine myself in the shoes of a young Ottoman villager at the end of the nineteenth century, for whom a window had suddenly opened onto the world and whose only preoccupation is escaping from his prison through this window.

What these words betray is that Botros already saw himself as a future émigré and that he considered the English language as essential "equipment" for the big journey across the sea.

With hindsight, the privilege of later generations, certain things become obvious that weren't obvious for contemporaries, and certain misunderstandings are dispelled. Indeed, the way I see things today, my grandfather was the victim of a misunderstanding. If his wish was to emigrate, as his words suggest, he should have done so immediately and not attended the Presbyterian mission school. For despite appearances, the missionaries had absolutely no intention of preparing young people to emigrate. They were eager to teach their students English so they could be better educated and help their own country benefit from whatever they had learned, not so they would go and open grocery stores in Detroit or Baltimore. The hope of these preachers was to create a little America right there in the Levant—virtuous, educated, industrious, and Protestant. In fact, they required that their young students first know Arabic to perfection. They themselves studied the language diligently in order to speak it and write it as well as the natives. After that generation of pioneers, few westerners were to go to this trouble.

Contrary to his wishes, at the school of these distinguished foreigners Botros did not become "equipped" to emigrate, but to resist the temptation of emigrating, and though the powerful call of the Americas never vanished from his field of vision, in the future he felt tied down by inextricable moral scruples.

My grandfather was twenty-six when he left the mission school, armed with a long, ornamented document that I found intact in the family archives. Stamped by the "Lebanon School for Boys in Souk-el-Gharb," it certifies—in English and in Arabic translation—that Botros M. "has completed creditably the course of study prescribed by the Syria Mission of the Board of Foreign Missions of the Presbyterian Church in the U.S.A., and in testimony thereof this Certificate is given to him the first day of July in the year of our Lord one thousand eight hundred and ninety-four." Signed, "Oscar Hardin, Principal."

There is no doubt that Botros was influenced and even to a large extent reshaped by his association with these ministers. He resisted following them in the realm that was of the greatest importance to them, however, since he never wanted to convert to the Protestant religion.

Skimming through his notebooks from that period, I even have the feeling that he remained impermeable to all the religious aspects of their teaching. While he was immersed in a milieu where the Bible was omnipresent, tirelessly read, reread, commented upon, and cited in all circumstances—where all you had to say was "Apocalypse, seven, twelve" or "Galatians, three, twenty-six to twenty-nine" for the audience to understand the allusion—Botros practically never used quotes from the Gospels, never in the five years he spent among the Presbyterians nor later in life. It just wasn't his worldview or his way of thinking. For him, a sentence from a book, whether the book was sacred or secular, could never replace a rational argument or excuse a man from thinking for himself.

But there were also other motives behind his estrangement from his masters. In his notebooks dating from then—there are two identical ones, both small, with squared paper, black covers, and red edges—I read this, for example:

Her breasts, ivory pomegranates,
In a stream of light,
Even covered, her bosom still spreads
A red brightness of dusk . . .

Evidently his intimate meditations strayed and didn't quite conform to the wishes of the venerable pastors.

At no point, however, does Botros let himself criticize his masters. A man of honor does not bite the hand that feeds him. Yet we have every reason to believe that after five years of associating with the missionaries every day in the classroom and the boarding school, he had come to be irritated by their moral rigidity as well as by their songs, gestures, sermons, prayers, and even the nasal sound of their voices. He champed at the bit until he received his diploma. Then he thanked them politely, turned on his heel, and walked away, promising himself never to return. Indeed, for many years he never saw them again. He took a very different, not to say the opposite, path.

It would take a betrayed revolution, a small war, and another greater one before he resigned himself to knocking on their door again.

TWELVE

If my great-uncle Gebrayel had followed the same path as my grandfather—who was nine years his senior—he would not have emigrated, and the Cuban chapter in our family history would never have been written. Things did not turn out this way. Both brothers, when they were young, probably had the same dream of one day leaving for an unknown, distant land. But they had very different temperaments. The younger brother saw no point in preparing for the big journey across the sea; he didn't make the detour to Abey or Souk-el-Gharb, and he made no effort to deepen his knowledge of languages. At eighteen, he simply boarded a ship leaving for America.

He had just finished school in the village, and he too could have enrolled in the mission school had he wanted to. This time Tannous would not have objected. But Gebrayal had no desire for that, and even Khalil, the preacher, didn't encourage him. Gebrayel was certainly clever, and he had a sparkling personality. He was also jovial, sociable, generous, and had a thousand other qualities, but he couldn't spend two hours straight concentrating on a grammar, rhetoric, or theology book. On the other hand, he was just as incapable of driving a pickax into the soil.

Moreover, Gebrayel didn't believe in the future of his native country or in his own personal future on the mountainside. He therefore had no qualms as he set off for the port of Beirut on foot, by night, under a full moon. He left without warning his mother and father, though he may have apprised one of his brothers.

More than a century later, we can still find traces in the family archives of the anxiety his departure caused. "If you receive a letter from Gebrayel, send it to me immediately. I'll be infinitely grateful to you," Botros writes to his parents twice. "It seems we received a letter from Gebrayel. Why wasn't I informed?" complains Theodoros, deep inside his monastery.

The oldest mention of the event is in the above-quoted letter Botros received from his father.

Concerning Gebrayel, I am sending you a letter I wrote to him, so that you will read it and send it on to him, since I don't have his address . . .

Several pages ago, when I first mentioned this one and only manuscript bearing Tannous's signature, I dated it as "late 1895." Actually, the letter is undated, and I put forward this hypothesis by crosschecking, using Gebrayel's departure as the basis for establishing a date.

For even if the family documents give no indication of the month or year of his journey, they contain one valuable piece of information. Gebrayel did not go directly to Havana; he first settled in New York. This led me to research the archives in Ellis Island, for decades the compulsory gateway to America for émigrés coming from Europe and the Levant. And thus one day I had the luck—and thrill—of seeing the silhouette of my long-lost great-uncle materialize on an old register.

His given name was spelled "Gebrail," and his family name was the one I myself am accustomed to using. There can be no doubt concern-

ing the identity of the young man who disembarked on the island of illusions on December 2, 1895.

Age: Eighteen.
Calling or Occupation: Farmer.
Ethnic background: Syrian.
Port of departure: Le Havre, Seine-Inferior, France.
Ship of Travel: Marsala (2,422 tons).
Final Destination: New York (long stay).

There was nothing unexpected in the manifest signed by the
Marsala's German captain, J. Lenz, not even the departure from Le
Havre. The trip to America was usually made in two stages; the first
leg was to Europe, often France; from there one boarded a steamship
and crossed the Atlantic. The only surprise I had was that Gebrayel
had not left the village by himself. His name, the ninth on the manifest,
is listed just before that of another family member: Georges, one of
Khalil's sons. The form is filled out in an identical manner for him,
starting with his age: eighteen.

I won't often talk about Georges—Gerji in the family documents
that are in the Arabic language—in these pages. I know very little
about him, just enough not to be indifferent to his being with Gebrayel. He left the country following a quarrel with his preacher father;
the quarrel was so serious that when Khalil died, twenty-seven years
later, they had not made peace.

I can't avoid comparing this estrangement with the one that occurred between Khalil and his own father, the priest Gerjis, a falling-
out that also ended only with the death of the father. I am reminded of
a statement traditionally ascribed to the Prophet of Islam, namely that
a man's worldly deeds, both good and bad, will all be added up after his
death—except for the way he treated his parents. For this he will be
punished or rewarded in his lifetime!

Far be it for me to condemn Khalil. Botros had feelings of gratitude
for him, and I myself owe him a great deal, as I shall have occasion to
explain in the following pages. But it has to be said that the "original

quarrel" between him and his father established a pattern resulting in a tenacious, recurrent family "custom": conflicts caused by religious quarrels lasting an entire lifetime.

I shall never know the exact reasons for the falling-out between Khalil and his son. I suspect it wasn't so much a matter of religious belief as way of life. This is just an assumption—it would be rash to assert anything after so many years. I should probably mention, however, that the atmosphere in the Presbyterian preacher's household was extremely austere, as is evident in the following childhood memory of one of Khalil's granddaughters. The grandmother and mother mentioned in the text are Khalil's wife and daughter.

When it was a question of personal expression of affection, as came to be showered on other children in the village, in our case it was virtually lacking. I, for one, didn't know what it meant to be hugged and kissed as a very young child. When I jokingly questioned my mother about that, she surprised me by looking flustered and saying that she did kiss me, but only while I was asleep. This, she said, was so as not to spoil us . . . My maternal grandmother . . . was an even more serious type of person, and wouldn't hug and kiss us as children—neither in our waking hours, nor when we were asleep . . . Her puritan personality stood in sharp contrast to the typical Lebanese village grandmothers.

This grandmother, whose name was Sofiya, appears in several photos in our archives. She is always wearing a long, dark dress, and there is never so much as the hint of a smile on her face. She was from Souk-el-Gharb and belonged to one of the first families in Mount Lebanon to be converted to the Protestant religion by the Anglo-Saxon missionaries.

In Souk-el-Gharb . . . we paid two visits to relatives, which were memorable, each in its own way. The first was to relatives of my mother . . . I looked forward with great anticipation to this visit, wanting to meet new relatives. After making the climb, we found the old lady of the house alone at home, sitting in front of their large mansion reading the Bible. When we arrived, she gave us a curt welcome, and right away proposed to continue her reading, but aloud, so we could "share" with her. We were in no position to object to her proposal and were thus submitted to a lengthy sitting, listening to monotonous reading to which I did not relate in any way. There was no conversation at all. We didn't get to enter the house or meet any other members of the family. All my high expectations of the visit were dissipated by the time we said goodbye and left the old lady to continue her reading. She being of close relation to my maternal grandmother, I would guess they had both been exposed to the same type of education and strict upbringing!

These memories fail to explain why the breach between Gerji and his father was so irreparable. But they shed light on why this eighteen-year-old was eager to run away from the family home and why, out of the preacher's eight children, seven ended up settling abroad.

Under Tannous's roof things were not as rigid. Though one might take dissimilar paths, become a priest, a pastor, or a Freemason, one was first and foremost father and son, brother and sister, brother and brother—inextricably bound for all eternity. When Botros left home in anger, Tannous immediately sought to make up with him, even if it meant jeopardizing his parental authority. And when Gebrayel emigrated six years later, Tannous wrote to him as soon as he could. I am not sure Khalil reacted to Gerji's departure in the same way.

The reason I am comparing the two households is because my origins can be traced back to both, two dissimilar streams that flowed into each other.

For the preacher Khalil was my great-grandfather too, just as Tannous was. My family story is about the merging of these two bodies of water.

Tannous would be the first of these two ancestors to die—in the first weeks of 1896, at about sixty-five, a short time after having written the only letter by him in my possession. This is probably why Botros had prized it and kept it.

On rereading what he wrote about Gebrayel, I wonder if the worried father received some kind words from his son before passing away. I would like to believe he did, but all things considered, I doubt it. Adolescents who left home were rarely in a hurry to write. In any case, it is too late, I'll never know.

It seems I shall not have much more to say about Tannous in the following pages. I have exhausted everything I was able to glean about him, and I am resigned to the fact that the rest will have to remain obscure. The harvest could easily have been much skimpier. Great-grandparents are distant figures. There isn't one person in a thousand who can tell you their great-grandparents' first names. Yet their roads lead all the way to ours, and I, for one, can't be indifferent to the fact that Tannous was the first of my ancestors to leave "me" a written trace of his earthly passage. Admittedly, it is unpolished, but this only makes his gesture all the more poignant.

THIRTEEN

Before taking the boat, Gebrayel probably had a long conversation with Botros. Some sentences in their subsequent exchanges suggest that the younger brother had tried to coax his elder into coming with him and that the latter had hesitated before turning him down.

My grandfather was already living in Beirut, and it is likely that he accompanied his brother and his companion to the port and waved goodbye as they sailed away.

He had moved to the future Lebanese capital a year before, in September 1894. He was taking courses—mostly in law, but also Turkish- and French-language classes and courses in accounting. And he was teaching, as was his habit. But he no longer did so in order to pay for his education and earn some pocket money, as he had done in Abey and Souk-el-Gharb. He had started a real teaching career.

In a Protestant school? No, in the most Catholic school

imaginable, the Patriarchate School, founded, as its name implies, by the Greek Catholic patriarch to promote education in his congregation. Thus, two months after an American pastor had personally handed him his diploma, Botros returned to his community's fold. He had probably grown weary—like others—of the austerity that prevailed among the Protestant preachers. Still, his ability to casually go from one rival denomination to another betrayed, above all, his deepseated indifference to religious doctrine. He studied wherever he could study, taught wherever he was offered a position, and believed this was both his right and his duty. As for the ministers and priests, they were free to pursue their own objectives, in their parishes or as missionaries.

My future grandfather lived in Beirut for three years; he loved the city and returned to live there several times in the course of his life. At that time it was in full expansion; the 1860 massacres had favored its development. Many people who had been dozing lazily in their Mountain villages, thinking themselves protected from the savagery of the world, were jolted awake by these events. The boldest among them chose to cross the seas; a huge migration began that continued uninterruptedly from then on. Initially, people left for Egypt and Constantinople; then they sailed farther and farther away, to the United States, Brazil, the entire American continent, and Australia. The least adventurous—usually those who were already burdened with a family—left their villages and "went down" to the port city, which gradually began to look like a metropolis.

In 1897 Botros had to leave Beirut for Zahlé, a city that was less open to the outside world, where he had solid ties. It was the birthplace of his mother, Soussène, and she had numerous influential relatives there. It seems he had been offered a position he found tempting, to become "teacher of Arabic rhetoric and of mathematics" in one of the best institutions of the day, the Oriental Greek Catholic Basilian Secondary School, founded by the Melchite monks of the order of Saint Basil, to which his brother Theodoros already belonged.

I don't know what my grandfather's status was at the Patriarchate School, but from his notebooks at the time, he clearly regarded his new position as the real beginning of his career, a career for which he had high hopes—too high, no doubt, disillusionment was ineluctable! He grudgingly admitted that it was a reasonably well-paid job, necessary for his livelihood, particularly now, for since his father's death he had to help provide for his mother and younger siblings. But he emphasized the fact that this position represented, first and foremost, a moral and noble political commitment, the beginning of a long struggle aimed at bringing about a profound change in the thinking of his compatriots, a modest but also unduly ambitious fight, since—as he wrote at the time, black on white—his ultimate objective was to "enable the East to catch up with the West and—why not—outstrip it." Outstrip it, no less.

When it came to what was wrong with the land of his origins, Botros's diagnosis was no less harsh than the one that had led Gebrayel to go into exile. Indeed, it may even have been Botros who had instilled his disillusioned view in his younger brother. In his writings at the time, certain expressions constantly recur, such as "the pitiful state of this country," "the decay of our Eastern lands," "corruption and negligence," "the darkening of the horizon." He too dreamed of freedom and prosperity, of America and Australia, as revealed by his naive praise of the English language. But his stay at the mission school had made him develop a scrupulous sense of responsibility. Rather than leave his country for another, where life would be better, why not work at making his own country better?

The first thing that had to be done to make it better was to fight against ignorance. Wasn't this ambition as good as his brother Gebrayel's? Wasn't this fight an even more exciting adventure than the journey to America? Wasn't it more commendable to build another America at home, in the East, on the land of our origins, rather than sail off to the one that already exists?

In Zahlé, in the streets of the old city and in the outdoor cafés along the Berdaouni River, Botros did not go unnoticed. Those who knew him at the time describe him as a stylish young man, tastefully dressed, with studied elegance and a desire to be provocative.

For one thing, he always went about bareheaded, which made people turn around when he walked by. In those days, most men wore

Oriental headgear, either the tall fez known as the tarboosh, the small fez known as the *maghrebi*, the Arab kaffiyeh, or embroidered bonnets. Men who wanted to follow Western fashion wore hats; many men changed from one to the other depending on the circumstances. But no respectable person went out bareheaded. Except for my grandfather. Some passersby couldn't refrain from whispering or grumbling, sometimes even shouting at him, but this didn't prevent him from walking around bareheaded to his dying day.

Then, perhaps as a way of asserting his originality even more, he always wore a sort of black cape around his shoulders, fastened in the front with a gold ring, and it fluttered behind him like a pair of wings. His suit underneath was black as well, and his shirt white, with a wide, full collar. No one else in the country had the same silhouette; he could be recognized from a distance.

In this peaceful, sleepy Ottoman town, halfway between Beirut and Damascus, Botros soon became a local celebrity. Not just because of his outfit, but as a teacher, poet, and orator. He took part in every festivity and ceremony. He wrote countless occasional poems, commemorating the accession of a patriarch, the visit of a governor or a bishop, marriages, funerals, jubilees—all of it wasted energy, in my humble opinion, but part of the prevailing custom.

Fortunately, during that period he also wrote more extensive pieces, such as a long play in prose and verse that was performed by his students. The manuscript can be found among the family papers—a large black notebook with an invitation card slipped into it: "Performances: July 19, 1900, at 14:30 for the ladies and July 20 at the same hour for the men."

The play is titled *The After-Effects of Vanity*. Its explanatory subtitle is *An Evocation of What Is Praiseworthy and What Is Reprehensible in Our Lands of the Orient*. It is the story of an émigré who returns to the old country, weary from many long years spent abroad, but everything conspires to discourage him.

In the very first scenes, there is a lively discussion centered on the inevitable dilemma: Should you leave or should you stay? The protagonists hurl topical arguments and age-old quotes at one another.

ONE CHARACTER: When your prospects narrow in your town and you're afraid of not being able to earn your living anymore, then leave, for God's earth is wide, both in longitudes and latitudes . . .

ANOTHER CHARACTER: You think you've prescribed the cure whereas you've just pointed to the disease! The reason the country has fallen so low is precisely because so many of its children choose to leave rather than reform it. I, for one, need to be among my relatives, so that they will share my joys when I am joyful and console me when I am in distress . . .

THE FIRST: Love of one's country is but weakness of character; have the courage to leave, and you'll find another family to replace yours. And please don't tell me that remaining one's whole life in one's birthplace is in the nature of things. Look at water! Don't you see how fresh and beautiful it is when it flows toward the horizon and how viscous it becomes when it stagnates?

FOURTEEN

So the exchange goes, at length, with a few nice flights of fancy, and one surmises that the audience was moved to see reproduced onstage, and thereby ennobled, the debates daily preoccupying most families—including, apparently, the author's.

At the end of the play, Botros gives the advantage to those who still believe in the future of their country. How could he have done otherwise? He was expressing himself in the presence of his students and their parents; the setting was the end-of-year celebration. The honorable teacher couldn't possibly exhort them to leave their land.

Yet his letters at the time reveal quite different feelings. For instance, the letter addressed to his émigré brother in April 1899:

> *My dear Gebrayel,*
>
> *After waiting a long time, I received your first letter from New York, which reassured me regarding your health and informed me of your intention to leave the city and go*

into business. I was delighted to learn that you want to escape from your wage-earner status and devote yourself to an activity that could lead you on the road to prosperity. On the other hand, I was upset to learn that you wouldn't be returning home for a long time, and that you would be settling in Cuba, where I know the war has created an unstable situation.

After spending three years in the United States, Gebrayel had just moved to Havana. His own letter being lost, it is hard to know why he decided to move. At the time, New York was the most natural destination for the émigrés in our family; many cousins already lived there, and they were kind and helpful to newcomers. But in those years the great metropolis was also the home of many Cuban émigrés, refugees from the war of independence who were preparing to return to their homeland as soon as it was liberated. We can presume that Gebrayel associated with them, heard their stories about their beloved island, and was talked into following them.

The dates coincide, at any rate. The last Cuban insurrection broke out in 1895, several months before my great-uncle's arrival in the New World; the treaty proclaiming the island's independence from Spain was signed in Paris in December 1898; the troops commanded by General Máximo Gómez took symbolic possession of Havana in February 1899. This was when most of the exiles started to return. The letter whose opening paragraph I just quoted was written in April, which leads me to believe that Gebrayel left for Cuba with the very first wave of returning refugees. Botros continued:

I was afraid you might encounter difficulties, and I was about to ask you to give up those projects, when I received the postcard you wrote from the steamship you had boarded. So I realized it was too late to try to get you to change your mind and that I had better entrust your fate to the Almighty and wish you prosperity and success. But I remained worried and unable to regain peace of mind until I received your letter from Havana telling me that everything was going very well for you. Then I thanked Heaven.

After that, I received your last letter, where you ask me insistently to join you and also to send you a few books. As concerns the books, I shall send them to you very soon. As concerns me, things are not so simple. You

must be aware of the fact that it is difficult for me leave under the present
circumstances.

Oh, if you only knew . . .

Of course, the letter I am transcribing here is one of those first
drafts my grandfather was in the habit of keeping. It could be that he
changed certain things when he wrote the final copy. But even if this
isn't exactly the letter he ended up sending, it certainly reflected what
he was thinking.

Oh, if you only knew how much I want to travel and how much I hate
teaching! But, out of decency, I can't possibly leave school in the middle of
the school term, when they are counting on me and there is no one to replace
me. And that's only the first reason. The second is that I distributed seeds
last summer, as usual, and that I won't be paid until next summer. The
third is that I am owed money that won't be reimbursed until July . . .

But let's forget these three reasons! Yes, I am willing to assume that these
three obstacles will be ironed out. There's still a fourth, and I'd like you to
tell me what to do about it. I'm referring to the present situation of our
house and our property. Yes, tell me, dear Gebrayel, how could I abandon our
possessions, and let them be ruined and plundered at the hands of strangers,
without any of us being on hand to make them yield a profit or defend them?
To whom could I possibly entrust them? To our poor mother, who is already
carrying a mountain of worries on her shoulders? To our young brothers and
sisters, who don't yet know what to do with their lives? To our older brothers?
You know them better than I do. Our common property is theirs when it's a
matter of dividing up the revenues; it is no longer theirs when it's a matter
of dividing up the responsibilities! And you would like me to travel?

Of course, I completely agree with you when you say that all the
property in danger of being ruined or plundered isn't worth much! I would
even add that everything we own is worth nothing, hardly enough to
guarantee the future of one person! But it wouldn't be honorable to let our
lands and our houses fall into a state of neglect, causing our mother, as
well as our brothers and sisters, great sadness, and creating reasons for
future quarrels among us all. Could we live abroad with tranquil minds
leaving such waste behind us—what do you think? Tell me!

FİFTEEN

I have reread these paragraphs over and over again ... I feel I can hear the voice of this grandfather I never knew, his voice from when he was a young man, wondering how not to ruin his life and whether it was sensible to stay home or honorable to leave. The same questions I had to ask myself three-quarters of a century later, in very different circumstances. But were the circumstances really different? We have always emigrated from our land for the same reasons and with the same feelings of remorse; we brood over them for a time while we prepare to bury them.

Here—as in his play!—Botros endeavors to clarify the dilemmas that a good number of his compatriots merely vaguely sensed and lived with. Yet his reasoning didn't reach its logical conclusion, as we see in the very last paragraph, which I find disconcerting. For at the end of his structured, well-articulated, unassailable argument, my grandfather concludes:

This is how things stand, dearest brother. So if you really think we should
leave, that success in Havana is guaranteed, and that we should remain
there for a long period of time, not just a month or two, please find a way
of entrusting your affairs to someone and come home, just long enough
to settle these problems, and then let's leave together. Or send power of
attorney to one of your brothers, certified by your country of residence.
Yes, that may be the simplest solution . . . If you hurry and send this power
of attorney, I could be at your door in three months, God willing! This
document must be sent right away, so hurry, hurry, and at the same time,
prepare suitable conditions so that you and I can work together in Cuba!
And I shall come, God help me, I shall come!

Your affectionate brother
Botros

Strange! Strange that this is the way the letter ends, as if in fast
motion! It takes the moral high ground in the beginning, prescribing
the behavior of a man of honor; then in the last lines it suddenly slides
into a scarcely concealed capitulation. Gone is the logically minded
older brother explaining to his younger brother why he can't respond
immediately to his pressing invitation; instead we see a febrile Botros
almost shouting and begging, "Hurry up and send me that power of attorney, and I'll be in Cuba in three months!"

How could power of attorney change what he had just explained regarding his obligations to their mother, their siblings, their lands, their
houses, and the secondary school where he was teaching? It is hard to
see how it could. What this last paragraph betrays is that hidden under
the mask of the wise adult, there was a distraught young man. A young
man who wanted to leave, who envied Gebrayel for having left, but who
didn't dare take the plunge. And he tied his own hands with all sorts of
moral arguments in order to justify his indecision.

Though there was great affection between the two brothers, there
was clearly also a profound dissimilarity. Not so much in their opinions
as in their temperaments and their life journeys, though I am unable to
say whether their journeys determined their characters or their characters determined their journeys—probably a bit of both. Neither of the

two had any illusions about what the future held for them in the land of their origins, given the state it was in. But Gebrayel had the spirit of a conqueror; he wanted to forge ahead in the world and carve out a place for himself. Botros, on the other hand, had not yet despaired of seeing his compatriots transformed thanks to the miracle of knowledge. Despite what he says, he had the soul of an educator and would never rid himself of it.

Yet when he wrote this letter, my grandfather seemed tempted to follow in his brother's footsteps. It is probable that the respected teacher carefully avoided proclaiming in too loud a voice "how much he hated teaching," but it is clear that at this point he was ready to exchange one life for another and one shore for another.

The proof of the matter is a letter he sent in October 1900 to a prominent person, whose name we don't know, in Zahlé. This man had apparently written Botros to ask if it was true that he wouldn't be teaching at the Oriental Secondary School in the new school year and to beg him to reconsider his decision. Botros responded as follows:

> In answer to your question, dictated by your paternal concern for me, I must unfortunately confirm that I have taken leave of the reverend father superior, having decided to leave the field of education and embark on another kind of activity either in Egypt or in the American lands. In fact I shall be leaving on a trip very soon, if God helps me. You may not approve of my decision, but if we had the opportunity to meet and I could explain my reasons for doing this, I am certain you would approve of me, and would be my best lawyer with the school officials who are constantly pressuring me to make me change my mind. They are being so kind that I ought to thank them by returning to the school and teaching free of charge! But I have made up my mind, and I am counting on your support and your understanding, which have never let me down . . .

Botros doesn't elaborate on the pressing "reasons" that led him to give up teaching and give in to the old temptation to emigrate. However, one thing seems clear: if he was getting ready to leave, it was not in order to rescue Gebrayel, as my relatives always believed.

Since this last letter was addressed to someone he seemed to hold in the highest esteem, had this really been the case, he could have pleaded a family emergency—a brother in distress—to justify resigning from the secondary school. He doesn't; instead he puts forward his own career choices and first gives Egypt as his destination, then "the American lands"—a vague expression. Nothing about what he says reveals an urgent reason for going expressly to Havana. He was just eager to leave.

Yet in the family, they still stick to their version of the story. I made it my duty to get the reaction of Botros's own son, his oldest son, my uncle, who is now ninety and lives in New England. His answer on this was unambiguous:

> I do remember Father saying that he was getting letters with burned corners from Uncle Gebrayel as a sign of emergency begging him to come and help him. I know that Father did go for a short time and that he was successful, but I have no idea what the nature of the problem was. Our father did learn Spanish on the way to Cuba . . .

I took note and was careful not to reveal to this faraway uncle that in one of the many notebooks left by his father, I had just discovered these few verses written in the same period:

> I received a gift from the loved one
> Which reminded me how generous her/his hands were.
> I brought the gift to my lips
> Because her/his hands had touched it.
> No doubt it is precious, the gift of the loved one
> But I myself had offered her/him
> The most precious thing I own,
> My heart . . .★

My future grandfather notes in the margin that he wrote these verses "upon receiving a gift sent by a friend who is in the American

★In French the gender of "the loved one" is ambiguous throughout the poem, as shown.

lands." A male friend? The words used in the poem, including the term "loved one," are deliberately ambiguous—an ambiguity that is customary in all Arabic literature, where it is considered almost crude to use feminine adjectives or pronouns in referring to the woman being wooed. In this particular instance, the ambiguity is tenuous; there can be no doubt that the male "friend" is actually a woman. There are at least two reasons why. The first is that the behavior described by the poet is clearly that of someone in love. The second is that the "friend" in question is not named, which makes no sense in Botros's case if the loved one were a cousin, nephew, or former schoolmate. My grandfather, always conscientious, carefully jotted down in his notebooks the precise circumstances of every story he told and every poem he wrote. Why would he have omitted the name of someone from whom he had received such a gift and of whom he spoke in such affectionate terms? Conversely, it makes perfect sense, especially in the context of the period, that he refrained from setting down in writing the name of a woman with whom he was in love.

I don't want to draw improper conclusions from these few verses. At most, they lead me to note that my grandfather's departure for the Americas must have been prompted by a number of motives. He already had many cousins and friends in the New World, and probably also an especially dear female friend whom he was eager to see again. And then, of course, there was his brother, who had been entreating him for several years to join him in Cuba.

Had Gebrayel been less persistent, I am certain that Botros would have hesitated for an even longer period of time. This I am more than willing to admit. But clearly the family legend fails to tell the whole truth. My grandfather did not cross the Atlantic in order to rescue his brother in distress; he set sail because he himself was in distress, the country of his origins bringing him only disappointments, and he was irresistibly tempted to go breathe the air elsewhere.

If more evidence is needed to confirm this intuition, let me quote some other verses that he sent that same year, 1900, to a very dear cousin who had just settled in New York and whose name was Salim:

My heart is already in the country where you are,
My eyes are constantly turned toward those distant shores.
There was a time when I saw in Zahlé a paradise
Now its land seems cramped,
I hate the life I lead here, and I hate teaching,
Sometimes I feel I am about to run away,
As though I were fleeing, ashamed, defeated . . .

SIXTEEN

Oddly enough, in the hundreds of pages bearing my grandfather's handwriting, I cannot find a single mention of his stay in Havana. Not even an allusion, an anecdote, or a couple of occasional verses. However much I skim his letters, his notebooks, and the countless loose sheets, I find not even one fragment of a sentence to confirm beyond all doubt that Botros set foot in Cuba.

I would have had to rely exclusively on oral legends if this interlude hadn't involved another witness: Gebrayel himself. He isn't very verbose either, but his silence is more porous, let's say, than his brother's. In the letters he wrote to my grandfather many years later, the ones my mother brought back from Lebanon for me and which I read before reading any of the other family documents, my Cuban great-uncle refers to Botros's trip two or three times. Though indirect and allusive, these comments are nonetheless enlightening. For example, just before ending one of the letters:

I am eager to clasp you in my arms on the gangway of the ship! I hope this
will happen soon, and I can promise you that this time you won't go into
quarantine and you won't have to deal with the Seguridad. And if I
weren't so completely taken up with my new shop, I would have set off with
my whole family to meet you halfway.

So Botros had had some unpleasant surprises just after disembark-
ing in Havana. Transported with the crowd of immigrants—probably
in a cattle cart, as was done in those days—to the faraway suburb of
Casa Blanca and locked up in the sanitary district, he had languished
perhaps not for the entire statutory forty days, but at least for a week
or two. Before being herded away, he had probably been subjected to a
humiliating body search by the criminal investigation department. We
can assume that he cursed the day when he let himself be convinced to
leave his nice Oriental Secondary School in Zahlé.

And this wasn't his only disillusionment. In the same letter, while
Gebrayel keeps insisting that his brother come—or rather return—to
Cuba, he says, in parentheses:

(thank God we now have a house where we will be able to live together like
all respectable people instead of sleeping in the attic as we did before) . . .

On reading these lines, I think I can better grasp what happened
and understand things from my grandfather's point of view. First,
when he arrived, he must have slept in a seedy medical facility and
then, for the rest of his stay, in a dingy attic. For him to be treated like
human cattle—he, the haughty dandy who put infinite care into dress-
ing differently from everyone else, with his long black cape fluttering
like wings behind him; he, professor, poet, acclaimed playwright, venerable and punctilious man of letters!

Given these circumstances, he probably didn't stay very long in Havana and probably didn't spend many nights in that attic above his
brother's store. Perhaps he was not cut out for emigration after all. The
immigrant must be prepared to swallow his share of humiliations
every day. He has to accept that life will treat him with disrespect and

that he'll be smacked and jostled with undue familiarity. Gebrayel had left at eighteen; he could put up with this. For him, a transient period of humiliation was a rite of passage or a tactic, a way of lying low. Not so for Botros; he was an adult whose soul was already set in its ways.

My grandfather must have been quick to draw the obvious conclusions from his misadventure: leave Havana, forget this episode as quickly as possible, and re-create a respectable image with a white lie or legend. His brother had appealed to him for help; he had left for Cuba, rescued him, and returned home. Mission accomplished. In the interim, he had learned Spanish . . . No one in the family ever heard any other version of the story but this one.

Did he bear his brother a grudge for this misadventure? Those who are still alive don't know. But now when I recall the story I always heard, I think it constitutes a settling of scores of sorts. Admittedly not a very harsh one, but a settling of scores nonetheless.

For what image of Gebrayel does this family legend convey? That of a turbulent young man whose escapades landed him in prison, or almost, and who never would have extricated himself without the wisdom, solicitude, and intelligence of my grandfather. Apparently, the truth was quite different. Seeing that his business was expanding and afraid of not being able to handle it properly, Gebrayel summoned to his side the person in whom he had the greatest trust: Botros. The latter left home, and though he probably gave Gebrayel a helping hand, he couldn't bear the living conditions his brother inflicted on him (inflicted on his own self too), about which Gebrayel had probably not been frank in his letters. Tensions may also have arisen between the dynamic young man of twenty-five, aggressive and reckless, and his elder sibling, more circumspect, but surely also a bit sensitive and disgruntled at being under his younger brother's orders. Hence the compensating legend invented by my grandfather when he returned . . . Hence, also, the silence in his archives.

Of course I can't exclude the possibility that the notebooks and letters pertaining to the Cuban episode were preserved by Botros and that they got lost before reaching me. However, it seems improbable to me. Certainly many documents were lost over the last century. I have no illusions about that. My family's past was not handed down to me intact in the archives. But having immersed myself in this motley repository for months, I now have the intimate conviction that the Cuban episode did not just vanish out of simple bad luck. Several of my grandfather's notebooks, especially those from his last years, include events and anecdotes related to various places and periods in his life. Surprisingly, not a single one of these takes place in Havana.

I can only conclude that Botros's trip to Cuba, though it remained in his descendants' memories as a mythical exploit, had been nothing but a regrettable misadventure for him.

SEVENTEEN

Fortunately for my grandfather, Havana was only one of the stopping places in his tour of "the American lands," and as far as the rest of his trip is concerned, concrete traces remain. The bilingual visiting card, for example: "Botros M." in Arabic; "Peter M." in English, with his title, "Professor of Arabic Rhetoric and Mathematics in the *Collège Oriental*," and his address, given simply as "Zahlé (Lebanon)." On the back, a sentence written by hand in English: "Traveling at present in the United States."

I came upon this discreet, barely yellowed card in my preliminary work on the family documents. Worried that it might get lost, I slipped it into a transparent sleeve. On the other hand, I completely overlooked a slim oblong booklet, so well preserved that it might easily have been mistaken for a recent address book forgotten among the relics.

When I came upon it again several weeks later, I noticed these words penned on the light brown leather cover in fancy gothic script:

United States Mortgage & Trust Company
In account with Peter M. M. . . .

It is the booklet of a savings account opened on April 21, 1904, in a New York bank located at 40 Nassau Street, not far from Wall Street. Amount deposited: $1,000; interest earned: $14.29 . . .

According to the booklet, Peter M.'s account was closed seven months later, so all the transactions fitted on one page. Leafing through the remaining blank pages, just to check, I fell upon a text in Arabic that starts like this:

> *First draft*
> *of some things I wrote in New York in 1904,*
> *recopied from papers that were in my pockets*
> *on board the steamer called "New York"*
> *on November 24, 1904*
> *in the middle of the Atlantic Ocean.*

This is followed by thirty-four pages, in small handwriting and careless penmanship, of recorded poems, anecdotes, and thoughts related to my grandfather's stay in New York. I now knew where his American journey ended and when, and was in a better position to gauge his state of mind in this period of his life.

The contents of this savings booklet, converted into a pocket organizer or memory organizer, suggest that Botros was quick to forget and make others forget the things he had written in his letters—to his brother, his cousins, and his friends—in the period just before his trip, namely that he hated teaching, found the land of his origins "narrow," and had decided to emigrate to "Egypt or the American lands." The attitude he adopts in his New York notes is not that of a newcomer looking for employment, but of a distinguished guest, a prominent person from the old country who has come to casually "inspect" the wonders of America and the miseries of the diaspora.

Thus, he is taken on a tour of a cigarette factory and given an entire carton as a gift to encourage him to write advertising slogans. The

assignment seems to amuse him, since he carries it out zealously, listing about ten possible slogans, in verse and prose, in his notebook, including the following:

> Why do so many people immigrate to America?
> Because that's where they make Parsons cigarettes!

Or:

> Yes, it's true, I decided to quit smoking. But that was before I dis-
> covered Parsons cigarettes!

Or again:

> The late lamented Cornelius Van Dyck told people for whom to-
> bacco was harmful to limit themselves to three cigarettes a day.
> Had he been familiar with Parsons cigarettes, he would have al-
> lowed them to smoke up to thirty-three!

The American missionary Cornelius Van Dyck, founder of the
Abey School, must have been a celebrity at the time, at least among
Levantine émigrés, since Botros felt he needed no introduction. When
I was I child, I heard about him constantly; my grandmother used to
quote him, and so did my father on occasion, though he couldn't have
known him, since the minister died in 1895. I discovered only belatedly
that Van Dyck was virtually unknown outside the milieu in which I
grew up. Even today I can't help but feel an absurd pride when I see his
name mentioned in a book about Orientalists.

My grandfather seems to have had a very pleasant stay in New York. On
every page of the booklet he mentions the gifts he received, the childhood
friends he met, and the banquets given in his honor, in the course of
which he improvised verses that were immediately printed in the many
Arabic-language newspapers published in the United States at the time.

He was asked to respond to the great events of the day, such as the conflict that had just broken out between Japan and Russia. It inspired a long poem titled simply "Concerning War":

*Aren't we, the people of the twentieth century, always criticizing those
who came before us?
Always priding ourselves on what we have invented, and which didn't exist
in the time of the ancients?
Our surgery allows us to cure a sick organ, so we boast
Of having relieved a man's suffering, but later, with our cannons we mow
men down by the thousands!
What is the good of promoting science and education, if it is only a way of
preparing us for war?*

And some lines below:

*War is aggression and pillage; it is destruction and carnage,
But it is a crime for which we forgive kings, whereas we make children
pay for it.*

EIGHTEEN

For the sake of truth, I must add that in this poem of 1904, which fills a good three pages in his booklet, my grandfather does not just curse all wars, the sufferings they cause, and mankind's hypocrisies. When it comes to the war in progress, he doesn't dismiss the belligerents without pronouncing his position; he chooses his camp unambiguously, siding with the Russians against the Japanese. In his opinion, the latter were clearly the aggressors. He develops an entire argument in support of his thesis, invokes the rights of people, and cites specific incidents and places that must have been familiar to his contemporaries.

To be honest, I don't think this is the real reason why he sided with Russia. He never mentions the real reason, but I know what it is. Like all children from my Mountain area, I know what it is. I have no tangible proof, yet I know with absolute certainty. I imagine that my Levantine explanations will fail to be immediately intelligible to people who grew up in a civilization that differs from mine. I shall try to explain nevertheless, for it may help to better decode the complicated world I come from.

A long time ago, our entire family belonged to the Orthodox Christian community, like the great majority of Greeks, Armenians, Serbs, and, of course, Russians, the largest in number. Then we had our own schism. This was not so long ago, probably at the time of Tannous's father or, at most, of his grandfather—in other words, sometime in the late eighteenth or early nineteenth century. For reasons that remain obscure, one segment of our family decided to join the Roman Catholic Church and recognize the authority of the pope. This did not happen peacefully. There were arguments, quarrels, and fights in every household.

There was even a notorious murder. A man from our family, nicknamed Abou-Kichk, assassinated a patriarch at the entrance to the village. He fled to Cyprus but was tricked back home and hanged. The murder is sometimes explained as a crime of passion; that's the explanation favored by storytellers. But serious historians have another, religious explanation: the patriarch was Catholic, and he had come to encourage the faithful to break away from the Orthodox Church, the church to which the killer belonged. The latter had hoped to put an end to the patriarch's proselytism by assassinating him.

Whatever the case, these events caused a deep rift. Even to this day, our family is divided in two—in fact, in three, if you add the small Protestant community.

At present, by and large, the wound has healed. But in the early twentieth century it was still painful. Botros, a Catholic by birth but deeply suspicious of religious quarrels, took every opportunity to show that he was above such disputes.

Let me return to the Russo-Japanese War of 1904–05. Its impact far exceeded the territorial stakes involved or the scale of the fighting. It caused a cataclysm in the minds of men; they suddenly had to revise their view of the world. To their astonishment, they discovered that an Oriental country equipped with modern weaponry could triumph over a European power. The consequences were worldwide and, by history's yardstick, almost immediate. In under ten years, the Russian, Persian, Ottoman, and Chinese empires underwent upheavals from which they never recovered. This was before the Great War came and swept away whatever was left of the Old World.

In my village, however, events were interpreted differently than in the rest of the world. People spontaneously reacted according to their religious affiliations. The Orthodox branch of the family was violently pro-Russian while the Catholic branch, in "mechanical" opposition, hoped for the czar's defeat and the mikado's victory.

By proclaiming his support for the Orthodox country and asserting that the Russians were within their rights, Botros, who came from a Catholic family, was "straddling" sectarian divisions among his kinsmen and taking an ecumenical, conciliatory position. His message to his cousins was that events had to be judged in the light of universal principles and not personal affiliation.

Though he followed the events of the Russo-Japanese War with passion, as did many of his contemporaries, Botros took up brighter themes too during his New York evenings, such as this poem where he mocks the imaginary exploits of a boastful hunter:

> *Youssef threatens the birds with his weapon,*
> *But the birds are safe and sound,*
> *They have no cause to worry,*
> *It has even been observed that they live longer,*
> *Since Youssef has taken up hunting.*
> *The lead from his gun is gentle*
> *Like raisins from Corinth . . .*
> *Is he training himself never to wound*
> *These weak creatures? Or do the game birds wear*
> *The relics of the Holy Cross around their neck?*

When he recopied the text of this poem, Botros was careful, out of politeness, not to identify the Youssef who was the butt of his joke.

But it so happens that the name of the cousin with whom he was staying in New York was Youssef. He was the same age as Botros, a dentist by profession as well as a shareholder in a printing firm he had co-founded with other cousins. It seems that they all tried very hard to get their visitor to extend his stay—and perhaps become their associate—but he refused. For him the die was cast. His trip to America was to be no more than a digression in his life; the time had come to round it off with dignity and go back home, head held high.

On the eve of his departure he invited the editors of the Arabic-language newspapers of New York to his cousin's house. If he is to be believed, these men spent their time quarreling among themselves, and he tried to reconcile them. Émigré men of letters from several Oriental countries were also present. He delivered an enthusiastic speech to them, predicting the spread of freedom of the press in the countries of the Levant and an inexorable increase in the number of readers.

Only yesterday, not even five percent of the population in our countries subscribed to newspapers; today that number is easily twenty percent. Soon, if progress continues and newspapers do not disappoint, the number of subscribers will be seventy or even eighty percent. Reading newspapers will then become an indispensable daily activity for our countrymen, just as it is among the most advanced peoples.

I have no idea where my future grandfather found these statistics, but they were obviously optimistic, and his predictions even more so. That said, his intentions were undeniably praiseworthy.

In concluding his speech, he uttered a final exhortation to the émigrés before sailing back home:

You are right to criticize the rulers of our countries, but don't confine yourselves to that; if the rulers are corrupt, this is because the population is corrupt as well. The rulers are merely the emanation of this generalized decay. The tree must be cured by its roots. Persons who express themselves in newspapers and books, and who speak in public forums, must devote themselves to that task.

As for me, this is precisely the mission I shall devote myself to from now on, as hard as I can, and to the end of my life, with God's help!

No doubt there was a touch of rhetorical flourish in Botros's comments and an understandable desire to leave majestically after the humiliating beginning of his adventurous trip. But this wasn't just idle talk. He devoted himself to these quixotic battles until the end of his life—changing mankind, fighting ignorance, and rousing the peoples of the Orient. These battles too brought their share of disillusionment and humiliation, so much so that he eventually regretted not having left the country when he had the opportunity. I am convinced that in his most difficult moments later in life he recalled his stay in "the American lands" with great nostalgia.

But for all his regrets, he never dared to leave for America again, for he had clipped his own wings with an "official line" fabricated as soon as he returned: he had never considered emigrating, never considered abandoning his family, his students, his country, to make a life for himself elsewhere. No, not he! The only reason he sailed across the Atlantic was to rescue his brother from a tight spot. Since he was geographically close, he took the opportunity to tour the United States; he then returned home to tackle the immense tasks incumbent on him. His nearest and dearest had all adopted this version of the facts. Had he been outspoken again about wishing to emigrate, he would have lost face.

It was only because I found his personal papers that I discovered that he had harbored many other temptations in his youth.

Enlightenment
Ideals

NINETEEN

Thanks to my grandfather's savings account booklet, I now knew the precise dates of his stay in the United States. If he opened an account on April 21, 1904, he must have arrived a short time before. This was confirmed by a belated investigation in the Ellis Island archives: a person by the name of Peter M. disembarked in New York on April 18 from a ship called *Vigilancia* coming from Havana.

In his answer to the questionnaire of the United States immigration officer, he calls himself a tradesman rather than a teacher, probably because he had just worked in his brother's Cuban company.

Age: 36
Nationality (Country of last permanent residence):
    Turkey
Race or People: Syrian
Able to read: Yes

Able to write?: Yes

Final destination: New York

Whether having a ticket to reach final destination: [Probably a
    question intended for people traveling to other cities in the
    United States, but the newcomer had replied docilely]: Yes

By whom was passage paid?: Self

If you compare the 1904 form to the one Gebrayel filled out in 1895,
you can't help noticing that the form had become significantly more
detailed.

Whether in possession of $50 or, if less, how much? [Botros's haughty
    reply]: $500

Whether ever before in the United States, and if so, when and where?
    September 1902

Whether going to join a relative or friend, and if so, what relative or
    friend; and his name and complete address: [Botros merely wrote]
    Hotel America, N.Y.

Ever in prison or almshouse or institute for care and treatment of the
    insane . . . ? No, no, no

Whether a Polygamist? No

Whether an Anarchist? No

Deformed or Crippled? No, no

Though the profusion of details is not particularly informative and
merely makes me shrug as my grandfather probably did, I am nonetheless pleased that I am finally able to date the different stages of his trip
in "the American lands"—Cuba from September 1902, more or less, to
April 1904; the United States from April to November. As for the time
periods before and after his American sojourn, the dates can be determined only hypothetically. Since there are no other documents in the
archives for the years 1901–05 except for the New York savings account
booklet, it is reasonable to assume that Botros was abroad for this entire five-year period. He may have visited Egypt on the outward journey, as intended, and stopped briefly in France or England on the way

back, but these are mere suppositions; he himself makes no mention of anything.

On the other hand, what can be substantiated from his correspondence is that he returned from his grand tour with his mind filled with dreams and ideals. He longed more than ever to change the world or to change the Orient, which comes to the same thing. This is evident in the following letter, dated March 18, 1906. From the sender's signature and his village of residence, we know that he belonged to the Hamadehs, an eminent Druzean family from the Mountains. He seems to have had a long conversation with my grandfather not long before in one of the few public places in the Beirut of the day:

> *I can't stop thinking about that evening on the terrace of the Star of the Orient. It was darkest night, and what we were saying had the precise purpose of clearing away the darkness and spreading light; which can only happen if people like you rally together and join forces. So don't let indecision override determination, for you are a free man, and a free man doesn't accept injustice. Go down the only path possible, the only one a man like you should take. I am telling you my most sincere feeling, because I find it admirable that you are in such a frame of mind, and that you want to remain in this country . . .*

This letter evokes the atmosphere of "significant evenings." Two Levantine men enamored of freedom and Enlightenment ideals conferred with each other on the best way of transforming the established order. Two youths sustained by a noble ambition and in love with life. I picture their faces lit by a flickering lamp while all around them the Ottoman city slept. They must have had the feeling that their whisperings would undermine the foundations of the Old World.

They were very much the product of their time, nourished on the promises of the nascent century, some of which would be kept and others forgotten, some hideously distorted. That same year, perhaps that same evening, throughout the Orient, thousands of educated persons, young and not so young, "conspired" this way, in the same hope of "clearing away the darkness." Some, like Sun Yat-sen or, later, Kemal Atatürk, became the reformist founding fathers of nations, while others remained foot soldiers or dreamers. But no particle of light is negligible, especially for those who are its distant beneficiaries—including me.

It is clear that Botros returned from his long trip with greater fighting spirit and greater militancy than ever. His friend probably gently reproached him for the indecisiveness he detected in him, but Botros had not returned home with his head bowed. Nor was he wounded, bitter, or downcast, in spite of the Cuban disappointment.

This fighting spirit already manifests itself in his New York booklet. Was it the exhilarating effect of his trip, his discovery of America, the welcome of his cousins and "friends," both male and female? I think his stay in the United States reinforced his long-held convictions, acquired in adolescence in Khalil's school and then later in the mission school, namely that it was both necessary and possible to build our own United States at home in the Levant, a federation of the different Ottoman provinces, where the diverse communities would coexist, where everyone would read the newspapers, and where corruption and arbitrary rule would no longer prevail.

But there was another factor that must have reinforced his self-confidence: for the first time in his life, my grandfather did not feel penniless. Those thousand dollars deposited in his savings account had probably puffed him up, to put it colloquially. To assess its value a century later, the sum must be multiplied by twenty or thirty. Someone visiting New York today with several tens of thousands of dollars in his possession would not feel pinched. Furthermore, Botros didn't even have to dip into the money during his stay; he withdrew it on the eve of his departure, which means that he had other funds in his pockets.

Where did the money come from? From his brother, apparently. Though he failed to keep Botros by his side, Gebrayel was certainly not going to let him leave in anger or empty-handed. He compensated his brother generously for the time spent working for him.

Thus Botros had been able to continue his trip in princely fashion. And when he returned home, he must have had a tidy sum left over, money enough to dine with his friends on the terrace of the Star of the Orient and smoke American cigarettes as they solved the problems of the world.

TWENTY

The exhilaration could not last indefinitely. The Havana nest egg didn't make my grandfather into a rich man who could live off his private income—as some people did in those days—while devoting his time to the hoped-for revolution. He had to start earning his living again.

Most opportunely, the Oriental Secondary School, never reconciled to having lost one of its best teachers, contacted him as soon as he returned. Botros wrote to his maternal uncle—Soussène's brother—who was a leading citizen of Zahlé at the time:

The father superior expressed the desire to have me return to the school. But I won't consider going back unless I have a better status and a better salary. I have other contacts in Beirut that will soon come through, so I asked for time to think. It might speed things up if you went to see him yourself. I am convinced that you will know how to

explain my demands to him better than I, and obtain from him what would
be in my interest and in the students' interest. Needless to say, if you reach
an agreement along those lines, I shall comply and obey you like a son . . .

His uncle's mediation must have paid off, since we next meet Botros
as "Director of Arabic Studies," a title he exhibited proudly, during
those years, in beautiful calligraphy on all his notebooks.

Such pride may seem inordinate in our day, in countries where there
are schools at every street corner, with attendance required for all children and an untold number of teachers and heads of departments. Now
that it is widespread and commonplace, teaching has lost much of its
prestige; this is also because of the distorted set of values that leads us
to respect financially profitable activities more than socially useful ones.

In my grandfather's day, a completely different attitude prevailed in
entirely dissimilar milieus. Among advocates of tradition, the person
dispensing knowledge, whether priest, pastor, sheikh, or mullah, had
influence and prestige within his community. For those who aspired to
modernity and freedom, the secular teacher—a newly "invented" person reflecting new times—was both a symbol and an irreplaceable mes-
senger of Enlightenment ideals.

Botros was conscious of his pioneering role, and he exercised it with
conviction, even solemnity at times. Graced with his new title, he
swiftly became an omnipresent figure in Zahlé, constantly invited to
speak, inaugurate a building, commemorate an anniversary, or sing the
praises of an illustrious visitor.

His speeches invariably followed the same pattern. First, a preamble expressing modesty. For example:

Those who came to this podium just before me have already said
everything. What could I add that would be useful?

Then, a long exposition, outspokenly militant and moralistic, denouncing fanaticism, corruption, and obscurantism.

Our Oriental people are lacking nothing, and have no failings, thank
God, except for one, which is ignorance. The great majority of people

are suffering from it, alas, and the symptoms are varied: incessant quarrels and conflicts, dissimulation and double-talk, treachery and deceit, violence and killing . . . This disease is not incurable, and the remedy is perfectly well known: it is genuine knowledge.

Finally, by way of conclusion, some didactic verses reiterating the same ideas, sometimes word for word, to imprint them in people's memory:

> *If you wonder what is wrong with the peoples of the Orient and why they are so often denounced.*
> *You will find that they have many qualities and only one shortcoming: ignorance.*
> *This disease is curable, but it is treated through knowledge, not emigration!*
> *Knowledge was born in the Orient before it migrated to the West, and it ought to return to the fold.*

This last theme is restated in all his speeches, tirelessly, passionately, vehemently, and with rage. At the end-of-term ceremony held in July 1907 at the Oriental Secondary School of Zahlé, for instance:

> *Children of my country, it is time to wake up, it is time to throw off the chains that are holding you back.*
> *It is time to catch up with the West, no matter how high above you it towers and even if it costs you your life.*
> *It was you who gave the West its knowledge; it was you who showed it the path.*
> *Moses and Christ and the Prophet of Islam were your kin, as well as Avicenna and others like him . . .*
> *Abandon your harmful traditions, and have no fear of those who will wrongly reprove you!*
> *Hold your head high, wear the clothes of your century, and proclaim: the time for turbans is past!*

When Botros attacked turbans, he fitted right in with the modernist revolutionaries of his day. Several years later Atatürk banned this traditional headgear, which he saw as a symbol of ignorance and obscurantism, and he proudly sported a Western hat, proof of modernity.

Though I don't mean to compare one of the great figures of history to my unknown grandfather, it is my duty to point out that the two men were at variance. Botros, as I have had occasion to mention, preferred to go around bareheaded—neither Oriental turban nor European hat. This was not just a whimsical fashion statement or an act of defiance. In *The Aftereffects of Vanity*, the play he wrote just before his trip to America, one of his countrymen says:

We constantly wear two faces: one to ape our ancestors, the other to ape the West.

This was his heartfelt opinion. He sometimes expressed it with bitter irony, as in the monologue he put in the mouth of another protagonist:

The Orientals see that the West has outstripped them, but they don't understand why. One day they see a westerner wearing a flower in his buttonhole. They say to themselves: so that's how they achieved progress! Let's wear a flower in our buttonholes and we'll catch up with them! Another time, they see a lock of hair falling over their foreheads and they think: so that's their secret! And they carefully comb their locks down to their eyes . . . When will you understand the difference between fundamental values and vulgar fashions? It is not enough to want to imitate the West; it is also important to know what is worth copying and what is not!

These words may partially echo the teachings of the Presbyterian ministers, who had their own personal criticisms of the West. As for me, I see them as the thoughtful rebellion of a free man, someone who fervently wished to see the status quo ruthlessly overthrown—but not any old way or for any old purpose.

TWENTY-ONE

 The restructuring of the Orient that my grandfather hoped and prayed for was much more
imminent than he imagined.

In the first days of July 1908, two young Ottoman officers, whose first names were Niyazi and Enver, took up
position in the mountains of Macedonia and called for
rebellion until there was the establishment of a modern
constitution. The two men belonged to a secret society
founded in the city of Salonika called the Committee of
Union and Progress, part of a wider opposition movement whose name would go down in history, that of the
Young Turks.

When the rebellion first broke out, everyone was convinced that the two officers would be brought back to
Constantinople in chains and made to suffer a punish-
ment that would serve as a warning. But when Sultan Abdul Hamid dispatched a regiment to subdue them, the
soldiers fraternized with the rebels. And when the sultan

ordered an elite division to march against the soldiers, they decided to disobey as well. In a matter of days, the Ottoman army was, if not in open rebellion, at least in a state of insubordination.

Incapable of quelling the movement, the monarch came to his own conclusions. Rather than wait for his capital and palace to be taken by force, he forestalled the rebels, dismissed his government, and appointed reformists into office. He also announced his decision to re-implement the liberal constitution drawn up in the first years of his reign, thirty years earlier, which had since been suspended. Fundamental liberties were to be respected, censorship abolished, and free elections organized.

There was an explosion of joy in most of the provinces. In Salonika, one of the first cities to have fallen into the hands of the revolutionaries, Niyazi and Enver were welcomed as heroes, and the latter—a young man of twenty-seven—addressed a jubilant crowd, proclaiming that henceforth there would be no more Jews, Greeks, Bulgarians, Romanians, and Serbs in the empire, "for all of us are brothers, under the same blue sky, all of us taking pride in being Ottomans."

Though Botros rejoiced over these changes, he expressed anxiety immediately. Invited to speak at a large public gathering in Zahlé, he began by congratulating "our valiant soldiers who shed their blood for the sake of freedom," but he then issued a warning to his compatriots:

> You are not unaware that for many years, the peoples of the world have viewed us with disdain and contempt. They consider us weak-willed and devoid of moral principles. They compare their advancement to our backwardness, their glory to our humiliation, their development to our decadence. More generally, they comment on our powerlessness in ways that are painful to hear. In response to these attacks, we would hide behind tyranny and say to people in foreign lands and to ourselves, "What do you expect us to do under such a regime?"
>
> Today we no longer have that excuse. And I feel that the whole world is watching us and saying, "The Ottoman people are no longer in chains. Now that the pretext they invoked to justify their

backwardness has been swept away, let's see what they'll do!" Well, if time passes and we don't catch up with the advanced nations, they will no longer regard us as human beings! They will be convinced that we were created only to be humiliated and submissive, and they will throw themselves on our property and our interests in order to devour them . . .

Odd that Botros was so worried when the revolution was still taking its first faltering steps. Perhaps this was related to his view of the society of his day, a view encapsulated by the words I quoted earlier: "if the rulers are corrupt, this is because the population is corrupt as well." There was, however, another, more immediate reason: very serious events were taking place, events that were ominous.

Indeed, while the monarch, a clever politician, had complied with the demands of his triumphant enemies, he had secretly started to call to arms all those who were worried by the changes. In traditionalist milieus, the agents of the sultan-caliph had no difficulty spreading the word that these revolutionaries were atheists and infidels, seeking to undermine the foundations of the faith and replace them with diabolic innovations imported from the West. If proof was needed, they said, one had only to observe the women. They used to dress with modesty, but now they ran around the streets showing their faces, demonstrating, and shouting angrily like men. The caliph had had to publish a special firman to call them to order!

Besides, whispered the monarch's envoys, look who has been applauding this movement from the start: the Armenians, the Syrian Christians, the Greeks, and, as might be expected, the people of Salonika! This last word was uttered with a wink, and everyone understood what was meant: the Jews. In the sultan's entourage, they blamed the British, the Italians, and especially the Freemasons.

Which was only half false. The movement had indeed started in Salonika, which was no great surprise to anyone, since Salonika was the capital of the Enlightenment in the Ottoman Empire. It had the best schools, and the different religious communities even competed among themselves, each priding itself on offering a better education than the others. Unquestionably, the first prize went to the smallest and most unusual community of them all, the one whose existence most people were unaware of—both in the Ottoman Empire and in the rest of the world: the Sabbataists. These were the distant followers of Sabbatai Tsevi, who had proclaimed himself Messiah in late 1665. He had aroused enormous expectations in all the Jewish communities, from Tunis to Warsaw to Amsterdam, and had also alarmed the Ottoman authorities, who ordered him to choose between conversion to Islam or execution. According to the chronicles of the period, he chose not to die, "wore the turban and took the name Mehemed Effendi." He was immediately abandoned by all his followers. Some historians believe that this traumatic disillusionment is what caused many Jews to turn away from messianism and become involved in worldly affairs.

When Sabbatai died, in 1676, there were only some four hundred families in Salonika still loyal to him. For a long time, in Turkish, they were called *dönme*, "those who turned," in the sense of "converted," a fairly contemptuous designation that was recently supplanted by, simply, Salonikans. They keep only vague recollections of their eventful past; their true faith at present is secular. Indeed, they were already staunchly secular at the end of the nineteenth century.

The reason I felt I should mention these men is because, unwittingly, though not really by chance, they played an invaluable role in spreading new ideas in the empire. Indeed, it was in one of their institutions, founded and directed by a man called Chemsi Effendi, that a boy called Mustafa Kemal—the future Atatürk—completed his primary education. His father, Ali Reza, didn't want his son to be restricted to a traditional Koranic schooling; he wanted him to attend an institution that would give him a "European-inspired" education.

This was the original spark that would set off a powerful blaze.

How did a seventeenth-century messianic movement transform itself, two centuries later, into a trailblazing vehicle for secularism and modernity? This is a subject that has fascinated me for years, like a body of water one walks alongside without ever taking the plunge.

I won't do so today either, for this is not where my origins lie. That said, I can guess—or at least sense, having the antenna of an eternal foreigner from a minority group—what life must have been like for these four hundred Sabbataist families: for Muslims they were not really Muslim, for Jews they were no longer Jewish, and for Christians they were doubly infidel. These families must have felt that the noblest, most honorable way out of the impasse was to rise above narrow affiliations. This required considerable commitment on the part of the community, as well as the rejection of other alternatives. For it could have closed ranks and hardened to guard against disintegration.

What saved the Sabbataists' soul—as far as I see it, at least—was, first, the spirit instilled by their founder. He has been endlessly mocked for choosing life over faith, but on quiet reflection, I think he had a point. Doctrines are meant to serve men, not the other way around. Of course, we can respect individuals who sacrifice themselves for an ideal, but we must also admit that too many people throughout history have sacrificed themselves for bad reasons. Let us praise he who chose to live! Let us praise Sabbatai's human instinct.

It seems to me that the other determining factor affecting the Sabbataists was Salonika, a city that already included scores of religious communities, all of them minorities, all more or less tolerated, all more or less marginal. Since most of these communities did not intend to predominate, they competed in terms of knowledge—in terms of wealth too, of course, but that is much more common. It was this environment that prevented the Sabbataists from becoming fossilized and drove them to put all their efforts, body and soul, into their schools.

What the Sabbataists wanted to accomplish in Salonika is similar to what men like Khalil and Botros wanted to accomplish at the same time and for similar reasons: to spread enlightenment and knowledge, to help the Orient to catch up with Europe so the Ottoman Empire could become a large and powerful modern state—prosperous, virtuous, and pluralistic—where all the citizens would have the same fundamental rights regardless of their religious or ethnic affiliations. A kind of American dream on the soil of the Orient, for generous-minded members of minorities who have lost their bearings . . .

TWENTY-TWO

In Salonika, this ideal was shared by an important part of the population, and they welcomed the 1908 revolution with enthusiasm. The Committee of Union and Progress, to which the rebels belonged, was far better established in that city than in the rest of the empire. Indeed, among its members were Sabbataists, but also "normal" Jews, city residents of Italian nationality, Bulgarians, Albanian Muslims—such as Niyazi—Circassians, and a great number of Turks, such as Enver, the leading rebel officer. It was easy for the sultan and his circle to point to the foreign elements and to ask their people by what right these foreigners, who had always been under the authority of the sultan-caliph, dared to meddle in the affairs of the empire. As for the brotherhood's Muslim members, the traditionalist insinuated that they were all Freemasons, hence atheists and renegades.

There again, this was a mixture of truth and falsehood. The Salonika Masonic lodges had played a significant role in developing and promulgating revolutionary ideas, but their role should not be overestimated. The desire for change, liberation, and a galvanizing force for the "awakening of the Orient" had been budding for decades in many provinces throughout the empire—even as far as my village. It didn't have to be "invented" one evening in Salonika in a meeting of Italian Freemasons.

But the work of sabotage by the sultan's agents had its effect on the population, and the climate deteriorated so much that by April 1909, eight months after having yielded to the rebels, Abdul Hamid decided that the time had come to take matters firmly in hand again. It was then that a growing number of suspicious incidents occurred everywhere in the empire, attributed at the time to the monarch's henchmen. Though this is not inconceivable, we can't be certain of anything. The worst unrest took place in Southeast Anatolia, particularly in the town of Adana, where riots broke out; these took a violently anti-Armenian turn, ending in a massacre—the first big massacre, but unfortunately not the last.

Several days later, there were demonstrations by soldiers and religious traditionalists in Constantinople, at the gates of the imperial palace, demanding a "return to true values." A few prominent reformists were lynched in the street; others—ministers, for the most part—were forced to go underground. Noting that the government of the Young Turks had ceased to exist, the sultan announced his compliance with the will of his people and the suspension of the constitution. We can rightly assume that compliance, in this case, did not go against his grain.

But, as in July 1908, no one foresaw the events that occurred next. Several army units, led by Enver and Niyazi, left Salonika and marched on Constantinople. They crushed the counterrevolution with minimal combat and seized the imperial palace. The country's highest religious authority, the *sheikh-ul-islam*, a man receptive to reformist ideas, immediately issued a fatwa calling for the deposition of Abdul Hamid "for tyranny, murder, armed rebellion, and violation of the sharia," thereby fighting fire with fire, so to speak. The parliament met the same day, and when the text of the fatwa was read to them, they approved it overwhelmingly.

The assembly sent the sovereign a delegation of four deputies to notify him of his deposition: two Muslims, one Armenian Christian, and one Jew, Emmanuel Carasso—a significant choice because Carasso was also a high dignitary in the Salonika Freemasonry. It was in that city, I might add, that the deposed sovereign was locked up under guard—in a sumptuous residence, but a prisoner nonetheless.

One of his brothers, whose given name was Rashad, replaced him on the throne, taking the name of Mehemet V. He was said to be in sympathy with the Young Turks, or at least unwilling to oppose them.

Botros celebrated his accession with a poem that created a sensation that year.

> I salute the era of Rashad, for he will restore what was destroyed in our
>   building!
> I salute Niyazi's and Enver's swords, I salute the brotherhood that
>   unsheathed them,
> I salute free men from all communities . . .

Apparently, proud partisans of the revolution declaimed these verses, not just in Zahlé, but also in Beirut, Damascus, Aleppo, and even Constantinople, though they didn't always know who was the author.

If there is some form of life after death and my grandfather were in this room, next to me, right now, watching me rummage through his archives, he would probably want me to stop quoting here and go on to another chapter. For I am approaching a territory that he would have preferred not to broach. In fact, I would prefer not to as well. But if I am to focus a beam of light on my forgotten grandfather, this is the price that must be paid: the truth cannot be controlled like a dog on a leash. I can't avoid pointing out that before hailing those who deposed Abdul Hamid, my grandfather's notebooks show that he had frequently sung the praises of that same sultan.

For the sake of accuracy, let me count . . . I have found at least eight laudatory, or at least deferential, mentions. If I really scoured his notebooks, I would find more. I won't quote them all, but I feel I should reproduce the following one, excerpted from a speech given in Zahlé:

> Of course, our first and last words of praise must be addressed to the person who is behind all beneficent actions, His Majesty Abdul Hamid Khan, our venerated sovereign, sultan, and son of sultan, may God extend his flourishing reign . . .

A bit further along, these few verses:

> *If you want to know what metal virtue is made of,*
> *Look to the Ottoman family.*
> *Destiny, which is often cruel, has shown its benevolence*
> *By giving us Abdul Hamid as sovereign . . .*

On the opposite page, Botros penciled in the following words:

> This verse must be changed.

In another notebook, my grandfather writes that he was attending the performance of a play titled *Saladin* when he heard the news of Abdul Hamid's deposition and the accession of Mehemet Rashad. He mounted the stage to say a few words about the deposed monarch, "on behalf of the Ottoman people":

> People trusted him with their lives, their honor, and their property, but he sold it all at a giveaway price. His name will be forever tainted, for instead of eradicating treason and corruption from the kingdom, he sent his agents out to spread hatred and sedition. This is why I say to this arrogant person . . .

A few particularly harsh verses follow, but enough, I shall stop here. It would be just as unfair to heap blame on my grandfather for not having had time to sort out his writings before dying, or because political changes affected his views. Let he who has never changed opinions cast the first stone.

Leniency is all the more called for when you consider that Abdul Hamid was a complex, ambiguous person about whom historians still argue today. It seems highly plausible that when he first became sultan, he really intended to reform the Ottoman Empire and make it into a modern state on a par with the European powers then ruling the world. The exercise of power made him more mistrustful and cynical, some say perverse or even paranoid. He was afraid of things slipping out of his control, as often happens when long-standing tyrannies begin to loosen their grip. What's more, the Ottoman dynasty was in a phase of swift, irreversible decline, a tendency that no monarch, no matter how clever, could possibly reverse. In another era, Abdul Hamid might have been a great sovereign; though he came too late, most historians believe nevertheless that he was the last sultan worthy of the title.

But beyond the monarch, I am primarily interested in my grandfather—what he condoned, when he compromised and when he didn't, his indignations and vacillations. Without wishing to defend him at any cost, I see a coherence behind his various political stands. My grandfather was not opposed in principle to the Ottoman Empire. He would have liked to see it change into a constitutional monarchy rather than disintegrate. He proclaimed proudly that he was an "Ottoman citizen," and his dream was to see a large state made up of many nations, in which all men would be equal, regardless of religion or language, and would exercise their rights under the leadership of an honest, benevolent sovereign. If necessary, this constitutional sultan could remain titular head of the majority "church," a bit like the king of England. History decided otherwise. "Our" empire crumbled, like the Hapsburg Empire, into scores of miserable ethnic states whose murderous rumblings have caused two world wars and dozens of local wars, and have already corrupted the soul of the new millennium.

History is often wrong, but in our cowardliness we mortals give learned explanations of why its decrees were just, why what happened was inevitable, and why our noble dreams deserved to die.

TWENTY-THREE

In that same year, 1909, while rebellion was brewing in the Ottoman countries, a letter was received in our village that eventually changed the course of several lives. It was from my great-uncle Gebrayel and was addressed to Khalil.

Many years had gone by since the two men had seen each other. The Havana émigré who had left the country at eighteen was now thirty-two. His former teacher was seventy-two, a respected figure, certainly, but a very controversial one as well. The Catholics in the village openly detested him, for even after all these years they still couldn't understand how the son of the good priest Gerjis could have espoused heretical beliefs and—to add insult to injury—brazenly converted the priest's house into a Protestant house of worship. On Sunday mornings, when the preacher rang the bell he had placed on the outside wall to summon "his" faithful to the service and a good number of villagers came streaming out of their homes in their best clothes, there were those for whom this was plainly the work of the devil, a sign that Heaven had abandoned this country of sinners for good.

Yet Khalil did not proselytize aggressively. He always avoided any confrontation with the other communities and merely doggedly followed his own path. In the family archives, most of the documents bearing his handwriting are lists of the needy. Indeed, he made it his habit to travel to all the Mountain villages and inquire after the most destitute; then he requested help on their behalf, either from the Anglo-Saxon missionaries or from a few wealthy men of his acquaintance. He took no account of the recipients' religion and never asked for anything in return. When these people, to whom no one else paid any heed, saw the diligence of this man month after month, they were eventually attracted by the sound of the new bell, and the Protestant community grew in number.

Teaching had long been Khalil's other activity. But after spreading knowledge for a few years, his pioneering school, which had benefited Botros, Gebrayel, and dozens of other children from our village and the surrounding area (including, incidentally, the family historian, Issa, author of *The Tree*), he had been forced to close it down. For Khalil this was worse than a defeat; it was the death of a dream.

As I have mentioned, he had completed advanced studies in Abey, Souk-el-Gharb, Beirut, and elsewhere, and had held various positions of responsibility in Protestant institutions. He then returned to our village and founded his school on the American model, receiving American aid as well as aid from Presbyterian missions from Scotland. This was a highly ambitious project. The missionaries were almost like people from another planet, and they had a golden rule, adopted by their local disciples, including Khalil: the pupils were not to be given a third-rate education; they were to be given exactly the same education as pupils in Boston and Edinburgh, and the teachers were to be just as demanding with them as with young people of the same age in the United States or Great Britain.

This meant that the new school would be unlike any previous school in the village. Until then, meaningless sentences were mumbled ad infinitum in the same droning voice—the same sentences that had been mumbled by generations of illiterate ancestors under the menacing stick and bored gaze of a priest. For Khalil, it was a point of honor to have the best textbooks sent to him, to recruit the best available teachers, and to impose the most rigorous standards on his students.

Alas, the experiment didn't last, in spite of the villagers' very favorable reception. Why did it fail? I won't dwell on the reasons here, for in any case, I was only able to get a rough idea. He had to contend with the Catholic clergy's hostility. After having been caught short, they eventually launched an effective counteroffensive. I shall come back to this later. He received only weak support from the missionaries, for they saw these kinds of schools proliferate throughout the mountain area and wanted to sponsor only the most successful, meaning the ones in the largest villages. For Khalil, however, the most serious setback was the fact that his own kin "deserted" him. Not one of his five sons seemed willing to take over from his aging father as headmaster of the school. In fact, not one was interested in teaching. Worse still, none of them wanted to stay in the village, or in the country for that matter. They all dreamed of settling overseas. Some had already done so; others were getting ready to do so.

Wounded in his pride, he decided to close down the school, bring his long teaching career to an end, and start a new career in . . . silk. Yes, raising silkworms. He planted white mulberry trees all around his house, for their leaves are the food of silkworms, and he built a silkworm-rearing house in an isolated spot, to keep the odors at a distance. According to *The Tree*, he applied "the method recommended by Pasteur" and produced "the most valued cocoons in the whole region."

I can easily believe this. Khalil was rigorous in everything he did—a quality I value, even if I can't help smiling as I describe his strange transformation. On the one hand, rigor counteracts laxness, mental nonchalance, carelessness, and vague approximations—in sum, all the scourges that have had a debilitating effect on the Orient for too long. On the other hand, rigor equals inflexibility and moral rigidity, attitudes that undermine the gentle art of living enjoyed in our lands.

To be more specific, the rigidity of the preacher and his wife was clearly a factor in their children's "desertion." It was also a factor in a few other serious family crises. That said, it would be ungrateful of me not to add that it was primarily thanks to this man and his short-lived school that the light of knowledge reached my relatives. I realize that it is always risky to suggest a beginning for things. Nothing is born of nothing, least of all knowledge, modernity, or enlightened thought; progress is made in tiny surges, in successive laps, like an endless relay race. But there are links without which nothing would be passed on, and for that reason, they deserve the gratitude of all who benefited from them. I feel personally grateful to the preacher, independent of the fact that he chose to be a preacher. It is possible to be indifferent to the Presbyterian faith and deeply question the motivations of the American missionaries, yet feel that only an education of the highest quality can produce citizens worthy of the name.

To be honest, I don't know if Khalil sought to educate good citizens or just good Protestant Christians. As he was a believer and a preacher, there probably wasn't much of a distinction in his mind. But whether with students or the needy, he was careful to practice charity without pettiness. He lavished knowledge on his pupils and prayed to the Lord that the children would make good use of it. In fact, some Catholic villagers had no misgivings; they entrusted their children to him without the slightest fear that he might treacherously lure them away from the faith of their fathers. Such was the case of my great-grandfather Tannous, who enrolled his children in the preacher's school one after the other, without any of them converting to the Protestant religion.

Well, that's almost true. Though no one converted directly as far as I know, a significant number of Tannous's descendants did become Protestant. His youngest daughter, Yamna, for one, whom I mentioned above when I excerpted the passage in Tannous's letter agreeing to her receiving a real education. She was surely one of the first girls in the village to have had this opportunity. It was Khalil and his wife, the austere Sofiya, both staunch supporters of women's education, who took her under their wing and encouraged her. Did they also convert her? It hardly matters, since she eventually became a de facto Protestant when she married the preacher's eldest son, Dr. Shukri.

. . .

Let me pause for a moment. This is the first time since I began this rapid trip down the river of my origins that I have come across a person whom I knew. I was tempted to write "whom I caught up with," for that would better reflect the feeling I have of running after ancestors who slip away, die too soon, or emigrate and never return. Shukri— "Dr. Shukri," as he was always called in the family—is someone I once met when I was a child. Not Yamna, who died before him—of her I remember only seeing a photo that day, glued to a black velvet support and hanging, framed, in the living room. This was the same living room that had formerly served as a place for the village Protestants to congregate and pray; in fact, there was still a rusted bell on the outside wall of the house, but at the time I had no idea what purpose it had served.

Today, this house is mine . . .

TWENTY-FOUR

Let me describe the day I went to visit Dr. Shukri. It occurs to me now that he probably asked to see me one last time before he died, for he was elderly and more or less confined to his room.

I have vivid images of that meeting, though I was at most five years old, perhaps only four. I can still see him, a sick old man, so gaunt that his face looked triangular and his eyeglasses too big and too heavy. But he had a lively gaze and nimble hands. He was sitting up in a four-poster bed, his back against a large embroidered pillow. He had a balding head, with a crown of silky, tousled white hair. He made me sit in a wicker chair very close to the bed, and he taught me a conjuring trick that I can still perform. Having placed a soup plate in front of me, he filled it halfway with water, took a coin from the chest of drawers, and dropped it into the liquid. The point was to pick up the coin without wetting one's fingers. "You'll see, it's very simple!" he said. He asked me to bring him an empty glass and an old newspaper; he tore off a piece of newspaper, crumpled it up, stuffed it in the glass, and set it on fire. Then he put the glass on the dish, rim down. As if by magic, the water immediately flowed into the blazing paper, and the bottom of the dish became dry. I marveled at this and never forgot my visit to Dr. Shukri's.

He died a short time later, before I could see him again—at least I don't remember any other meeting. He was often mentioned in my childhood as an erudite man with an adventurous mind, though no one ever went into detail, and when I got older, as far as I remember, he was never talked about anymore. Fortunately, *The Tree* gives him a comprehensive biographical note, but only up to the age of thirty-seven, when the book was published. I now know that he was born in 1871, attended his father's school, and then pursued his studies, predictably, at the American school. He was well versed in various sciences, including astronomy, botany, meteorology, and toxicology, and he wrote dozens of articles in specialized journals. This was before he realized, relatively late, in his thirtieth year, that he was passionately interested in medicine. The author of *The Tree* was a friend of Shukri's, and was very interested in his career. Issa writes:

> He received his diploma from the Ottoman commission in 1904 and started his medical practice with success. But he was tempted by travel and set off for Egypt on February 23, 1906; there he enlisted as an officer in the army and was sent to Sudan, where he still is at press time.

In all likelihood his marriage to Yamna was celebrated between the two dates mentioned, in late 1905 or early 1906, in any case soon after Botros returned from his American trip. Right afterward, the newlyweds left for Khartoum, where Shukri had obtained a position as military physician with the British army.

This union between Tannous's daughter and Khalil's son brought the two families even closer, for now they were not just friends and neighbors with a vague common ancestry. Botros was surely delighted. Not so his brother Theodoros, who had been ordained as a priest shortly before his sister's marriage and for whom this marriage into a family of "heretics" was mortifying, particularly since Shukri was a militant Protestant and virulent in his hostility toward Catholics. The fact that his own sister became the wife of this man and that they went to live among the English must certainly have distressed Theodoros. But he didn't do anything to prevent its happening—or maybe he couldn't.

Still other ordeals awaited my great-uncle the priest. For Gebrayel's 1909 letter to Khalil also mentioned marriage, though allusively. Very allusively, you might say, since, in the very last lines, after writing about a thousand other things, Gebrayel requested that his former teacher "send his respects to his virtuous daughter, Miss Alice."

Though this was not a formal marriage proposal, the sole fact of mentioning her separately instead of including her in his general greetings—when he hadn't seen her since she was a little girl—was a way of sounding things out.

Khalil remembered his student Gebrayel as a cunning, resourceful boy, jovial, but too concerned with his appearance, impatient with academic work, and having no great interest in religious matters. Many years had gone by since then, and he had heard various rumors concerning Gebrayel's true situation in Cuba. Like everyone else, Khalil had been told that Botros had gone to Havana to get his brother out of a tight spot. What exactly was that all about? Was it true that Gebrayel had had problems with the law? In what way? For a responsible father, these are questions that had to be clarified before he could consider marrying off his daughter . . .

Before answering the letter from Havana, the preacher opened his heart to Botros, who was very embarrassed by this mark of trust. On the one hand, he had been taught by his own experience not to take his brother's promises at face value. He couldn't very well conceal this from a person like Khalil; he couldn't say to him, "You can give Gebrayel your daughter with complete confidence," when he himself was still smarting from his Cuban misadventure. What if the unfortunate young woman ended up sleeping in an attic as he had? On the other hand, he couldn't possibly betray his own brother by advising the preacher against giving him Alice's hand in marriage.

None of the relatives still alive today know what the two men, both of whom died long ago, said to each other. Anyhow, they would probably have been uncommunicative on a matter like this. The fact is, after his conversation with Botros, Khalil decided to bide his time and not give an affirmative answer. He wrote Gebrayel a courteous, well-written letter, thanking him for his concern regarding the health of his family members, adding that he would like to inquire about his health and business and make sure that everything was now going well.

Gebrayel, whose bookish intelligence didn't match Botros's, but who was more astute in everyday matters, immediately grasped what was whispered in the village, and he decided to retaliate in his own way. Someone else might have made a long list of all his successes, itemized his property, and given details of his revenues. My Cuban great-uncle knew that he was dealing with an austere Presbyterian preacher, and he decided it was preferable to approach things another way. He replied with a rather concise letter in which he merely asserted that he was an honest worker, that he slaved around the clock, and that he would work even harder when he had a family to support. Then he casually mentioned that he had noticed a beautiful Presbyterian church a few steps away from his house.

The preacher liked the tone of the letter and wasn't at all indifferent to this last detail; nor was Alice, who feared ending up in an island with a dense Catholic population. Two or three more letters were exchanged; then Khalil gave his consent. His wife, Sofiya, sailed to Cuba with their daughter a few months later. Gebrayel lodged them in a small apartment, furnished expressly for them, right above his shop, in the center of Havana.

The marriage was performed without pomp, but there were two successive ceremonies, one in the Catholic church in the neighborhood, the other in the Presbyterian church. A short time later, Sofiya returned home, confident about her new son-in-law; she had seen that, though papist, he was hardworking and virtuous. Indeed, Gebrayel devoted all his time to his business; as for Alice, she divided her days between domestic chores and prayer as she waited—but not impatiently—for Heaven to grant her the blessing of a child.

TWENTY-FIVE

Gebrayel and Alice's first child was born in Havana on January 30, 1911. Among the family documents is a luxurious, hand-painted christening announcement, with the picture of a lilac branch and, in the background, a landscape with two sailboats. We learn that the parents held the ceremony on July 16 in their home, at number 5 Egido Street, and that the officiating priest was the "parish priest of the church of Santo Cristo del Buen Viaje." The persons mentioned are the two parents, "Gabriel" and "Alicia"; the godfather, whose name was Fernando Figueredo Socarrás; and the godmother, a certain Carmela Cremate, who was apparently unable to attend, for she was *"representada por la Señorita Rosa Martinez."*

Included with the announcement is a photo of the baby, lying on his stomach, bare bottom, on an embroidered sheet. Cut to fit into an oval frame, it must have been taken on the day of the christening; nothing is written on it except the name of the printer in tiny letters: IMP. CASTRO, HABANA.

I was not particularly surprised that the Presbyterian preacher's daughter had agreed to have her child christened by a Catholic priest. Had she asked her father, this is probably what he would have advised. In his twilight years, Khalil had adopted a moderate attitude on these issues, which he lacked in his youth. In the later documents of his that I own, he almost always signs "Khalil, son of the priest Gerjis," and adds, in small letters, "Servant of the evangelical community." This was an elegant position to take, illustrating his desire for reconciliation and peaceful coexistence, and furthermore it showed tact and cleverness. The Protestant community was a recent, tiny minority where he lived; he had a duty to preach by example and convert only those who came to him eagerly requesting it.

Since his son-in-law Gebrayel was not Protestant, his newborn child wouldn't be either. If the son later expressed a desire to convert to his mother's religion, he would be free to do so. For the time being, let the priest christen him. One of the boy's given names was even Theodoro, in homage to his uncle, the Catholic prelate.

Hence two persuasions were brought together around the crib. Digging a bit deeper, I discovered a third, for one name on the announcement held my attention: "Socarrás." I was certain I had come just recently across the name. Was it when I read up on Cuban history after my mother brought me Gebrayel's letters from Lebanon? Working my way backward, I was pleased to find the following paragraph, which had left a trace in my memory:

On January 28, 1895, José Martí celebrated his forty-second birthday in New York; it was to be his last birthday. The following day, he signed the order for the general uprising that would lead to Cuba's independence. On February 2, the document was given to Fernando Figueredo Socarrás, who rolled it up and inserted it inside a cigar that he placed among four other identical cigars. Then he left for Key West and Cuba. The war of independence began on Febrary 24. In the interval Martí had gone to Santo Domingo to meet Máximo Gómez . . .

When I read this text for the first time, I was primarily interested in the person mentioned last, whose house my great-uncle bought. I already knew the name José Martí, at least as author of the famous "Guantanamera," but I wasn't aware of how revered the poet is by his compatriots, for whom he is the founding father, in a certain sense, of the Cuban nation. On the other hand, I knew nothing whatever about Figueredo Socarrás and the part played by his cigars in the war of independence. How had this person become the godfather of my great-uncle Gebrayel's son?

It seemed incredible, yet I would be lying if I said that I was completely astonished. No, I had my own theory. But to confirm it, I had to immerse myself in some reference books as well as in the family archives. What linked Gebrayel, émigré from Mount Lebanon, and Figueredo Socarrás; the latter and José Martí; and Martí and the Dominican officer Máximo Gómez, commander in chief of the revolutionary forces, was that all four were Freemasons. The membership of three of these men is extremely well documented in the books that recount their careers. As for my great-uncle, whose name never entered the history books, one need only read his letters. Actually, you don't have to read them, you merely have to glance at his envelopes, or the heading of his stationery, to see printed in the left corner, just under the logo of the shop and just above the address, the words *"Distintivos masónicos"*— "Masonic insignia"—which means that he was authorized to supply the different objects—medals, ribbons, aprons, sashes, necklaces, etc.— used in the ceremonies.

All of this squared with the things I had heard whispered in the family. Namely, that my great-uncle Gebrayel was a Freemason, and so was my grandfather. Had the two men influenced each other? And at which point in their lives? I must confess that I can't be certain about this, even if I am slightly less ignorant after having read our archives.

As far as Gebrayel is concerned, I would imagine that he was initiated after his departure for the New World, either in Havana or earlier in New York, and if so, probably by Cuban exiles and Martí supporters. This is just a hypothesis, but it seems much more plausible than my great-uncle's being initiated at eighteen in a village in the Lebanon mountains.

As to my grandfather, I was unsure for a long time and groping in the dark. I could make many assumptions, but none of these constituted proof. For example, the previously quoted letter, written to him shortly after his return from America by the friend with whom he had had a long conversation in Beirut on the terrace of the Star of the Orient:

It was darkest night, and what we were saying had the precise purpose of clearing away the darkness and spreading light; which can only happen if people like you rally together and join forces. So don't let indecision override determination, for you are a free man, and a free man doesn't accept injustice.

I would think it's not irrelevant to point out that the expression "free man," in the singular and particularly in the plural, *al-ahrar*, is commonly used in Arabic as a way of designating *al-massouniyoun al-ahrar*, "the Freemasons" . . .

Let me read on in this letter.

Go down the only path possible, the only one a man like you should take. I am telling you my most sincere feeling because I find it admirable that you are in such a frame of mind, and that you want to remain in this country . . . I hope to get an affirmative answer from you so I can raise a toast in your honor, though I am not in the habit of drinking.

I shall soon send you the book of doctrine I mentioned . . .

This man, whose tone is that of a close but recent friend, was evidently encouraging Botros to join a brotherhood. Given the situation at the time, March 1906—two years before the uprising of the Young Turks—it could only be a secret society, or at least a "discreet" one.

Now let me reread the poem my grandfather wrote when the counterrevolution was crushed and the sultan Abdul Hamid was overthrown.

I salute the era of Rashad, for he will restore what was destroyed in our building.

The symbolism of the destroyed building that has to be restored is typically Masonic. Is this proof? Not really, just one more assumption. All the more so since the poem continues as follows:

I salute Niyazi's and Enver's swords, I salute the brotherhood that
*   unsheathed them,*
I salute free men from all communities . . .

Each time I reread those verses, it reinforced my conviction. I could accept that "the brotherhood" saluted here is the Committee of Union and Progress, or the Young Turks, rather than the Freemasons; however, here again the reference to "free men" sounded to me like an allusion for the initiated.

I made other connections and dissected other parts of sentences. I asked some friends who belonged to the Freemasonry thousands of questions. They patiently filled the enormous gaps in my knowledge concerning its history, ideals, rites, and allegiances, though they were unable to enlighten me regarding my grandfather's career. In the end, I resigned myself to not knowing for sure. To console myself for this absence of proof, I told myself that if Botros, contrary to Gebrayel, had chosen to keep this aspect of his life in semidarkness, there was a reason. As a Levantine, he had to mask his true convictions, both out of fear of the authorities and wariness regarding prevailing opinion—including that of his relatives. Perhaps I should refrain from looking beyond what he wished to reveal.

And then one day, proof arrived. In a letter signed by a friend, a high-ranking Freemason dignitary who had taken my research to heart:

May Heaven grant that the information I send you today be the
information for which you have been waiting for so long! Indeed, in the
archives of the Scottish Lodge No. 908, I just found the following:
*   "Name of candidate: Botros M. M.*
*   Date of Acceptance: April 6, 1907.*
*   Age: forty.*
*   Registration number: 327."*

If the age matches his, then we found it: "Brother Botros" was a member of the Assalam Lodge, which was founded in Beirut in 1905 under the jurisdiction of the Grand Lodge of Scotland. It was one of the most active lodges in the past and to our day.

If I refer to what you told me in your previous letters, namely that your grandfather returned from America in late 1905 or early 1906, and that he lived in Beirut until the autumn of 1907, the dates seem to tally.

This time, yes, all doubt was dispelled. And even though I had formed my view a long time ago, this confirmation gives me the feeling of entering a new phase of intimacy with the man with the forgotten face, despite the generations, and despite the shifting frontier that separates the living from those who lived before us.

TWENTY-SIX

July 24, 1909, the first anniversary of the promulgation of the Ottoman Constitution, was declared Liberty Day and celebrated throughout the empire; it was not unlike the Fête de la Fédération, organized in France one year after the taking of the Bastille on July 14, 1790. Indeed, the similarity doesn't end there, as is clear from the speech Botros delivered on this occasion before the population and authorities of the city where he lived.

After paying tribute to the new sultan and the revolutionary officers, he resorted to his favorite device—the falsely modest preamble:

I would have devoted my speech to explaining the three essential concepts in the motto of our Ottoman Constitution, namely Liberty, Fraternity, Equality, by comparing the true meaning of these words with the way most people interpret them, but the previous speaker did this better than I could have . . . Therefore, so you won't have to listen to the same thing twice, allow me to just tell you about the conversation that took place yesterday evening between an Ottoman and an *ajnabi* . . .

I've reproduced this last word in the original because it calls for clarification. It could be translated as "foreigner," provided its special connotation is kept in mind. *Ajnabi*, or the feminine *ajnabieh*, usually refers to a "European" person in the ethnic sense of the term. In the Levant, a Moroccan, Iranian, or Greek will never be called an *ajnabi*; nationals from these culturally close countries are usually referred to by the name of their specific country. An *ajnabi* is someone who comes from more distant lands—Europe, America, or, more rarely, the Far East. For my grandfather and his audience, the word probably summoned a Frenchman, a Briton, a German, or an American. I could therefore have translated it as "European" or "westerner," instead of "foreigner." After hesitating, I finally opted for "foreigner," so that the term would not be rendered explicit improperly, for it isn't explicit in the culture of the old country.

That said, the explanation I just provided is largely superfluous, inasmuch as the "Foreigner" and the "Ottoman" in this fictitious conversation were actually one and the same person—my grandfather himself, who must have felt that his comments would go down better if he attributed them to two imaginary interlocutors.

THE FOREIGNER: I notice that your public spaces are decked with flags, and the inhabitants look joyful . . .

THE OTTOMAN: That's because tomorrow is a big national holiday, called Liberty Day. We are going to assemble; there will be speeches and articles in the newspapers, just like in France or America, and in other free countries on such occasions.

THE FOREIGNER: The nations you mentioned do indeed organize holidays to celebrate the accomplishments they are proud of. As for you, could you tell me what accomplishments you're celebrating?

THE OTTOMAN: We're celebrating the proclamation of our constitution, which advocates liberty, fraternity, and equality. Isn't this an accomplishment we can be proud of?

THE FOREIGNER: Liberty certainly warrants a holiday. But I don't quite understand what you mean by "proclamation." If you're celebrating the publication of a text, I happen to know that it was published about thirty years ago, and I don't see the point of this belated celebration. And if you're celebrating the actual implementation of the constitution, the actual implementation of the principles of liberty, fraternity, and equality, in other words the fact that every citizen really enjoys the rights to which he is entitled, well, it is my duty—from having frequented various administrations, and various civil, religious, and other institutions—to tell you that these principles are completely disregarded and that most of your leaders can't even imagine that they might one day be applied. From that point of view, I think it's a bit early to be celebrating . . .

THE OTTOMAN (indignant): Are you making fun of our great men? Of our constitutional sultan? Of Niyazi and Enver? Are you one of those defeatists?

THE FOREIGNER: Calm down, dear friend, and try to understand me. I am speaking to you in your own language, and I am not a defeatist. And if I weren't the most sincere of free men, I would not have spoken to you so frankly. I know a thousand things that you don't know about the qualities of your sultan and some of your great men. Your sovereign is a just and virtuous man, and none of our kings is better than he. As for Niyazi and Enver, they are courageous heroes. You can be sure that we at home honor men of that caliber more than you do here. And above all, don't think that I am trying to warn you against the constitutional system of government; in my opinion there can be no other. However, to have meaning, the constitution must be imprinted in the mores, not just on paper. What I mean by this is that people must learn to behave like citizens; everyone should enjoy his rights and attend to his occupations without worry. Is that the case? The fact is that your mores are still those of your ancestors—Arabs in the age of ignorance, who practiced insult and aggression and banded together in clans in order to attack and plunder one another. Even those among you who claim to be civilized, notables and leaders, have no qualms about using barefaced lies and calumny to achieve their ends. They tell you that black is white and white is black, that a lion is a fox and a fox is a lion, while you, you follow them blindly and pray Heaven to grant them victory. Well, be aware that if you don't change your behavior and don't get rid of these leaders very soon, your constitutional government will become corrupt. Yet this is the last government you can still test; you won't have any other. You will fall into foreign hands and be treated like slaves. Come out of the pride of ignorance, stop scorning candor and truth, stop supporting those who lead you to your ruin, and put an end to those celebrations and festivities that make no sense!

The Ottoman bowed his head and became pensive, expressions of joy vanished from his brow, and tears began to flow from his eyes. He looked around him, searching for someone who could console him. Then he broke into these verses . . .

The masks of the two interlocutors—which had become increasingly transparent as the dialogue progressed—have just fallen. The "Foreigner," who sometimes described himself as "the most sincere of free men," now starts talking the way Botros talked a year earlier, while the "Ottoman" is about to recite a poem written by the same Botros and dealing with the same themes.

It is in order to celebrate their victories that the nations of the earth
  organize holidays, but our holidays are a mere mockery.
Tell me, what is there to celebrate? What rich province have we conquered?
  In what way have we improved the lives of our countrymen?
One sultan has abdicated, another has mounted the throne, but power is still
  exercised in the same way.
We are a fickle nation, blown this way and that by the winds of
  passions . . .

TWENTY-SEVEN

These words, spoken in public one year after the Young Turks' rebellion and scarcely three months after Abdul Hamid's downfall, weren't just the result of a fit of bad temper and impatience. Though in the dialogue both the Ottoman and the Foreigner pretended to defend the new sultan and the revolutionary officers, the mere fact of speaking about these leaders in a cavalier manner was significant. Botros was feeling a growing disappointment. He was more and more aggrieved, and he took advantage of the newly acquired freedom of expression to let it be known.

What exasperated him, first of all, was that the administration's way of running things and the behavior of the local civil servants, whether governors of provinces or the lowest-ranking clerks, were still those of the old regime. But one had to be very naive to expect these things to change overnight on the mere publication of a decree.

Another thing that distressed him, even if he couldn't be explicit about it, was that he was beginning to realize that nothing had been settled, or would be, concerning what he felt was the most crucial issue.

That issue was the "empire's minority groups." I've borrowed this term from the history books that deal with the problems of the Orient, but it falls short of explaining the most important thing. For defining the rights of minorities is not what is most important. As soon as one formulates the issue that way, one enters into the hateful logic of tolerance—that is, of protection bestowed condescendingly by the conquerors on the conquered. Botros didn't want to be tolerated; nor do I, his grandson. I demand that my prerogatives as a citizen be fully recognized without my having to disown the many affiliations I possess. This is my unalienable right, and I turn away haughtily from societies that deprive me of it.

What Botros was interested in—but the word "interested" is too weak. I really should say: what governed all his emotions, all his thoughts, and all his actions was knowing whether he, a member of a minority group, a Christian whose mother tongue was Arabic, could have the status of a full-fledged citizen in a modernized Ottoman Empire and not have to pay for his birth throughout his life.

He had good reason to believe that the revolution of the Young Turks was moving precisely in that direction. All the minorities who had applauded the movement from its inception and sometimes actively contributed to it, these "free men from all communities," were bound to have the same hopes as he.

But before long, there were some unsettling events. For instance, general elections were held that should have heralded an era of liberty and democracy, but they were marked instead by manipulation and rigging: all means were justified to ensure the election of the largest number of representatives supporting the revolutionary officers and their Committee of Union and Progress. These members of parliament came from all the different nations in the empire, but an alarming pattern became apparent: with every vote, the "unionists" divided into two clans, Turks and non-Turks.

The same split emerged within the ruling body. The minorities, "non-natives" as well as Freemasons, were gradually removed from power and supplanted by an ultranationalist group, led by Enver Pasha. He dreamed of a new Turkish empire that would extend from the Adriatic to the borders of China—a single nation, with one language and one leader. It was hard to believe that this was the same Enver who had inspired a wave of enthusiasm throughout the country when he addressed the crowd from the balcony of the Olympia Palace in Salonika and proclaimed that henceforth there would be no more Jews, Greeks, Bulgarians, Romanians, and Serbs in the empire, "for all of us are brothers under the same blue sky, all of us taking pride in being Ottomans."

Those who had formerly applauded his inspired oratory wondered now if they hadn't just heard what they wanted to hear. They began to find it significant that Enver had said there would be no more Greeks, Serbs, Bulgarians, Muslims, Jews . . . but among these groups he hadn't included Turks. And they began to wonder whether Enver didn't have a hidden agenda, whether equality and fraternity weren't just pretexts for revoking the specific rights enjoyed by the different peoples of the empire up until then.

There had obviously been a grave misunderstanding, and it was to weigh heavily on my grandfather's destiny, as well as on the destiny of the empire that was his birthplace. Botros was a patriot, whereas the officer whose sword he had hailed so bombastically at the dawn of the revolution was a nationalist. All too often we tend to equate the two attitudes, with the assumption that nationalism is an acute form of patriotism. In those days—and in other eras as well—this could not have been further from the truth: nationalism was the exact opposite of patriotism. Patriots dreamed of an empire where diverse groups could coexist—groups speaking different languages and professing different beliefs, but united by a common desire to build a large modern homeland. They hoped to instill a subtle Levantine wisdom into the principles advocated by the West. As for the nationalists, when they belonged to an ethnic majority they dreamed of total domination, and of separatism when they belonged to a minority. The wretched Orient of our day is the monster born of the two dreams combined.

At this late date, I deserve no credit in making these assertions. History has made me a witness to so many eloquent events. But in my grandfather's day, the hopes raised by the rebel officers were growing slimmer month after month and were soon swept away. Enver pushed his country to enter the First World War on the side of the Germans and Austrians, for he nourished the dream that a Russian defeat would enable Turkey to acquire the Russian possessions in the Caucasus and in the Turkish-speaking provinces of Central Asia, commonly known as Turkistan. It was, however, the Ottoman Empire itself that was defeated and dismantled. The indomitable officer then went and offered his services to Lenin, before turning against the Red Army and dying under fire near Bukhara in 1922 at the age of forty-one.

By then my grandfather was no longer interested in this man. I don't even know if he heard about his death. It wasn't much of a topic of conversation in the Mountains in those days. Enver's death in combat, which might have had an epic aura for the peoples of the Orient a few years earlier, had become insignificant. The memory of the glorious rebels of 1908 had been eclipsed by the emergence of another Turkish officer, who had played only a minor role in the events of the empire up to then: Kemal Atatürk.

Botros would be filled with enthusiasm for him too, impassioned even, beyond reason. He not only wrote a poem hailing his sword but also committed a folly in his honor—one more folly, but one that was unforgettable. I shall return to it in due course.

In 1909, with rising tensions in all the provinces and increasing numbers of unpleasant incidents, there was an Ottoman notable who decided, in a fit of rage, to leave Istanbul forever.

He was an Ottoman judge, originally from Sidon, in the south of present-day Lebanon, but his Maronite Christian family had been living on the banks of the Bosporus for many years. One summer Sunday, at the end of the traditional family meal, he quietly ordered his wife and thirteen children to pack all their belongings in trunks. He had just purchased tickets for the family and the domestic help, and they were to board the next ship bound for Alexandria.

The judge's first name was Iskandar; his youngest daughter, Virginie, was seven years old at the time of the exodus. She was born in Istanbul and spoke only Turkish. Later, in Egypt, she learned Arabic and French, but Turkish always remained the language dear to her heart. Her family lived in the delta of the Nile for many years. It was there that, at seventeen, Virginie married an émigré from the Lebanon Mountains whose name was Amin. And it was there that she gave birth to her first daughter—my mother.

My maternal grandmother died of cancer at fifty-four and was buried next to her husband in a Cairo cemetery. I barely knew her; I have only a vague memory of having once caught a glimpse of her.

She never taught her children a word of Turkish, and she told them very little about the sea journey and the exodus. But she sometimes described to them the family house in Istanbul, until she fell silent with a lump in her throat. I have inherited both the need to conceal and the nostalgia. Of Turkish, which so many of my ancestors spoke with pride, I know only the words that have survived in Lebanese dialect. However, I did grow up daydreaming about "our" house in Istanbul. I visualized it as a white-columned palace, which it probably wasn't, and for many years I avoided going to the former capital of the empire lest the mirage vanish into thin air. When I went there, late in life, I spent my first days looking for the traces of my ancestors and the address of "our" house in telephone directories dating from the beginning of the century. Then I decided to give up my obsession and finally walked around the city with the eyes of an adult.

My grandmother said very little about her father's reasons for going into exile, and her children avoided quizzing her, for they sensed that every word on this subject was a torment. I sometimes think that if she hadn't died so young, she might have told me the reasons. But I'm not sure. After all, my other grandmother lived to the age of ninety-one without losing her memory or an ounce of good judgment, yet there are a thousand questions I didn't find time to ask her. It's easy to blame death. But in this instance, as in many others, when I really tried to find out, I did. The truth is rarely buried; it is merely lying in wait behind veils of modesty, pain, or indifference; the one necessary prerequisite is a passionate desire to lift the veils.

In my case, I should have had the desire at a much earlier age, when I was still wearing short pants. A cousin from that side of the family had come to the village one summer day to visit my parents. I had never seen him before, and I never saw him again. He was a physician in a working-class suburb of Beirut, an affable, affectionate, courteous, diffident man. I can still see him as I did then, sitting in the drawing room, chatting with my father. Suddenly, in the middle of a sentence, the visitor had a brief but disturbing trembling fit, as if he were under the effect of a violent electric shock. My parents, who were apparently used to this tic, tried to behave as though they hadn't noticed anything. As for me, I was fascinated; I couldn't take my eyes off him; I stared at his chin and hands, waiting for the next spasm. They occurred, without fail, every two or three minutes.

When the cousin left, my mother explained that when he was a child in Turkey, "in the days of the massacres," a soldier had grabbed him by the hair, put a knife to his neck, and nearly slit his throat. Fortunately, an Ottoman officer happened on the scene and recognized him. He yelled, "Let go of him, you scoundrel! He's the son of the doctor!" The killer threw down his knife and ran away. Indeed, the cousin's father had been a physician too, and he had practiced with dedication in a working-class district, often without charging a penny. The boy was saved, but the fear he experienced that day had lasting aftereffects. In 1909, when the tragic incident occurred, he was six years old. He must have been fifty years older on the sole occasion when he visited my parents, but his body never forgot.

The survivor was my grandmother's nephew, though he was nearly her age, as he was the oldest son of her older sister. This is an important detail; he was the first son of the new generation, and his grandfather, the judge, idolized him as any typical Levantine grandfather would. Because of this child, and the tragedy that had been barely avoided, my great-grandfather decided to leave Istanbul with his entire family. The blade of hate at his grandson's throat was a warning signal; he was not going to act as though he hadn't heard it.

I've been told that many people were alarmed at the time to see a prominent person like my grandfather—an influential, wealthy, and respected magistrate—leave so hastily. Many other members of the Maronite community began to wonder if they shouldn't leave before it was too late. This is just one example, among many, of the convulsions undermining the dying empire.

In the last few years I have learned some interesting things about my great-grandfather from Istanbul, whose itinerary determined my own. This whetted my appetite but didn't satisfy it—perhaps one day I shall find bits and pieces of archives. I learned, for instance, that he had lost his eyesight and used to sit in court with an assistant by his side—usually one of his eight sons—who read him the documents presented to him and whispered in his ear to describe a plaintiff or a gesture.

The theatrical aspect of this situation must have appealed to him; though he was a judge, he had grown up near the footlights. His family had founded a well-known theater troupe, which played a pioneering role in several countries of the empire. His uncles, Maroun and Nicolas, were the first to give performances of Molière and Racine, whose works were translated by their good offices, and their sister Warda had been the most celebrated actress of her day. As a child, the future judge occasionally accompanied them on their tours.

One can't help noticing that the ease with which he decided to get up and go with his entire family—leaving behind his seat on the court, his house, and his status—and start a new life in Egypt is the kind of reflex more easily associated with a troupe of actors than with a bourgeois dynasty.

Apparently there was something of the traveling performer in my great-grandfather's soul, and it took over at the decisive moment.

TWENTY-EIGHT

To return to Botros and how he was affected by the Ottoman Empire's terminal phase, I feel I should make it clear that though his disillusionment could be partially explained by political events, there were also more personal reasons behind it.

Now that I've written this and reread it, I have to admit that when it comes to disillusionment, I find it impossible to separate the political from the personal. This is true for my grandfather, and it is true for Gebrayel and so many of their contemporaries. All those who emigrated, all those who rebelled, and even all those who dreamed of a more equitable world, were chiefly motivated by the fact that they couldn't fit into the social and political system that governed their mother country. Then, assuredly, there was a contributing individual factor that determined each person's decision, whether one brother left, for example, while another stayed behind.

In Botros's case, the fact of not leaving the country, of

wanting to believe in its future, was due as much to his convictions as to his family situation and his temperament—for he was insubordinate, quick-tempered, impatient, indecisive, and riddled with scruples. His was a risky choice, and he always knew it. He had constant doubts about the emergence of this new Orient he longed for, as well as constant doubts about his chosen profession. He usually hesitated to act on his doubts, but occasionally he did.

Thus, in July 1909, when he gave his speech involving the disillusioned dialogue between the Ottoman and the Foreigner, he had just made an important decision: once again he was going to resign from the Oriental Secondary School and give up teaching. It seems a disagreement with the religious men running the school was one reason for his decision, but he was also motivated by a thorough reexamination of what direction he wanted his life to take in the future.

This is clear from the following letter, written one year later, in June 1910, to his friend and brother-in-law, Dr. Shukri, who was in Cairo at the time, still in the British army's medical corps.

> *While I was thinking about you and your little family, and what you must be enduring in these days of great Egyptian heat, your finely phrased letter was delivered to me; it reassured me and made me regret that we weren't all together . . .*
>
> *You are a thousand times right to be furious against your parents for not writing to you. But put your mind at rest, the only reason you haven't heard from them is that they are completely absorbed by their preoccupations with the sacrosanct silkworm. I went to see them recently, in the village; you have no reason to worry, they are all feeling fine; we feasted together and drank to your health.*

Before broaching the subject of the school, Botros gave news, as he often did in his letters, of some members of the family. Usually I disregard this, but this time I wanted to keep the passage, for a specific reason.

> *As for our dear Theodoros, he was transferred from the Baalbek monastery, where he was an assistant, to the Mar Youhanna monastery, where he became the superior. Before me is a letter from him that contains*

only good news; I plan to reply later, and I shall send him your regards . . .
The émigrés in our two families are well, too, thank God, but I have no
recent news.

In a certain sense Theodoros was the leader of the Catholics in the family, while Shukri was a fierce "anti-papist" Protestant, much more so than his father, the preacher. Apparently, in this letter—and in several others—Botros was trying to be the conciliator, or at least appease the religious quarrels that threatened his family.

After this preamble, he gets to the main point:

As far as what you heard concerning my return to the Oriental Secondary
School, be aware that this is false. They did indeed contact me again,
through various intermediaries, to offer me a raise, but I turned down their
offer and explained to them that if I decided to give up teaching at the
beginning of last year, I certainly wasn't going to start again this year. I
even showed them that I had received various offers from Beirut, which I
also turned down, because I intended to devote myself to my own business.
It is true, believe me, I have nothing against this particular school. In fact,
my relations with the heads of the Oriental Secondary School have
improved; we visit one another regularly, and they constantly ask my advice
on various matters. It seems that the students and parents ask for me, but
I don't want to become tied to that institution again, or to any other.
Actually, I've had more than my fill of work in schools, at least the way
things are done at the moment. And I think back with bitterness on all
those years I lost between notebooks and inkwells in a country of futility
and superficiality! (My pen got carried away, dear brother, so forgive me,
and forget what I just said) . . .

Botros says that he intends to devote himself to his own business— but what business? The impression one gets from the archives is that he was turning many projects over in his mind; they pop up in his letters, then vanish immediately without leaving a trace. In the course of my reading, I see that he thought of starting a newspaper; of buying shares in a bookstore; of managing a large Beirut hotel, the Hotel of America; and of going into an import-export business with friends. At the same time, he was negotiating with a printer for the publication of his various writings—a dictionary of proverbs, a history of ancient languages, collected poems, his play titled *The Aftereffects of Vanity*.

None of these projects was brought to fruition, but there was one that he did try to launch. My grandfather never mentions it himself, at least not in the letters that have been preserved, and it is only thanks to the indiscretions of his correspondents that I was able to figure out what it was about. Take, for example, this bit of sentence in a letter from Theodoros:

> *You wrote in your last letter that you had just bought twenty thousand square pics,* ★ *but you didn't tell me where this plot of land is located, or what you plan to do with it, whether it has buildings on it or not, and if you intend to build on it yourself . . . Plus, you'd like me to intercede with our brothers and ask them to contribute to this purchase! Don't you know that they've had a bad crop, have no ready cash at all, and are hardly able to make ends meet?*

Then a bit further on:

> *You would really like your brothers to leave the village and go settle in Zahlé with you? Allow me to tell you that I think this would be difficult, if not impossible. You say you should all be together. Fine, but wouldn't it be easier for you, who is alone, to go live close to them, rather than tear all of them away from their village? In spite of this, I promise I'll discuss it with them when I see them . . .*

What purpose could this plot of land possibly serve? And why did Botros want his brothers to give everything up and come work with him? It was a cousin's ironic remark that first gave me a hint of his plan:

> *I've learned from the newspapers that women are beginning to smoke too. It seems that most of them like this intoxicating and soothing ingestion. This*

★One "pic" is equal to 68 centimeters.

*can only contribute to your prosperity. I hope you earn even more money
with their cigarettes than with the men's!*

These lines were written in 1912. Several months later, Botros received another letter on the same subject, this time from Gebrayel.
There was no irony in its tone, but no indulgence either. It is one of the
three letters my mother brought back to Paris from Lebanon, when I
first started my research and still knew very little about my grandfather and almost nothing about his Cuban brother. I had already seen
the passage below, but the handwriting was not very legible, so I didn't
spend time on it. I returned to it only later, after I had been able to
piece together the biographies of my relatives. And this was only after
reading the cousin's baffling taunts, for his letter was less damaged.

But let me return to the letter from Havana. It is dated May 19,
1912. Gebrayel writes, on the first page:

How happy I am to hear that you succeeded in growing tobacco . . .

So that was it! Botros had come up with the idea of growing tobacco, not far from Zahlé, in the rich Bekáa plain, and he had bought a
hectare of fertile agricultural land to get the experiment under way. It's
easy to guess how this idea insinuated itself in my future grandfather's
mind. He had marveled at the success of this crop in Cuba. This explains why he wanted to visit a cigarette factory during his stay in New
York and had tried his hand at inventing advertising slogans for the
Parsons trademark. Afterward, he wondered why the same thing
couldn't be done "at home"—a question that comes up constantly in
his writing, like a leitmotif and an act of faith. Whether it was a matter of politics, pedagogy, or industry, he always worked on the assumption that if something succeeded in the West, it could succeed in the
Orient, all men being fundamentally the same. If we put in the required effort and judiciously applied tried-and-true methods, why
couldn't we succeed where others had succeeded?

Indeed, why couldn't we reproduce the Havana miracle at home?
Wasn't the soil here just as good? Gebrayel's answer to him will be fairly
cruel.

TWENTY-NINE

How happy I am to hear that you succeeded in growing tobacco, but I'm sad when I think of the time and effort you spent in a land that won't pay back the price of your sweat or give you any outlet for your production. If only this same effort had been made in a tobacco-growing country like Cuba or Egypt! Yes, of course, in these countries you don't inhale the smell of the homeland or the bracing air of Lebanon, but the material compensations and the ease of communications make you forget your fatigue because here you obtain infinitely more than what our dear mother country can give you, especially in its present state . . .

Indeed, the émigré brother's words are pure common sense: the quality of the soil and its suitability for growing tobacco aren't the only factors. Other important considerations include prospects for export, whether the authorities in the country provide opportunities or not, and, above all, "the general state of the country," a recurrent expression everywhere in the family archives, so much so that it takes on an obsessive and violent overtone, becoming more corrosive than the words "decline," "arbitrary," "tyranny," "darkness," "rottenness," or "decay." Indeed, it is these neutral words, these plain authoritative assessments, that are most revealing: "the general state," "the present situation," "the circumstances everyone is aware of . . ." The sentence is cut off, for a few seconds of silent mourning, and after a sigh, one goes on to the next paragraph.

These disillusioned words are found in both Botros's and Gebrayel's writings. But of course the two brothers no longer experienced their disillusionment the same way. One brother still lived in this Orient with no prospects, while the other had turned his back on it once and for all. Admittedly, the émigré's letters still contained a few nostalgic allusions to his country; he missed breathing its air and the family reunions, but he never dwelled on these, for his choice had been made. His life would be in Cuba and nowhere else.

This island, where we were given our lucky opportunity, is progressing, and one day it will become one of the most important places on earth, materially, politically, and morally.

These words date from 1912 as well. I think that more letters were exchanged between the two brothers that year than at any other time in their lives. Gebrayel was making a last attempt to convince Botros to join him in Havana. And it would seem that my future grandfather was no longer hostile to the idea. Otherwise, why would the émigré have made the following remark:

Oh, if only the Lord would inspire you to get on a boat even before receiving the letter I am writing to you!

This appeal came after a very long period of silence. I have reason to believe that relations between Gebrayel and Botros had cooled after their friction in Cuba in 1904. I even think they stopped writing to each other. They resumed their exchanges only eight years later.

As I recently explained in a letter to our brother Theodoros, my business has really become much too large for me; there is now room for others . . .

If the émigré felt the need to confide in Botros about this, it meant that they hadn't been very much in touch in the intervening years. I assume they needed time to recover from their bad mutual experience. But it would also seem that for a time, Gebrayel had wanted to conceal his real situation from those who were near and dear to them. What were his reasons? I don't know for sure, though frankly, I can venture a guess from having known many other émigrés, both in our family and from other parts of the Mountains. The myth of the villager who sails off with no baggage except two loaves of bread and six olives and ends up the richest man in Mexico ten years later is a story I've heard a thousand times, in many a bedazzled variant. Such stories are a constant source of pressure on those who emigrate and often weigh heavily on them. They may be living in the remotest part of the Sahel or the Amazon, but they never escape the gaze of the relatives they left behind, for everyone in the family keeps a watchful, judgmental eye on them. And when they have a touch of pride—a widespread commodity among my countrymen—they don't dare return home without having proved their worth, or else they return just to go into hiding and die. In fact, a great many of them prefer to die in a distant land rather than return defeated.

As for Gebrayel, who had left against his family's will, had probably never made peace with his father, and had clashed with his brother when he came over, it was imperative that he have an impressive success before facing his relatives again. He attained this objective in around 1909, about ten years after establishing his business enterprise, La Verdad. That's when he decided to reestablish contact with the village and request Khalil's daughter in marriage. At that point, my great-uncle could no longer conceal things indefinitely. Though he did do so for a while, as the story I heard from three people in the family shows.

On the day after his marriage, Gebrayel moved Alice into a modest apartment above his shop, where she was expected to do most of the housework herself. Several months later, looking contrite, he came and asked her whether she was disappointed by the life he was making her lead. She looked at him, baffled by the question.

"Why would I be disappointed? We're in good health, and we aren't going hungry!"

"Don't you wish you had more? A bigger house? Someone to help you? A car?"

The preacher's daughter replied with complete equanimity, "I don't wish for more than what Heaven will grant us."

"Well, Heaven has granted us more!"

It was then that Gebrayel revealed to her that he was wealthy, that they could afford to live like a king and queen. He also told her that he was having a splendid residence built in the best neighborhood in Havana, and soon they would be moving into it.

THIRTY

Apparently, my Cuban great-uncle had a sense of drama. Indeed, at this point in his life, his whole way of presenting himself changed, as did the appearance of his envelopes. Until then, prior to April 1912 to be precise, his envelopes were plain, with no more than his name printed discreetly in a lower corner. Thereafter the print was like a fireworks display: the name "Gabriel" was splashed all over it in bold letters, with a long description of his activities—"Importer and representative in silk fabrics, hardware, cutlery, jewelry, and all novelties"—and a list of the foreign trademarks for which he was an authorized dealer: Kremenz, The Arlington Co., La Legal . . . Surrounding the printed matter was a profusion of drawings representing, among other things, the La Verdad shopwindow and its interior, the inkwells, jewelry, scissors, and razors of his own manufacture, engraved with his name, not to mention the globe struck with his initials, or the inscription *"Distintivos masónicos."*

Perhaps this sudden display was also tied to the fact that he hoped once again to convince his brother Botros to come and join him. His letters on this subject were passionate and insistent.

> *There is an urgent need here for a wise and competent man like you, who could help me run this enterprise and trim it as one trims a tree that has grown too fast. Yes, we urgently need a man endowed with a piercing gaze who could clearly see which branches are the best, and make them grow, and which are least useful, and should be cut back.*
>
> *I suppose some people will wonder why I don't do this work myself, since I am right here, and it is my area. I'll answer that I am swallowed up by this work every hour, every minute, to the point where the tiniest detail takes on enormous proportions for me and I'm no longer able to see things in perspective, as a critical observer might, especially one with the wisdom of a man like you.*

Upon reflection, I think it is quite possible that Theodoros acted as an intermediary between the two brothers. He may have written to Gebrayel: "Botros gave up teaching; he has embarked on a project of tobacco crops and is in danger of squandering his own money and that of the entire family; perhaps you should convince him to come work with you . . ." This scenario cannot be excluded, particularly since it is in keeping with the priest's ways. I have another instance in mind, which I shall mention in due course . . .

That said, it is also perfectly plausible that Gebrayel was acting on his own initiative, because he did have a genuine and urgent need for help.

> *Unless you come, I shall have to reconsider my activity, because if things continue at this pace, my health will be ruined, without a doubt. This has been going on for years, and I honestly can't bear it anymore. If, unfortunately, you were to choose not to come, I would have no choice but to give up part of my work . . . I would concentrate on a small number of sectors, I would remain in charge of the factories for which I am the representative, and the products registered in my name, and leave the rest to other people, under some kind of arrangement—partnership, public*

company, or something . . . I would have a smaller income, but I would be able to rest a little, and I would have more time to devote to God and to people, especially my family, and to myself as well, for all the health problems I've had of late come from this constant pressure on me, these worries that continually accumulate, and this expenditure of energy that is exhausting me. Of course, I have people to help me. I have four in the office, four in the warehouse, four who travel around the country, three at home, plus those who handle the customs, many intermediaries, and people who supervise the factories. But you know me, I have to check everyone's work myself. Believe it or not, I have to write an average of twenty-five letters a day, as well as dozens of invoices, orders, etc. etc. I am simultaneously boss, secretary, employee, overseer, arbitrator, and if I hadn't become accustomed to this ages ago, my brain would have disintegrated in half a day.

This is what drives me to request the help of a man who can share this burden and guide me with wisdom toward the best solution. Then, if this man feels that what we are doing is acceptable, he will share the profits with me; and if he feels that some things have to be improved, he will help me do so, and this will benefit everyone.

You should know that the work I expect of you will open a door for all our relatives, particularly since the present situation makes it clear that emigration has become inevitable for them . . .

The full array of arguments is there: rational analysis, emotional blackmail, and financial advantages. Above all, Gebrayel tries to dispel Botros's usual scruples: you won't be doing this just for your good, he says in essence, but for the good of all our relatives, who have no prospects in our country of origin but do here in Cuba!

These arguments were bound to have a persuasive effect on my grandfather. But though he gave the Havana option serious thought, he preferred another alternative. For instance, he would have wanted his brother to open a large branch of his store in Beirut, which he and a few partners could have managed. The family business would then have had two large branches, one in the Levant, headed by Botros, the other across the Atlantic, headed by Gebrayel. A lovely idea, but it didn't at all correspond to the latter's plans, and he retorted:

I'm not seeking to extend my activities even more; what I need is help, help in what I am already doing here, in Cuba!

Another thing Botros would have liked was for his brother to buy up his plots of land in Lebanon so that he would have capital and could become his partner. Gebrayel's answer:

What would be the point of my buying plots of land at home when I am here and will remain here? That said, I might have done it anyhow, just so as not to turn you down, if I hadn't just acquired the Máximo Gómez house. Now, I'm sorry, I can't!

What Gebrayel didn't seem to understand was that Botros no longer wanted to work for someone else. He had congratulated Gebrayel for "escaping the salaried condition," and he longed to escape it as well. He didn't want to be answerable to a headmaster anymore, or to the manager of a business, and certainly not to his younger brother. He didn't want to be his employee or be indebted to him. If he could sell Gebrayel his plots of land, he would at least have the feeling of contributing and not just receiving; he would invest his money in a business and be one of the partners; and if he didn't have enough capital, he would bring in friends as other partners, so he wouldn't find himself in an inferior position.

Gebrayel, who was usually very considerate of his brother's hypersensitivity, and flattered him, praised him, and reassured him constantly, failed to gauge, this time, how important this matter had become for him. Naïvely, he made the following offer:

From the time you leave Beirut, to your arrival in Havana, I shall pay you a monthly salary of thirty English pounds; thereafter, your salary will be fifteen pounds a month, since you'll live in my house (thank God we now have a house where we'll be able to live together like all respectable people instead of sleeping in an attic as we did before) . . .

This was a faux pas! Precisely the thing that he shouldn't have said. Gebrayel thought he was eliminating the last material obstacles to his brother's arrival, but he had overlooked the foremost obstacle, his brother's desire for independence and his extreme touchiness on this point.

I wouldn't go so far as to say that it was blunders like these that ultimately dissuaded my grandfather from leaving for Cuba. Throughout their correspondence, it seems to me, Botros was more hesitant than his brother wished to believe. Indeed, even suspicious, as can be seen from this enigmatic passage in Gebrayel's letter:

My trust in you, in your devotion to work and to the family, has always been great and never stops growing from day to day, and in my mind there isn't the shadow of a doubt as far as this goes. This is why I'm very surprised by the allusions in what you wrote to the fact that some members of the family don't trust you. Tell me, who are you referring to? Are you thinking of me, by any chance? If so, let me tell you, dear sir, that if doubt has crept into your mind on this subject, it is the fruit of your imagination, or the fruit of a misunderstanding. And if you have someone else in mind, I can only advise you to exercise your usual magnanimity and spirit of forgiveness toward that person.

The tone remained polite, diplomatic even, as was usually the case in our family correspondence. But it is clear that at this point, regardless of what Gebrayel says, there was a serious lack of trust between the two brothers. Botros must have sensed that Gebrayel and Theodoros were consulting each other behind his back on the best way of finding a suitable occupation for him and persuading him to give up the shaky projects he had embarked on.

I find it very understandable that my future grandfather was sensitive and touchy at this stage in his life, particularly in his exchanges with two younger brothers, both of whom had "made it," each in his own area: the priest had become the superior of his convent, and the businessman had amassed a fortune. As for Botros, he had yet to "make it" in any field.

Indeed, while he was pursuing these long-distance negotiations, he never stopped asking himself what direction his life should take next, his feelings of anxiety being all the more acute in that he wasn't twenty or thirty anymore, but over forty-four. It wouldn't have been easy for him to leave his country and adapt to another society and another way of life. To give up his work and start out in a completely different profession, from the bottom rung, like an apprentice. And it couldn't have been easy for him to confront the fact that he didn't have a home of his own, didn't have a wife or children, while his youngest brothers and sisters were all married.

He had probably seriously considered leaving for Cuba in the year 1912. I don't have his letters. If he made copies, they are lost. The only letters I have are those of his brother, and they suggest that at one time his departure was taken for granted and imminent. But I am not surprised that ultimately Botros decided not to go. If he hadn't been able to bear emigration when he was younger, how could he put up with it now? Moreover, his departure would have seemed like a defeat, a disavowal or betrayal of all the people he had constantly lectured on the obligation to stay and contribute to progress at home. He could never have accepted losing face in this way.

In the end, he didn't leave. He informed his brother of his decision at the end of that summer. Gebrayel was disappointed and remained so all his life, but he had no choice but to resign himself to this. In any case, it was too late for the two brothers. Their paths had diverged irreversibly for too long, and blood ties alone had kept their dialogue alive, a dialogue devoid of true complicity. Though they still shared the same ideals, from then on, each brother would remain on his own shore and would walk down his own road, at his own pace, to his own demise.

Wars and
Battles

THIRTY-ONE

As it turned out, 1912 was one of the most decisive years in Botros's life, and this had nothing to do with Cuba. As I write, I realize that I
am presenting a somewhat biased view of my grandfather's biography. But I find it difficult to be coldly objective in relating the encounters that brought me into the
world, without which this narrative would have no raison
d'être. And from my point of view, 1912 was the year of
a crucial meeting.

While he was still discussing with his brother the ap-
propriateness of a second trip to Havana—plagued, as he
so often was, by scruples and indecisiveness—Botros had
a flash of inspiration. He went to see Khalil and solemnly
announced that he had come to ask his daughter's hand
in marriage.

The daughter in question was Nazeera, the youngest.
During a recent family reunion my grandfather had had
the opportunity to exchange a few words with her and

had been struck by her insight, determination, and serene beauty. During the following days and nights he frequently found himself tenderly recalling her penetrating gaze and soothing voice. Initially, he didn't want to acknowledge that the young girl was becoming important to him. But as the days went by, a certainty began to take root in his mind—not unlike the one Tannous, his father, had once felt about Soussène: the certainty that he could no longer do without her; he wanted her as a wife. To Botros, this must even have seemed like his last hope. For there he was, constantly wondering what career to engage in next, deciding obstinately to remain in the mother country though he had lost all faith in its future, discussing expatriation once again though he lacked the courage for it. Indeed, he had lost his way, and now, lo and behold, his path was suddenly lit up. The calamitous year was going to be the year of happiness. The more he thought about it, the more this union seemed like a lifesaving miracle.

Moreover, a rational miracle, which seemed in harmony with the natural order of things. When my future grandfather made his request to his former teacher, he didn't doubt for a moment his response. Hadn't there already been two marriages between Tannous's children and Khalil's? Gebrayel and Alice, most recently, and before that, Yamna and Shukri. In fact, Nazeera's older brother Shukri had been one of Botros's best friends for a long time. He was convinced that the preacher would welcome him with open arms, for he had been his most brilliant disciple, whose opinion he had solicited before consenting to Alice's marriage.

But that's not the way things turned out. Khalil reacted evasively and with embarrassment. He didn't have the strength to look Botros straight in the eye and turn him down, but he had no desire to give his consent.

Nazeera had just turned seventeen; her suitor was forty-four. He had many years of teaching, travel, and writing behind him and had acquired a certain fame. The age difference alone would not have been a sufficient reason for a rejection: in those days, husbands were regarded as second fathers; there was nothing unusual about their having graying temples. Slightly more unusual was the fact that at his age Botros was a bachelor and not a widower. Usually men who were marrying at forty were not marrying for the first time—such as Khalil himself, whose first wife, Hanneh, had died in childbirth and who had then married his late wife's sister, Sofiya.

Why hadn't Botros "settled down" by then? To those who dared criticize him for this, he was in the habit of responding by giving various commendable reasons: his obligation to first take care of his younger brothers and sisters; his teaching load, which left him very little time for himself; wanting to be sure he was in a decent financial position before making a lifelong commitment . . . If Léonore is to be believed, these were nothing but excuses.

"The truth is, your grandfather couldn't stand women. Oh, he liked them, but he couldn't stand them, if you see what I mean."

My cousin Léonore tried to explain, and I tried to understand. Apparently, Botros wished women were educated and that they worked, spoke in public, laughed, smoked . . . He liked them as they should have been, in his view, and as they might have been, but he hated them as they were: agents of social conformity and clippers of wings. As someone who went around with his cape fluttering like two wings, he mistrusted anything that might fasten him to the ground. He was restless; he felt as though he were suffocating as soon as he saw himself tied to a house, a job, or a person.

Léonore continued. "You should be aware that your grandfather had a vile temper, God rest his soul! I'm sure no one's told you that; we're much too polite in this family. He was very demanding and used to get angry as soon as he saw behavior he didn't like. With women, men, children, students . . ."

According to her, this didn't mean that he was capricious or unpredictable; quite the contrary, everything he did was logical and scrupulously fair. But that's just it—too logical, too implacable. He never overlooked the slightest peccadillo.

"In a country like ours, can you imagine? A country where people usually accept everything with a shrug! A country where people keep saying, 'Don't try to straighten a curved cucumber!'; 'Don't carry the ladder horizontally!'; 'Nothing happens that hasn't already happened!'; 'If you can't break a hand, kiss it and ask God to break it!'; 'An eye can't fight against a drill!'; 'Any man who takes my mother will become my stepfather!' . . . Every day, Botros had thirty occasions to vent his anger. He was in a perpetual state of rage. How could he ever spend his days and nights with just any ordinary village woman? He wouldn't have been able to bear it, and she wouldn't have been able to bear it. He waited until he'd found an extraordinary woman who would understand him, share his ideals, his whims, and his rage. Who else could that be but Nazeera . . ."

I don't know what this tardy explanation of Botros's protracted bachelorhood is worth. I am only partially convinced by it. It is quite possible that the moral rigor that distinguished the preacher's household attracted him at this stage in his life. I am also prepared to believe that he waited a long time for a suitable woman, the only one who would understand his moods and put up with them. But while waiting, he didn't exactly lead an ascetic life. I found many clues suggesting that he didn't dislike being single and that he had an eventful love life.

Such things are not discussed in our family when it comes to venerable departed relatives, or if they are, only in a low voice, and of course, they aren't on exhibit in the family archives. However, skimming the notebooks left by my grandfather, I came across passages that were highly revealing.

> *I should have had two hearts, the first, numb, the second, constantly in love.*
> *I would have given the latter to the ladies for whom it beats, and lived*
> *happily with the other.*

I am delighted to see that despite his scruples and disillusionments, his youthful years were not dull. Elegant, brilliant, admired, engaged with the ideas of his day, at ease in different languages, traveling around the world with a pocketful of dollars, he must have been attractive to women, and in no hurry to "settle down."

> *I spent my life speaking of love,*
> *And my own words are all that remain of my love affairs . . .*

True enough, Grandfather! But isn't this the common lot of all mortals? Our sole consolation, before being laid to rest, is to have loved and been loved, and perhaps to have left a personal trace.

Occasionally, out of a sense of propriety and a form of dandyism, he claimed that the contents of his verses were unrelated to his life, that his romances didn't include physical love and it was all just a poets' game:

Of course, if I had listened to my heart,
Of all those madly in love, I would have been the most madly in love of all.
But all I desired from them were smiles,
But all I obtained from them were smiles.
And may the earth swallow me up if I am lying!

Perhaps he wasn't lying completely. Among the many pages of love poems in his notebooks, the most daring verses were probably not intended for a lover; they were probably just literary reminiscences or writing exercises, such as these, already quoted:

Her breasts, ivory pomegranates,
In a stream of light . . .

But at other times he relates specific circumstances and quotes verses addressed to ladies who were important in his life. For instance, the woman whom he nicknamed *mouazzibati*—literally "my persecutor":

One day she got mad because I had criticized her harshly, and she didn't want to talk to me anymore. I was annoyed at myself, and a woman neighbor, who had noticed what happened, said to me, "That's how one learns! Next time around, be more cautious!" I answered, "Next time I'll crawl out of my mother's womb muzzled!"

Then, the other day, my persecutor met me in the street in her neighborhood, and against all expectations, she greeted me with a welcoming smile. So I recited these verses . . .

As might be expected, all of this is heavily cloaked in anonymity; in those days, naming the loved one was out of the question. But occasionally, thank heaven, traces remain. Thus a first name has survived in one of the documents in our archives. Probably because it was recorded on a sheet that included important things that had to be preserved at all costs—namely, the letter I've already cited more than once, that Botros received from his friend Hamadeh in March 1906, the day after the evening they spent together in Beirut on the terrace of the Star of the Orient. His correspondent alludes indirectly to secrets they exchanged during their conversation; then he expresses these cryptic wishes:

May the electric flux of memory never cease to turn (and may God keep Kathy for you!) . . .

THIRTY-TWO

I shall never know, from the last survivors or the departed contemporaries, who this Kathy was, rescued from complete oblivion in a parenthesis. Was it she who had sent that mysterious gift from the United States that my grandfather covered with passionate kisses because she had touched it? Had she been one of the reasons he had left for the "American lands," or had he met her during the trip he completed that year?

I don't feel that I have any right to speculate or build castles in the air. In any case, the suitor's love affairs were not what made Khalil hesitate about giving his daughter away—except insofar as these affairs revealed a "fickle" tendency that manifested itself in many different ways and made him seem not very dependable, at least not as a future husband and family man. We should remind the reader that when Botros asked for Nazeera's hand, he had been unemployed for three years and had no permanent residence; he had also been hatching dubious projects that most people probably laughed at and his close relatives must have viewed with anxiety.

Once again, I can't help comparing his career with that of his brother Gebrayel. Gebrayel left for New York at eighteen. There he met Cuban exiles with whom he became friends, so much so that he adopted their language and their struggle, followed them to Havana, and settled among them for good. In 1899 he founded his Havana company, La Verdad, to which he devoted every minute of his time, and it eventually became one of the most prosperous businesses on the island. Steadfastness, more steadfastness, and determination. And what was my future grandfather doing during that time? First, he couldn't make up his mind about whether to remain in the mother country or leave. Then he finally decided to leave, only to return four or five years later, lambasting emigration and claiming he had never contemplated settling abroad. After that, he went back to teaching, a profession he claimed to hate, in Zahlé, a city he cursed for being small and provincial. And predictably, after only three school years teaching at the Oriental Secondary School, he couldn't stand it anymore. Once again he inveighed against his profession and bitterly regretted all those years "lost between notebooks and inkwells."

From Khalil's point of view, the two suitors, though brothers, were completely different, even quite apart from Gebrayel's social success. As a future son-in-law, the émigré offered a sense of security; Botros did not. He was unstable, irascible, unemployed, and already relatively old.

Nazeera's father had made up his mind; he wasn't wavering between yes and no. He worried only about how to turn Botros down in the least hurtful manner.

When he broached the subject with his wife, he was not surprised to find that she was even more opposed than he, and actually frankly hostile. For Sofiya, the suitor's unreliability and vile temper were mere trifles compared with his other grievous—indeed unforgivable—fault: his lack of religion. Coming from a rigid and humorless Protestant family, she didn't at all like Botros's cavalier attitude toward matters of faith. And this was before she even knew what he was "hatching" on this score.

The preacher asked his wife not to reveal her feelings and to leave the settling of this thorny matter to him. He went to Beirut to see his daughter, who was a boarder at the American School for Girls, and he had a long conversation with her. He explained to her his and her mother's point of view in detail, and he was relieved to find that she wholeheartedly agreed with them. On his way home to the village, he worked out a satisfactory answer in his mind, a way of turning down Botros's proposal without humiliating him.

As soon as he saw his former pupil, he told him, in the same prim tone of voice he used for his homilies, "My daughter is a gifted student, and she has vowed to pursue her studies as long as possible. I am sure that an eminent educator like you can only encourage such diligence."

Botros didn't immediately grasp that he had just been rejected. When he deciphered the message a few seconds later, he almost exploded. Then he mastered himself, managed to look impassive, nodded his head politely, and said, "I'd like to talk to her . . ."

"She's bound to tell you the exact same thing. I just saw her!"

But the suitor insisted on having a conversation with her, and Khalil couldn't refuse, given their long-standing friendship and their more recently forged ties of close kinship. In any case, Khalil had no fear; Nazeera had made her decision after giving it careful thought, and she wasn't the kind of girl who changed her mind overnight.

Botros had a face-to-face conversation with her a few weeks later when she returned to the village for the summer vacation. At the end of their talk, she told her parents that after careful reconsideration, she was in favor of this marriage. The parents were trapped, particularly since their daughter made it clear that this time she wouldn't change her mind. Khalil felt he couldn't withhold his consent, regardless of his misgivings. His wife, on the other hand, never resigned herself to it.

I shall never know for sure what Botros could possibly have said to Nazeera to convince her to marry him. These kinds of intimate exchanges, so distant in time, are seldom passed on in families, and even less in mine. However, on rereading the old documents, my guess is that the suitor did not set down a long misty-eyed poem at his beloved's feet. This would not have swayed her.

It is probably outrageous on my part to think I can analyze the feelings of a young girl of seventeen on the basis of what I know of the grandmother she later became. But a thoughtful person stays on course; she doesn't meander from one soul to another, like a hermit crab changing shells. We can trace a line from her earliest youth to her final mature years, and near this line she will always be recognized as true to herself, for better or for worse. When it comes to Nazeera, here is the sequence of images I see: the studious adolescent among her classmates and teachers at the American School; the young bride sitting on the grass for a holiday lunch; the wife surrounded by her husband and children, holding her youngest on her lap; the more mature mother surrounded by her children, now young men and young girls, her husband already gone, but her mother, Sofiya, standing erect by her side; the young grandmother, with me in short pants leaning proudly against her knee; and then the very old lady holding her great-granddaughter. Throughout the sequence, we know it's she. We're never confused, we recognize her, her soul hasn't changed . . . And these images blend in my mind with all those that weren't captured in photos—the first being the image of her on that Sunday in August when I went to hold her hand and grieve with her over the death of her child, my father. No cries, no wordy lamentations, none of the vulgar tantrums sanctioned by bereavement.

From everything I know of her, there is one thing I am certain of: Nazeera did not waver on a whim or a change of heart; she committed herself to a plan for life, a plan that was meaningful to her. Botros had suggested they open a school and run it together. A modern school as had never previously existed in the country. A school that would serve as a model for all the others and cast such a powerful beam that it would light up the whole Orient.

A school? Why is this a groundbreaking plan? Isn't that exactly what Khalil had done thirty years earlier—started a new kind of school, such as the Orient had never seen before?

True. But since then the project had come to a standstill. As pointed out earlier, the preacher had become old, and not one of his eight children—five boys and three girls—had wanted to take up the torch. All except Nazeera had left the country and were scattered to the four corners of the earth. The eldest, as we know, was a physician in Egypt, and one of his younger brothers, named Alfred, had followed him there; a third son was a pharmacist in Puerto Rico, and the other two had settled in New York. As for his daughters, the eldest and her husband lived in Texas, and Alice now lived in Cuba. The only one still living in the country was the youngest daughter, Nazeera. For her, taking up the torch, ensuring the permanence of her father's initiative, and consoling him for having been deserted by all the others—this was a plan that was bound not to leave her indifferent and one that the preacher couldn't reject either.

Doubts could certainly be raised about Botros's character, the fact that he liked being provocative and tended to be unstable, but no one had ever questioned his qualities as a teacher. If there was one man in our village who could revive the age-old dream of civilizing the country, it was he.

THIRTY-THREE

I couldn't find the exact date of my grand-parents' wedding, but in all likelihood it took-place during the second week of October 1912, in two successive ceremonies: a Protestant ceremony in Beirut and a Catholic ceremony in our village church.

The wedding must have been organized in haste, because Gebrayel wasn't informed of it. He wrote two letters and a telegram to his brother in October of that year; I found all three filed away in the same enve-lope. There is no indication that Gebrayel knew of the marriage. Not one word of congratulations or the slightest allusion to it. Quite the contrary, he is more insistent than ever that Botros come join him as soon as possible.

The first letter starts as follows:

I have only just received the letter you sent me on August 18, and I can't understand the delay. I am answering you

hurriedly, just so you'll understand why I didn't write to you sooner. I'll
send you a longer letter in a few days, with detailed answers to the various
questions you raise.

I would also like you to know that I am about to buy the house I told
you about, General Máximo Gómez's house. The signing will take place this
week, God willing, and I promise I'll send you a telegram the same day to
tell you the news. In that case, this letter will arrive later, by way of
detailed explanation.

The price we agreed to is sixty thousand riyals . . .

A note in passing: the "riyal" just mentioned is actually the American dollar. It is not unusual to find the U.S. currency rebaptized this way in letters of the period. This orientalization is very relative, for the word "riyal" is of purely Latin origin. It comes from *real*, or "royal"; similarly, "dinar" comes from the Roman *denarius*, and "dirham" from the Latin *drachma*.

As I went through the family archives, I was constantly struck by the fact that in the past, all the names were easily and unhesitatingly translated according to the languages used. Thus, when Botros expressed himself in English, his name became Peter; when he received a letter written in French, it was addressed to Pierre. In Cuba, Gebrayel became Gabriel, and Alice became Alicia. In America, the names sometimes lost syllables in translation: Tannous became Tom, Farid became Fred, and Nadim Ned.

Some names of countries underwent a similar transformation; the United States was translated as *al-Wilayat al-Muttahidah* because *wilaya* was the Ottoman equivalent of "province" and the name stuck.

When it comes to the currency, even in the 1960s I sometimes heard elderly émigrés back in the village talk about American "riyals." This brought the ghost of a mocking smile on their interlocutor's face, and gradually the habit was lost.

But let me return to Gebrayel and his letter to his brother announcing his purchase of the Gómez house.

The conversion of the building, originally conceived as a residence, into
a commercial space, will probably cost ten thousand riyals, or slightly less;
I shall therefore have to pay out seventy thousand in total—this is the
maximum sum I can do without at present. I shall be a bit short on liquid
assets, but I can't pass up this kind of opportunity. It is 815 square meters
of land worth over one hundred riyals a meter, not even counting the
building. This location is the best in Havana; the new government palace is
going up directly across the street, and the train station that serves the
entire island is already in the street behind it. I got such a good deal that
all those who heard about it were thrilled for me if they were friends and
choked with jealousy if they were rivals.

You'll understand that under these conditions, I'm not in a position to
buy the plots of land you hoped to sell me. But if your goal in selling them
to me was to acquire capital, come here, I beg you. You and I will discuss
this quietly; I'll fill you in on all the aspects of my business. I'm ready to
make you a partner in any way that suits you!

Oh, if only the Lord would inspire you to get on a boat even before
receiving the letter I am writing to you!

Though Botros, by now, had taken a completely different path and
never felt "inspired by the Lord" to set sail for Cuba again, three other
members of the family were tempted by the journey.

The first to leave was a young man by the name of Nayef. He is not
spoken of kindly in the family correspondence; everyone seems to
think of him as the black sheep, a mischief-maker, someone whose example should not be followed—though what he had done wrong is
nowhere explicitly stated.

He was Botros and Gebrayel's nephew, the son of their older
brother Youssef. I haven't talked much about him; I don't own a single
letter signed by him. I presume he had had less schooling than his
brothers. One of the few stories still being told about him concerns the
circumstances of his marriage. So many of my ancestors' memories in-
volve weddings, epic duties, brief moments of incandescence in their
obscure lives!

The story about Youssef dates back to 1880. His older sister

Mokhtara was about to get married, and Soussène, his mother, was expecting a child. This made Soussène anxious, and one evening she complained to Tannous, her husband. How was she going to cope with all her children and her newborn, since her eldest daughter would no longer be at home to help her? "Don't worry," Tannous replied. "I have an idea. We'll marry Youssef off, and his wife will help you instead of Mokhtara." They considered all the different girls in the village and settled on Zalfa, a neighbor whom Soussène was fond of. "If you're sure she's who you want, I'll go talk to her father right away . . ."

The father welcomed Tannous, as is the custom in the village. He asked him to sit down, had refreshing drinks served, and made small talk before they got to the reason for the visit. "I came to ask for your daughter's hand for Youssef," said the visitor. "She will be his!" was the host's immediate response.

The young woman was already getting into bed and had just let down her long hair when her father called out, "Zalfa, do up your hair again; we've married you off!" This sentence has remained in the villagers' memory, even among people who no longer know who said it or in what circumstances. In referring to a precipitate, hasty, and fairly dictatorial marriage, we sometimes quip, "Do up your hair again, we've married you off!"

Having done up her hair again and put her clothes back on, Zalfa came in and appeared, head lowered, before her father. He said, "We've promised you to Youssef. Are you glad?" She uttered a shy, submissive yes, and didn't seem too displeased. Then Tannous went home and found Youssef fast asleep. He had qualms about waking him, so he told him only on the next day that they had decided to marry him off, that they had selected a wife for him, and that she had consented. The bridegroom wasn't even eighteen.

I owe this story to the man who, over the years, probably told me more than anyone else about our large family. Born in 1911, he is Youssef and Gebrayel's nephew. He is Botros's nephew as well, and also his student, protégé, and admirer. A lawyer, public speaker, and womanizer, he once held high political office. Those who know the family and our country will easily guess who he is. In these pages, however, I shall simply call him the Orator, since I adopted the rule of not giving the real names of relatives who are still living when the book is completed.

According to the Orator—though I read this in *The Tree* as well— shortly after marrying Zalfa, Youssef set up a tannery at the entrance to the village. I never saw it when it was in operation, but the building is still standing, intact. Most of my childhood walks with the other children in the family led us to that building. This was also where the car road from the city ended; beyond, people had to continue on foot.

Youssef ran this business with occasional help from his brothers. Later he was assisted by his eldest son, Nayef. But the work was difficult, unpleasant because of the smell, and not always lucrative. There is no question that it didn't offer very tempting opportunities, particularly for the young people in the family, and it certainly didn't prevent their training their gazes further, beyond the sea that can be glimpsed at the horizon when you sit on the tannery roof, as I often did as a child.

I don't know whether Nayef left for Cuba on his own initiative or at his uncle Gebrayel's express invitation. What I do know is that the two men didn't like each other at all. Very soon they became rivals and even downright enemies. The nephew opened his own business in Havana, a stone's throw away from his uncle's.

In a letter to his brothers, Gebrayel complained about Nayef's "questionable activities" and had very harsh words for the family; instead of sending him someone he could trust like a son, who would relieve him in his work, they had sent him a poisoned gift that only added to his worries and troubles.

These remarks upset Youssef, and to make up for Nayef, he promised to send one of his other sons to Cuba—Nassif, a dreamer but a thoroughly honest and affectionate boy.

Gebrayel welcomed him without any hostility or prejudice and saw that he was indeed different from his brother. But, because Gebrayel was a demanding company head, this was not enough. In one of his letters to Botros, he complained in a tone that was both paternal and despairing.

As for our nephew Nassif, he is still the same. His health is good, but he makes slow progress, contrary to what we expected of him.

I see only two reasons for this. First, his keeping company with Nayef and his acolytes, though I categorically prohibited him from seeing them, but he doesn't listen to me. Secondly, the letters he receives from home that disrupt his mood. One day, he receives a letter saying, "Our dearest child," or "Our dearest brother, the work here is not going well, the hides are too expensive, good workers are scarce, and buyers are even scarcer. With the wars, the turmoil, and various misfortunes, life here is becoming impossible, everyone is sad. Work well where you are, perhaps one day we will all come and join you there . . ." After that Nassif concentrates on his work, he becomes serious, assiduous, and it is a pleasure to watch him.

Then another letter arrives: "Our child" or "Our brother." "We're happy to tell you that everything is going well here, our country is better off than America, our business has never been as prosperous, we're earning a lot of money; there's so much demand that we can't handle it anymore. It would be good if you could come help us out!" Right away, Nassif can't concentrate on his work anymore; he starts talking to me about going back.

That's how he's been since he arrived. Every day we have to scan his face to see what kind of mood he is in. He's always thinking about home, he doesn't travel around the island, he doesn't want to see anything, and he doesn't want to learn anything. I keep telling him he's wrong, sometimes gently and sometimes not so gently, but nothing can be done. And this has been going on for three years! Three years that he's been in this state of indecision and melancholy! Three years that he's been suffering from this ailment whose symptoms I've just described, and he refuses to undergo treatment!

I haven't written to his father yet, because I know he hasn't recovered from the suffering that Nayef's behavior caused him, and I don't want to heap more grief on him. On the other hand, I'm sure you'll agree with me that I cannot tolerate this state of affairs indefinitely. That's why I'm writing you, so you'll tell me, with your wisdom, how I should solve this problem!

My feeling is that it would be best for this boy to go home, because he clearly has no desire to make headway here in spite of everything I have done to make his work easier. Things that were completely within his reach! For example, I put him in charge of the store's food department, with the job of supervising it, and nothing else; in exchange I gave him half the profits. This is how he earned almost one hundred French pounds last year—net for him!—and this year he'll earn even more. If he were more motivated and made better use of his intelligence, if he knew how to adjust the orders according to his customers, he could have earned four to five thousand riyals in this sector alone, seeing as there are nearly six thousand sons of Arabs on the island who all come to our stores to buy the food products they are accustomed to, and we have no competition in this sector.

Furthermore, in order to reward him for the help he gives us in other areas—packaging, etc.—I pay him forty gold riyals a month; and I keep an eye on him constantly for an encouraging sign that would allow me to go into a full-fledged business partnership with him . . . So tell me, dearest brother, don't you think I'm treating him decently?

I've asked Nassif more than once to write to his father to explain the situation to him with the same candor, and ask him whether he should stay here or return home. But he never has, either because he can't make up his mind or for some other reason that he hasn't told me. Or else he would prefer me to do it. Well, so now I have! Now it's up to you to explain the situation to his father. He can think about it with complete freedom and then convey his instructions to me. I shall do whatever he wants and whatever will comfort him, but I can't be expected to resign myself to this waste of time and fecklessness that leads nowhere. This is no way to reap the fruits of emigration!

After this long plea, a line added in the margin, written from top to bottom in pencil:

I showed dearest Nassif what I just wrote to you about him. He read it attentively, found it truthful, and didn't raise any objections.

THIRTY-FOUR

 Except the nephew did feel the need to take up his pen four days later—on November 1, 1912— to give his own version of events.

To my uncle Mr. Botros, may God preserve him,

I kiss your hands, though from afar, and send you my feelings of affection while asking the Almighty to unite us soon. I've been on the verge of writing to you more than once to outline the reality of my situation here; what prevented me from doing so was lack of time. But today they are electing the president of the republic, and the stores are closed, which allows me to devote my time to writing to you. I shall try to do so honestly, without any exaggeration, and starting at the beginning.

I arrived in New York on October 28, 1909. My uncle Gebrayel was there, he came to the island [Ellis Island presumably], got me out, and treated me exactly as if he had been my father. Then we went to Havana together.

*As soon as we arrived on the steamer, the boatman came to see my uncle
to criticize my brother Nayef's behavior, which was very instructive
for me.*

*Then I started working here right away. That wasn't easy, particularly
since I don't know the language. After six months of suffering, I
understood that you were right to tell me that I was too young to become
an expatriate, and I began regretting that I had come. So I decided to leave,
either for New York or for home, but my uncle stopped me and put me in
charge of the Syrian food products sector. I took care of it, within the
limits of my abilities, while continuing to work in the rest of the shop as
much as I could. At first my salary was thirty riyals a month; later it
became forty. But you know how expensive life is here; and of course I
had to send a bit of money to my parents. All in all, last year I was left
with 390 Spanish riyals from my salary and my grocery earnings.*

I assume the young man really means Cuban pesos . . .

*I haven't yet done my accounts for the current year. In any case, I am not
denying what I owe my uncle Gebrayel. I appreciate his advice, and I'll
never forget how he welcomed me and everything he has done for me. But
what I'm personally most interested in, before anything else, is staying
healthy, and one doesn't stay healthy in this country—you know this better
than I! Earning money isn't the only thing I'm interested in, as Uncle
Gebrayel is; I also care about leading a healthy life. That's why I'd rather
return and work with my brothers. This is the conclusion I've come to after
thinking about it for a long time. The work here is fine for people who are
used to being locked inside, but I'm not. I've made up my mind now; I'm
coming home at the beginning of the summer. When I informed my uncle of
my decision, he wrote to you to complain about me and to tell you that I
didn't know what I wanted. Now that you know the truth, I'll let you be
the judge, and I'll accept your decision.*

*I don't agree with my uncle when he says that he asked me to write to
my father and explain how my work was going and that I refused to do so.
I wrote my father a long letter a year ago and I even showed it to my uncle;
you can check with my father. The letter was posted on October 17, 1911,*

and it described in detail my experience since I arrived here. That's why, when my uncle tells you that I change my mind like a feather in the wind, it's not true. I have a head on my shoulders, my behavior hasn't changed, and I represent our family honorably, certainly no better than my uncle, but as well as he. It's not true that associating with Nayef and his kind has corrupted my morals. When I go see my brother, it's to give him wise advice and to try to make him admit his mistakes, not at all to take inspiration from his behavior.

The young man then conveys Gebrayel's invitation to his uncle Botros, very tactfully—without implicating himself too much.

In short, I am determined to return home in the beginning of the summer, perhaps even earlier. So if the family thinks that there is a good future in the work I was doing here, one of my uncles should come and take over as soon as possible. I'm sure he'll succeed at it much better than I. And he could really earn four to five thousand riyals a year from it, half of which he could keep, according to what my uncle Gebrayel tells me. Think about it, and do what seems appropriate to you!

Then he returns to the subject of Nayef and brings up a question that worries him.

When you write to Uncle Gebrayel, remind him that Nayef is his brother's son and that he should feel responsible for him regardless of his faults. Because they are behaving with each other like enemies, not relatives, and I won't hide from you that I fear the worst!

In conclusion, Nassif greets Botros on behalf of all the émigrés in the family, mentioning Gebrayel, Alice, their son, and also "my brother Nayef." Then—returning the courtesy—he shows the letter to his uncle, who adds in his handwriting:

I'm delighted to read what our nephew has written. First of all, because most of the things he says are true. Secondly, because I note that my letter

*unsettled him and forced him to express himself in responsible fashion. And
I hope that this appendix, which I am writing at his request and in his
presence, will allow him to see the errors he committed and correct them.*

*I don't doubt that our dearest Nassif wrote these pages with
commendable intentions and a pure heart. And I don't hold it against him
that he expressed himself with candor. Since I see him as a promising boy
who knows how to behave honorably, I pointed out the sentences in his letter
that contained errors; so he excused himself and promised to correct them
below, which will reassure you on his situation and allow you to make good
decisions for his future. You can therefore view this letter, as well as the
one I wrote, not as complaints and accusations, but as complementary
testimonies that will allow you to form an opinion with full knowledge of
the facts.*

Indeed, after that comes a last passage in Nassif's handwriting:

*There is an error in what I wrote above concerning how Uncle Gebrayel
treats Nayef. In fact, he continues to behave patiently with him. He has
tried by every means to bring him back to reason, and has got him out of
several tight spots. But my brother doesn't listen to anyone and views as an
enemy anyone who tries to give him advice for his own good, even his own
father. I don't know where all this will lead, for Nayef has obstinately
strayed from the straight and narrow and is involved in several very serious
lawsuits.*

*As for the letter I wrote to my father, my uncle Gebrayel says he now
remembers I had given it to him, but he didn't have time to read it then and
had completely forgotten about it.*

*When it comes to the grocery profits, there's no contradiction between
my uncle's figures and my own. He was talking about total receipts and I
was talking only about the amount that I had left. There! I apologize; one
sometimes makes mistakes . . .*

THIRTY-FIVE

I have quoted from this correspondence at length because it has helped me understand many things that were always unspoken in the letters between Gebrayel and Botros. Namely, the feverish atmosphere that prevailed in "our" business enterprises in Havana and the difficulty some persons had adjusting to it. Botros had probably not been treated the way his young nephew was, but Gebrayel's aggressive professionalism, which explains his dazzling success, also explains his inability to keep his relatives with him. In fact, this energy played a part in his premature death.

It wasn't the fact of being far away from home that Nassif couldn't bear, it was the life his uncle was making him lead. As a matter of fact, several months after this exchange, he returned home, married one of his cousins, and promptly emigrated with her to another destination: Utah. There, it seems, he became completely integrated into the Mormon community. His children, grandchildren, and great-grandchildren still live there, and I sometimes call them to find out how they are getting on.

Nayef, on the other hand, never left Havana. As his brother predicted, it wasn't long before the worst happened: one day the family was told that he had died. In the family, his fate remains cloaked in mystery to this day. Originally everyone kept silent because they felt uneasy about him; today it's for the simple reason that no one knows anything about him anymore. All I managed to learn, from one of his nieces, is that he had enlisted in revolutionary organizations and had made a name for himself in these circles. This could not have helped his uncle's business: one man built up connections with politicians and high-ranking government officials; the other put all his energies into fighting against them. On rereading what Gebrayel says about him, I think this interpretation is the most plausible.

It seems that Nayef was killed during one of those measures of mass repression that took place regularly in Cuba at the time of the First World War. I don't know if he was judged and executed or shot summarily. An enigmatic verse written by Botros on this occasion suggests, in veiled terms, that his body didn't receive a proper burial.

After the feud with Nayef, Nassif's "flight," and Botros's nonappearance, Gebrayel turned to another member of the family, with whom he finally established a good, long-lasting relationship. This relative, who eventually became his right-hand man, was one of Khalil's sons, Alice's brother Alfred.

This collaboration is first mentioned in a letter written by Dr. Shukri to Botros and sent from Sudan on August 6, 1913.

> *Alfred wrote to us from Alep to tell us he had been hired on a temporary basis by the Baghdad Railway Company, but had just resigned because he received a telegram from our dear Gebrayel asking him to come to Cuba. He had had some health problems after his departure from Khartoum, but he says he has completely recovered now. Since he seemed in a rush to travel, I assume he has already embarked. If you want to write to him, address the*

*letter to Gebrayel, who will pass it on to him. That's what I'm about to do
in any case . . .*

What Shukri didn't know was that his young brother had changed
his itinerary to fulfill a last-minute "formality": getting married.
These words make me smile somewhat, but not for the reason that first
springs to mind . . .

In July 1913 Alfred had received an invitation from his brother-in-
law and was getting ready to leave for Cuba. He had just spent two
years with Shukri in Egypt and in Sudan, where he had worked as
a civil servant in the British army. Since he was contemplating leaving
again for a long period of time, he returned to say goodbye to his
parents, Khalil and Sofiya, and his young sister Nazeera, my future
grandmother, who had just given birth to her first child, my eldest
uncle—the very uncle who, sixty-seven years later, told her over the
phone, in my presence, that my father had died.

When he visited Nazeera, Alfred met her best friend Hada, who was
helping her take care of the newborn baby and standing in for Nazeera's
two older sisters, who by then had emigrated to the Americas.

Hada was taller than the other women in the village, taller even
than most of the men—at least taller than Alfred—and her shoulders
were broader than his. She might have seemed masculine if she hadn't
had delicate features and great maternal tenderness in her gaze and
gestures. Nazeera loved her dearly; since she had great affection for her
brother Alfred and knew he was fragile, while Hada was solid as a rock,
she took it into her head to bring them together. Of course they already knew each other. All the villagers consort with one another from
the day they are born, and they are all cousins, more or less. Alfred and
Hada didn't have to be introduced to each other, but they had never
had the opportunity to talk to each other alone before; therefore this
meeting was decisive, and Nazeera played an undeniable part as an
intermediary.

Nevertheless, the circumstances hardly seemed propitious for marriage. Alfred was merely stopping at home to stay goodbye and was
about to leave for a destination halfway around the globe for an indeter-

minate period of time. Apparently the feeling of urgency incited them to speed things up. They decided to marry right away. The young bridegroom would leave for Cuba alone. If he didn't like Cuba, he would return immediately; otherwise, Hada would join him there. The Presbyterian rite of marriage was celebrated on September 6, 1913. Alfred took the boat two days later, promising his young wife that in a year, if not sooner, they would be living together in their own house, either in the Orient or in the Americas. She waved her handkerchief on the quay until the ship vanished in the distance; then she returned to the village and waited.

I have in front of me the facsimile of the form Alfred filled out when he got off the boat at Ellis Island, the inevitable route, apparently, for the men in my family. Reading it, I learn that he stopped in transit at Piraeus, where he boarded the steamer *Themistokles;* he reached New York on November 11, 1913; he was twenty-eight years old; he wasn't a polygamist, a cripple, or an anarchist; and he listed Turkey as his country of origin. Next to his name, a printed inscription by an official and the stamp NON IMMIGRANT ALIEN. Indeed, Alfred had stated that he was merely in transit, since his final travel destination was Cuba, where he already had an address, "c/o his brother-in-law Gabriel M., Monte Avenue, Havana."

When he arrived in Cuba in late November, he wrote a first letter to Hada, telling her that he missed her and suffered from her absence every minute, that he wouldn't be able to live so far away from her for long, and that he was tempted to drop everything. In a second letter, posted in February 1914, he complained of being constantly sick. He was certain that he couldn't spend his entire life on that island. His wife shouldn't be surprised to see him suddenly return one day. However, in his third letter, written in May, he told her that in the end, he didn't dislike his work and was getting along well with Gebrayel, who was considering giving him important responsibilities and doubling his starting salary. In the fourth letter, he told her, euphorically, that he had become his brother-in-law's right-hand man and that Gebrayel couldn't do without him. His mind was made up; he was going to set-tle in Cuba for good and rent a large apartment in the center of the city, very close to the La Verdad shops—now located in General Gómez's former residence. It was high time for Hada to come join him.

This letter was the last one she received. Posted in Havana on June 12, 1914, it arrived in the port of Beirut on July 24. Four days later, World War I began. There were no more ships, no more mail, and no more trips. The married couple couldn't be united.

THIRTY-SIX

Meanwhile, Botros was laying the foundations of his new life. Would he one day wish he hadn't given up his various projects—particularly his tobacco plantation—and ruled out so many possible futures in order to follow the ordinary path he had always wanted to avoid: settling in the village, burdening himself with a family, spending the rest of his life "between notebooks and inkwells"? For the time being, in any case, he had no regrets; his life consisted only of joys, satisfactions, and accomplishments.

In the days following their wedding, Nazeera and he enjoyed a long period of family celebrations, banquets, and poetry competitions, and they received many messages of congratulations, some in prose, others in verse, all duly preserved and in my possession. And then, when the first child was born, a mere ten months after their marriage, once again there were competitions, panegyrics, and banquets.

I am looking at a photograph from that period. It must date from the autumn of 1913, because the trees have shed their leaves and Nazeera is holding a baby in her arms. On the grass in front of the young mother are two bottles containing a dark liquid; it could be syrup, or wine purchased from the nearby monastery. In the background, a little girl is playing with an upside-down parasol. The scene is a picnic in a spot called Khanouq, which I've already had occasion to mention. In addition to the infant, whom you can make out but can't really see, there are thirteen people—eleven women of all ages, including my very young grandmother, and only two men: her father and her husband. Khalil is sitting on the grass in front of her, in the foreground on the right; with his unobtrusive eyeglasses, light-colored mustache, and American-style hat, he looks like a pastor from the Midwest. Botros is standing behind his wife, gazing into the void. He is wearing a three-piece suit, but his shirt is open. He is bareheaded, of course, and his hair is short, though abundant. He has a thick black mustache. His appearance recalls that of the fiercely secular French schoolteachers who used to be called "the black hussars of the Republic."

If he looks pensive, it is probably because he couldn't take his mind off his school, which had opened a few days earlier or was about to open. The initial response had been very encouraging. Many inhabitants of the neighboring villages had promised to enroll their children in the school as soon as it opened its doors. Botros and Nazeera were beginning to fear that the demand would be too great and they wouldn't be able to honor their commitment for lack of space. Given their limited means, they had been able to convert only one room on the lower floor of their own house; they themselves lived upstairs with their child, on a floor that was also just one room.

Despite these modest premises, the institution was baptized "Universal School," no less. The brief inaugural ceremony, in October 1913, caused a minor revolution that delighted some, amused others, and shocked the majority of people. No one had understood, at first, that "universal" meant, among other things, that the school was for boys and girls. Not two separate schools, one for boys and one for girls, or classes for boys and classes for girls, as Khalil had timidly started when he still had his school. No, this was different from anything that had been done up until then: boys and girls were to sit side by side in the same classroom, and that was final. My grandparents made the rounds of the houses in the village to explain to the dumbfounded parents that everything would go well: "You'll see! Trust us!"

And everything did go very well—both as far as this sensitive matter was concerned and the education itself was concerned. The students were delighted; they ran down the paths to come to school and left only reluctantly in the evening. And they made rapid progress, particularly thanks to a method that became the Universal's specialty: the best students in each class were given the responsibility of explaining what they had learned to their schoolmates. This created a chain of knowledge that developed a sense of responsibility and a spirit of solidarity among all the pupils. The effect, it seems, was miraculous; even now the alumni of the school who are still alive talk about it with wonder and gratitude.

The success of the system was so great that enrollments had to be reopened in the course of the first school year, as can be seen from this memorandum dated February 28, 1914, a copy of which has been preserved in the archives:

Respected compatriots,

Some among you have asked us in the past to accept their children in the school, but we had to present our apologies because we had no more available seats in the room we converted for teaching. But now, at the start of the second semester of the school year, we felt it was necessary to admit new students, which led us to set up a second classroom.

Thanks to this, the Universal School is in a position to announce that anyone who will grant us their trust during this semester will be welcome, and we will serve him as best we can, God willing.

Warning

In a previous memorandum, we said that our school would not concern itself with denominational rites. Some persons understood this to mean that we refuse to teach anything related to religion, whereas the school's

*principal concern is to inculcate the precepts of Christianity. It was even
founded specifically in order to reinforce the Christian virtues.*

The Headmaster of the school

Botros M. M.

This "warning" points to the beginning of a long and painful battle. Actually, the battle started much earlier, but this episode would be
the most trying.

When Khalil founded his school thirty years earlier, the Catholic
clergy had responded with hostility. In their sermons they had fulmi-
nated against the heretics and promised eternal fire and brimstone for
their followers—particularly those who sent their children to the
school of those demons who didn't believe in the Virgin Mary, the
Host, or the saints. But the villagers, even the most devout among
them, didn't obey their church blindly. As long as the Protestant school
was the only school, they sent their sons there no matter what. Better
the risk of heresy than the certainty of illiteracy.

The diocese inferred from this that it was time to open its own
school. Its headmaster was a priest from Damascus by the name of
Malatios, a clever and by no means uneducated man who had the specific mission of bringing the stray souls back to the fold. The counter-
attack turned out to be effective. Up until then Khalil, the preacher,
had seemed like the champion of enlightenment fighting the dark
forces of ignorance. Now the scenario changed: it was the Catholic
school versus the "heretical" school; and when Khalil started to grow
old and had to close down his school because none of his sons wanted
to take up the torch, even some Protestant families enrolled their children with Father Malatios.

The war of the schools ended with the victory of the Catholics.
The first war, I should say. The second war started when my grandparents opened their Universal School.

In spite of being Catholic, the brother of a Catholic prelate, a former teacher at the Patriarchate Secondary School and the Oriental
Greek Catholic Basilian Secondary School, Botros was in their bad
graces. One reason for this was that he was the preacher's son-in-law.

Another reason was that he had attended the American mission school, and so had his wife. But these weren't the only reasons. There was something much more serious: his own beliefs. He probably wasn't Protestant, but then what was he? He was never seen at Sunday mass or at Khalil's "prayer service," for that matter. People in the village whispered that he was an atheist. He always vehemently denied it—and admittedly, there is no hint to that effect in his intimate writings. However, almost everyone was convinced of it, even among his nearest and dearest.

So when my grandfather sent his first circular to the families in Machrah and the seven neighboring villages formally announcing the founding of the Universal School and stating, among its features, that girls and boys would be admitted in the same classes and that it "would not concern itself with denominational rites," his opponents went wild. Not only did this man want to pervert their children's morals, he also wanted to de-Christianize them! Hence Botros's firm but defensive response: though the school refuses to get involved in the quarrels among the various communities, it is Christian. Essentially his message was this: parents, don't think you have to choose between a school of nonbelievers and a school of good Christians; in fact, the choice is between an institution open to all denominations and a school for Catholics alone, indeed for the most obtuse among them. In those days, the population in these eight villages and throughout this area of Mount Lebanon was exclusively Christian, but it included Greek Orthodox Christians, Melchite Greek Catholics, Maronites, and—more recently—Protestants. Botros hoped to attract students from all four denominations to his school. In the Levant, the first meaning of the word "universal" is being above community quarrels.

My grandfather went very far in his desire to bring people together. Thus, all the students, regardless of denomination, had to recite the same prayer every morning, the prayer being the Paternoster. They were all supposed to learn it in four languages: Arabic, Turkish, English, and French. In fact, among the family papers I found a silver plate with the Arabic version of the prayer engraved on it. I set it down on my desk, as it probably was on my grandfather's desk, and took the time to recite it slowly out loud:

Our Father which art in Heaven, hallowed be Thy name. Thy kingdom come. Thy will be done on earth as it is in Heaven.

Indeed, there is no word that might offend a Protestant, Catholic, Orthodox, or Freemason—which is what my grandfather was—or a Muslim or Jew, for that matter.

Give us this day our daily bread. And forgive us our trespasses, as we forgive those who trespass against us. And lead us not into temptation. But deliver us from evil. Amen.

No. Even in this second part there is nothing that might shock believers of any religion. It is probable that given the choice, their wording might have differed, but there is no mention of any controversial dogma, no Trinity, no pope, no church, no Virgin Mary—in fact, no Jesus . . . It is simply a monotheistic prayer, a "universal" prayer, like my grandparents' school.

In spite of this ecumenical aim, Botros never succeeded in appeasing his detractors. All the more so since this open-minded, unifying man was also a man of principle, and a stubborn one at that. He furnished a striking proof of this in the coming years; it delighted his opponents, embarrassed all his relatives, and was a trauma his descendants never overcame. He obstinately refused to baptize his children.

THIRTY-SEVEN

Whereas his brother Gebrayel, also a Free-mason married to a Presbyterian, had no compunctions about calling on the Catholic priest of his Havana parish and then choosing a high-level dignitary in the Great Lodge of Cuba as his child's godfather, Botros dug in his heels. His children would choose their religion, or no religion, when they came of age; till then, they would be free of any commitment. It was a beautiful idea that testifies to his seriousness in approaching these questions: a community of believers is not a tribe to which one belongs from birth, and it shouldn't be viewed as such. One should be allowed to seek, meditate, read, compare, and then freely join a chosen faith according to one's convictions. It was a truly noble idea, especially in that country, where the sectarian massacres were still vivid in people's memories. In our village, however, this was a major scandal. You could voice this kind of opinion in an evening discussion, but to act on it and go to such extremes was unthinkable, unprecedented, almost monstrous. It was assumed that this was one of "*moallem* Botros's" passing whims, for he never wanted to be like anyone else. He went around bareheaded when no respectable man did, and he wore black three-piece suits and a long cape when his own brothers still wore village clothes. Everyone knew he was eccentric, but since everyone agreed he was exceptionally intelligent, this made up for it. People joked and shrugged their shoulders: that's Botros, you have to take him as he is.

But in this instance it was no ordinary eccentricity. Several of his relatives tried to dissuade him—first among them, his brother Theodoros, who took it as a personal affront. But nothing could be done; my grandfather never baptized his children. He stood by his decision, cost what it may. Furthermore, to preserve their freedom of choice, he didn't give them the names of archangels or saints, as had been the case for his brothers, himself, and most of the villagers in his day. His children were given names evoking human qualities or aspirations: pride, conscience, hope, victory, or perfection. He avoided attaching any permanent religious label to them from birth, whether Christian, Muslim, or Jewish.

For his opponents, such as Father Malatios, this was a true godsend. There was no need to argue, denounce, or warn the faithful, for the nonbeliever had unmasked himself. To which my grandfather used to reply, "I believe in God, I believe in the Christian virtues, but I also believe in freedom of choice, and I'm opposed to denominational schisms." "He's lying," Malatios used to say. "This man believes neither in God nor in our Savior. He says this to lure you!" But Botros retorted, "Do you really think I'm two-faced, that I believe one thing and say the opposite? Don't you think, if I'd really wanted to dissemble, I could easily have avoided the hard time I'm given? Everyone should understand this once and for all: I believe what I say, and I act according to my beliefs. If everyone in the country behaved this way, we would never have sunk so low."

In spite of the accusations leveled at him, thanks to his devotion to his work and the effectiveness of his teaching methods, Botros succeeded in earning the esteem of many villagers, and though they never went along with him on the issue of baptism, they sent their children to him nevertheless, both boys and girls, so he would make them better prepared to confront the new times. But the controversy never died down.

Malatios's school and my grandfather's were not even two hundred meters away from each other, as the crow flies. Malatios's, at the very top of the village, was recently restored; it is now a beautiful massive building in ocher stone, with a red-tiled roof in the shape of a pyramid. It still belongs to the diocese. "Our" much smaller school is now just a ruin. But it hasn't been for long. In the early 1960s, I sometimes used to go there in the summer with my grandmother. She would take a big key out of her large handbag and open the door upstairs, pick up two or three objects that were lying about, and leave with a deep sigh. God knows if it was a sigh of nostalgia or relief.

As for the first floor, which our family still calls *l-madraseh*, "the school," its doors have been missing for a long time, and the floors of the two vaulted rooms are cluttered with disintegrating desks, broken chairs, pallets, and nanny-goat droppings, having been used as a shepherds' refuge for many winters.

The older generation in the village has never forgotten the war of the two schools. It divided most of the families. Even among Botros's brothers, there was one who fought for the cause of his "opponent" Malatios.

"My uncle Semaan wasn't on our side," one of my uncles recently told me in a low voice, as if the seriousness of the matter had in no way been attenuated by the intervening eighty years.

And Father Theodoros, was he "on our side"?

"He was neither for nor against us. He was the most upset of all of us; it kept him awake at night. We were the cross he had to bear . . ."

Indeed, it must have been agonizing for him—a rebellion against the church, with his own brother leading the insurgents! As a clergyman, how could he see in these events anything but a calamity sent by Heaven to test him? On the one side was Botros, supported—except on the baptism issue—by the majority of his brothers and sisters and many of his cousins; on the other side was the clergy, where he, Theodoros, was a rising figure. It was rumored that he might soon become a bishop, for he had all the necessary qualities—erudition, presence, eloquence, manifest piety, and a sense of authority. But how could someone coming from a family like this be appointed prelate, given the circumstances? On the one hand, the war of the schools; then, even more troubling, the controversy concerning the children's baptism; and, in addition, the fact that three of his siblings married the children of the Protestant preacher. It was too much! Far too much.

Theodoros's first reaction was dramatic. When he learned of his brother's decision not to baptize his first child, he left his convent and returned to the village, obsessed with one thing. One morning, when Botros and Nazeera had gone out and left the baby in the care of its grandmother Soussène, the priest showed up at the house with two "accomplices." He quickly slipped his stole on and took his big rosary and oil flask out of his pockets; then, declaring that his nephew looked sickly, he said he should be baptized immediately lest he die a pagan and remain in limbo to the end of time.

He had already undressed the child and was about to dip him in a basin of lukewarm water when Botros, alerted by Protestant neighbors, stormed into the house and flew into the rage you would expect. Theodoros said nothing in reply, shrugged his shoulders, left the house with dignity, and set off for the seclusion of his monastery on the other side of the Mountains!

Apparently the brothers made up soon afterward. The priest promised never to do this again, even if the eternal life of his nieces and nephews was in jeopardy, and Botros forgave him—just this once—grudgingly.

THIRTY-EIGHT

While Theodoros may have given up his strong-arm tactics, he wasn't resigned to letting a situation he considered intolerable go on forever. Though he never broke off relations with his heathen brother or disowned him publicly, he tried more than once to convince him to put an end to his rebellion. Didn't Botros often say he hated teaching? Didn't he want his whole family to leave their village, where they had no prospects? So why persist in this exhausting venture when he could be highly regarded somewhere else and much better paid? Whenever the Universal School faced difficulties, Theodoros tried to persuade his brother to put an end to the experiment and seek another career.

Proof is the letter he wrote on November 14, 1915, shortly after the start of the third school year. What he calls "chance" can also be seen as a subtle maneuver.

To my dear brother Botros, may God prolong his life,

After fraternal greetings and prayers, I am writing to tell you of a conversation I just had, at his Excellency emir Malek Chehab's, with his honor Youssef Bey Bardawil. This meeting was unplanned, but chance is sometimes subtle and efficient. The conversation centered on the best-qualified candidate for the position of investigating magistrate at the Zahlé court. And the first person whose name the emir mentioned was none other than yours. Which gave me the opportunity to intervene and describe the kind of man you are, and the aptitudes you have for public service. I also mentioned the fact that one of your fellow students at law school was presiding judge so-and-so . . .

Parenthesis: This confirms, for the first time, that Botros did indeed have legal training, which makes the family legend about his going to defend Gebrayel in the Cuban courts a little less absurd. However, although this new element sheds light on the genesis of the legend, it doesn't confirm the facts. Until proof to the contrary, I shall stand by my belief that my grandfather left for Cuba in order to go into a business partnership with his brother and not in order to defend him in a court of law.

End of parenthesis and back to Theodoros's letter.

From time to time, I called on Youssef Bey for corroboration; he confirmed my statements and backed them up forcefully. So much so that the emir acknowledged that logically, you should be appointed presiding judge directly—a position that will soon be vacant; but since regulations prohibit anyone from holding that position prior to having been assessor or investigating magistrate, he thought you should first be appointed to the latter position. This is a very important position, I should point out, for the man who holds it is independent and can deliver sentences on his own initiative.

Hence the emir promised to appoint you investigating magistrate, if you agree, with the understanding that, not too long afterward, you will be promoted to a more important position.

Parenthesis again, to avoid a misunderstanding: the emir in question was not the reigning prince—at the time, there wasn't one—but a high-level Ottoman official from the family of the former emirs of Lebanon, and he still bore the honorary title. As for the other person present, also an Ottoman official, he belonged to a Christian family that probably dated back to the Crusades, since Bardawil is the Arabic transposition of Balduinus or Baudouin.

So, if you would like to obtain this position, you should come to the emir's immediately, for the only thing that kept him from appointing you on the spot was the fear that you might not accept . . .

My greetings to our relatives, and may God keep you . . .

Obviously, the priest is afraid that the intractable Botros will say no. He humors him; he recounts the scene without ever making his brother look like a job applicant and he is quick to hold out the prospect of rapid promotion should Botros not find the job offer good enough.

Indeed, it seemed like a propitious moment. The year 1915 had been one of the most calamitous in the history of Mount Lebanon. First there was the war, the Great War, which the Sublime Porte had entered, in November 1914, on the side of the German and Austro-Hungarian empires. Enver and the Young Turks expected from this a miraculous renaissance of the Ottoman Empire, but ultimately, as we know, it led to its disintegration.

At the beginning of the conflict, the theater of operations was far away, and Mount Lebanon wasn't directly affected. Though some goods imported from France and England started to become scarce and émigrés could no longer send money to their families, people were still able to cope. One commodity was replaced by another; people eliminated nonessentials; brothers, cousins, and neighbors helped one another out; and everyone prayed the ordeal wouldn't last too long. Few people understood that a whole world was in its death throes and that everyone, great and small, would eventually share in the common suffering.

· · ·

Providence made its will known to the population by sending a biblical scourge: locusts! In April 1915, swarms of migrating locusts suddenly darkened the sky, swooped down on the fields, and devoured every-thing—"the green and the dry," to use the local expression.

This would have caused food shortages in normal times, but in wartime, with all the privations people were already enduring, it caused a great famine, the worst in Lebanese memory. The estimated number of deaths is one hundred thousand—which comes to almost one in six inhabitants. Certain villages were virtually depopulated. There had been many other famines in the past, but none left such a lasting impression on people. Even today you sometimes hear people say that the wave of emigration was caused by the great famine of 1915. This is untrue, of course, because emigration had already begun by then—to Egypt, to various "American countries," as well as to Australia—and had been going on for several decades. But it gained momentum, and the horrors of famine provided justification for those who left, silencing guilt and remorse.

In this ordeal, Botros managed once again to call attention to him-self. Usually, the grains for the next harvest were sowed in early fall. Those who had a surplus supplied grains to those who ran short. The family correspondence abounds in accounts of this sort: so many boxes of grain delivered to x, and so many to y . . . However, in the fall of 1914, when my future grandfather heard that war had broken out, he decided he wouldn't sow that year.

"He's crazy!"

This wasn't the first time he was called crazy. He had an inex-haustible—and for his relatives no doubt exhausting—propensity to never conform to common sense or the prevailing wisdom. Once again, he had well-honed arguments: if there were food shortages, the grains set aside for the sowing period would enable one to survive for a few months.

But what would he do the following year? If he didn't sow, he would have nothing to harvest, and with the food shortages caused by the war, no one would have a surplus to sell him . . . or if they did, they would ask a small fortune.

The madman! Always pigheaded about doing things differently from everyone else!

The wheat grew in the fields, the ears bulged and grew heavy, and Botros was pitied and jeered at, for his fields lay fallow.

And then the grasshoppers, the locusts appeared!

The sky darkened at noon, as in an eclipse, and the tiny voracious insects spread by the thousands over the fields, harvesting for their own benefit, devouring, razing, and cleaning everything.

In the meantime, people had already exhausted part of their reserves; by consuming sparingly, they could make their supplies last until November, at most. Botros was the only person who had enough to feed his family for the rest of the winter. An enviable position, admittedly, and proof that he was worth listening to more often. But wasn't it a curse to be "enviable" in such times? It isn't easy living in a village where people are dying of hunger when you yourself have enough to eat. Had Botros owned silos of grain, we can assume that he would have made it a point of honor to feed anyone who came and requested it. But he had kept only the part of the harvest meant for sowing; this enabled him to support his wife; his eldest son; his younger son—my father, born in October 1914; his elderly mother, Soussène; and possibly his youngest brother, with his wife and three children, including the son I call the Orator in these pages. This was a lot of people; he couldn't take on more. So what was he supposed to do if a cousin, a neighbor, a student, or a parent of a student came by requesting the bread that would save him from death? Slam the door in his face?

At the Universal School, the fall term began in a doomsday atmosphere. How could the pupils concentrate on studying when they were hungry and expected to go through the entire winter without food? And how could one possibly request tuition from their families? Given these circumstances, it is understandable that Theodoros thought it was an opportune time to try to get Botros and his family to leave the

village and—*force majeure!*—close down the school, in favor of a prestigious and lucrative appointment.

What should have made the proposal all the more acceptable was
the fact that the rival school, Malatios's school, had been forced to
cease its activities a short time earlier and wait for better times. Hence
no one could have claimed that the duel had resulted in Botros coming
out as the loser.

My grandfather didn't keep a copy of his reply to Theodoros in his
archives—or else the letter is lost. He obviously turned down the offer,
since he never shut down the school and he never became an investigating magistrate. But I don't know what arguments he used in his reply. I
assume he made a point of mentioning his scruples about shutting
down the school overnight when the school term had just begun. This
was the kind of behavior he would have found disgraceful. "Carting
off" his wife and children, running to safety with sacks of food supplies, and letting his fellow villagers die? Abandoning students and parents to their fate? If he had been capable of such desertion, he would
have left the country long ago. When he hesitated about emigrating,
hadn't he been constantly motivated by his scrupulous, nit-picking
assessment of what he saw as responsible and honorable conduct?

THIRTY-NINE

Though I don't have Botros's *direct* reply to his brother, there is an indirect one that is in the archives, written three days after he received Theodoros's proposal. It is addressed not to his brother, but to the Ottoman authorities, asking them to include the Universal School in the list of institutions eligible for public aid.

Written in the deferential style of the period, it begins by describing the undersigned as a "Lebanese Ottoman from the village of Machrah, having spent nearly twenty years in the service of educational institutions," among which he specifically mentions, first, "the Ottoman Secondary School." This institution isn't mentioned anywhere in the family documents, but I suppose my grandfather taught a few courses there and considered it clever to highlight it in this particular petition. He then lists the subjects he has taught, including mathematics, logic, astronomy, Arabic literature, various natural sciences, and, more vaguely, "a touch of foreign languages." In those times of war, suspicion, and xenophobia, it was evidently wiser not to lay too much stress on that aspect of things.

Following those years of teaching, a number of notables from the villages near my birthplace selected me to set up a national school for the education of the new generations in the spirit of brotherhood and equality among the different communities, and the exclusion of anything that goes against the interests of our holy fatherland.

I therefore yielded to the pressure of my compatriots and, three years ago, accepted the request to open a school based on these principles in my native village of Machrah, a location that seemed suitable to me because it is close to seven other villages, none more than a mile and a half away. These villages have a total population of about six thousand souls, and every student is able to come to school in the morning and go home at night without inconvenience or fatigue, in summer as in winter.

All those who have observed our undertaking over the last two years have noted that we have accomplished our task successfully and with complete loyalty to the Ottoman fatherland. This is confirmed by the large attendance our school has known this year. But the number of poor families in the population is great, and the locust episode that people suffered from, as you know, has made them incapable of paying tuition. I am therefore having enormous difficulties pursuing my activities and am fearful I may have to put an end to them.

The person to whom this request was addressed was a high-level official who had just been appointed governor of Mount Lebanon by the Ottoman authorities, and who had promised, on taking office, to get funds from Istanbul for expanding education. This explains why Botros, who had never before considered it worthwhile to inform the authorities of the creation of his school, wanted to make a bid in that direction. He summoned all his tact:

When I learned that you had stated your intention of entreating the sultan's graces for the creation of school institutions in our homeland,

*Lebanon, I said to myself that your spirit of equity and generosity
would not tolerate that our eight villages alone be deprived of the imperial
benefits that will flow over the vast Ottoman territories. That is why I
wished to present this petition, in the hope that an order be given to include
our school in the list of institutions you plan to create, and that you award
a share of the royal subsidies to it so that these villages not be put at an
unfair disadvantage compared with the other villages in Lebanon, and so
that our project, which has begun to bear fruit, not be condemned to
failure . . .*

The petition was timely: since the new governor had promised to
found schools, it was an opportunity for him to boast of having
founded one in a remote corner of the high Mountains. Who would be
so malicious as to point out to him that the school already existed? In
fact, my grandfather would receive a huge ornamented firman solemnly
announcing that a certain Botros M. M., Ottoman subject from the village of Machrah in Mount Lebanon, was authorized to create a teaching institution for boys and girls under the name of Universal School.
The firman is dated February 1917, fifteen months after the mailing of
the letter to the governor, forty months after the founding of the
school. Financial aid was promised, but predictably, it never came.

My grandfather was much too familiar with the Ottoman administration to stake his school's destiny on this kind of appeal. He wrote
the letter to show off and because it was the proper thing to do; as a
citizen, he felt it was his duty to appeal to the public authorities of his
country, regardless of who they were. At the same time, he went
knocking at another, more promising door: that of the American Presbyterian Mission. This was a door he had tried to avoid until then, because he hoped to keep his independence regarding the different
religious denominations and also because he had mixed feelings about
his own educational experience with the Anglo-Saxon missionaries. But
in those calamitous times you had to survive at any price, and he was
prepared to grasp, with gratitude, any helping hand extended to him.

A document in the family archives eloquently spells out the nature
of this aid, and what these times of war were like for my relatives. It is

a memorandum dated August 29, 1917, and reproduced by a mechanical process using purple ink; only the name "the honorable professor Botros M. M." is handwritten:

To respected brother pastors, preachers, and educators,

After a fraternal greeting, we would like to tell you that we never stop thinking about your situation and the difficulties of life at the present time. Also, after lengthy consultations, we have decided the following:

We will continue to pay the initial salaries, one-fourth in coins and three-quarters in bills; then, instead of raising salaries, starting October 1, as a way of giving special aid to every unmarried employee and to the members of the family of every married employee, we will provide a supply of wheat consisting of six okes per person a month, except for children aged six or less, who will receive three okes. But if one among you would prefer, for personal reasons, to receive the base salary and a second complementary one, as is the case now, rather than the base salary and the wheat, the decision is up to you, and we would be grateful if you would notify us as soon as possible.

The reason for this aid is to protect employees from the great famine threatening them, and from death. Furthermore, we reserve the right to judge if a person does not need this aid, in which case we will pay him the two salaries as we do now.

We hope that this subsidy will prevent you from being exclusively preoccupied with providing daily bread, and will allow you to devote yourself again to your missionary and educational work so that you can seize the spiritual opportunities in spite of the present situation. On this point, we call your attention to the words of Paul in his Second Epistle to the Corinthians, chapter VI, verses 1 to 10; and in his First Epistle to the Corinthians, chapter IV, verses 1 and 2, so that you will meditate on them deeply, and so that the Lord, who works in all of us who work with Him, will guide you and fortify you with His holy spirit and bless your work.

With our greetings to you all
from your brothers in the Lord
George Shearer, William Friedenger, Paul Arden

Even if these last exhortations were directed at the pastors and preachers more than at a secular educator like Botros, he must certainly have been grateful to these missionaries. For if, thanks to his foresight, he had not had to suffer the full effects of the famine in the winter of 1915–16, he would have been no better off than the other villagers if he hadn't received wheat and money from the Presbyterian donors in 1917 and 1918.

The subsidy was a piece of good fortune, and Nazeera still prided herself, sixty years later, in my presence, on having helped as many people as possible around her to benefit from it: the students, who received a good meal every morning when they arrived in school; Nazeera's and Botros's siblings and their families; their neighbors; and even some people whom they didn't really know. "One day an old woman showed up with her iron, begging me to give her a loaf of bread in exchange. I gave her the loaf of bread without taking the iron, of course, but a few days later I learned that she had died of starvation all the same."

No one was more worried about the poor than my great-grandfather the preacher. He had already been taking a census of the needy for years, and during the war years he devoted himself to this task body and soul.

A document dated 1917 bears his signature, "Khalil, son of Gerjis the priest." Written across the width of a double sheet, obviously torn out of a school notebook, is the heading:

List of the poor having an urgent need for food in the village of Machrah and the surrounding area

Below are six columns of unequal width, separated by vertical lines, listing the head of each needy family by name, age, home village, religion, and number of dependents, followed by "comments." Thus:

Head of family: Haykal Ghandour's Widow.
Age: 65.
Dependents: seven.

Village: Machrah.

Religion: Evangelical.

Comment: "has sold the contents of her house and has nothing left
to sell."

Or:

Gerjis Mansour's widow, 38, five dependents, Machrah, Catholic;
"her husband and some of her children have died of starvation."

Eid el-Khoury, 11, three dependents; "owns nothing."

Habib Abou-Akl's widow, 44, five dependents; "owns plots of
land but hasn't succeeded in selling them."

Khalil writes at the bottom of the page, ironically and angrily:

Altogether that comes to thirteen homes, including forty-nine
people who have been rejected by the angel of death himself, and
who are the neediest in the region . . . Here is the list you requested. I hope the Almighty will support you in your effort to obtain a bit of help for them. If you succeed, please be so kind as to
send this assistance through my son-in-law Botros effendi, head of
the school, and he will distribute it, because I am no longer able to
do so myself . . .

The reason my great-grandfather could no longer distribute aid
himself was because he had just turned eighty—he was born in 1837—
and his health was deteriorating. In fact, his handwriting looks un-
steady. But he was still passionate, fervent, lucid, and eager not to
show any religious sectarianism, which, in the face of such misfortunes, would have been not only petty but criminal. In the list I just
mentioned, the way the needy are divided up by community is beyond
reproach: there are three "Evangelical"—i.e., Protestant—families,
three Maronite families, three Orthodox families, and four Melchite
Catholic families. The preacher couldn't possibly have been more equitable. Even "the opponents," namely those who had sided with Malatios the priest, sometimes benefited from the aid Khalil managed to

obtain from the Presbyterian missionaries, which Botros and Nazeera were in charge of distributing.

During that period it seems that my grandparents dreamed of putting an end to their quarrel with the Catholic school once and for all. Thanks to the good offices of his brother Theodoros, Botros made a first attempt at reconciliation with the clergy. Thus, in that same year, 1917, he went to a Greek Catholic monastery, sat quietly through a solemn mass, and delivered a speech over dinner to an audience of clergymen on the theme of the harmonious coexistence of opposites.

When he returned to the village, he jotted down, in pencil, on a piece of paper:

> *When will man see the error of his ways? When will he wake up? When*
> *will he find the road to wisdom again?*
> *Imagine what would happen if the white of the eye refused to coexist with*
> *the black of the eye under the same eyelid?*

In an introductory sentence, my grandfather states that he had been inspired, in writing these verses, by the misfortunes caused by the Great War. No doubt. But these feelings may also have been inspired by his little war with the nearby school.

Then the other war—the real one—finally ended, and Botros felt relieved, temporarily. But only temporarily, because, from the first months of the postwar period, he would have to face other dangers, other humiliations, other unfair bereavements, so much so that his memory of the years of famine would soon take on a strange glow of nostalgia. It was nostalgia for a heroic period when mortals valiantly fought against calamities together, instead of enduring the hostile dictates of Heaven. Like a bull led in shame to the slaughterhouse who misses his days in the bullring, when at least he could die butting and charging.

FORTY

 Excerpts of a letter written on large pages, bearing Botros's signature and dated December 4, 1918.

Dear Alice and dear Gebrayel,

I wrote to you last month to tell you that the horrible war, which led to the deaths of hundreds of thousands of people and made us all live in terror, had come to an end. Thank God, without any loss being recorded in our two big houses.

(This designation refers to the descendants of Tannous and those of Khalil. The following paragraphs concern the latter, even though he is never referred to by name.)

Our father and father-in-law never stopped thanking Heaven for allowing us to get through this calamitous period with the persons dearest to us spared. In fact, he wrote you a letter to that effect last Saturday, November thirtieth, and on Sunday he celebrated mass with joy and energy, as if it were the greatest of holidays. In his sermon, he recalled the words of the aged Simeon when he said to the Lord: "Now, let your servant depart in peace!" explaining that as he went through this painful period, he constantly asked the Lord to keep him alive so that he could see where all these catastrophes, all these calamities, would lead, and so he could put his mind at rest concerning the fate of his children and their families. He added, "It is my turn to say, like the aged Simeon: Now, Lord, let your servant depart in peace!" He uttered these words with tears in his eyes, and all those who were there started to weep.

After prayer, he nevertheless finished the day in a good mood, and on the following day, Monday, he came to see us at home and at school. He joked with everyone and laughed, especially in the company of his two grandsons. Then he asked Nazeera to remove a bothersome hair from his right eye, and she did so immediately. Then he said, "My eyesight has become much worse; today I can hardly see anything with my left eye, and I have no more strength. I think my time has come." Then he cried and made us cry. We tried to cheer him up as much as we could. When he wanted to leave, we insisted that he stay, but he excused himself, saying he wanted to go to the fields to supervise some workers who were planting something for him. I offered to go in his place, but he refused, saying that this kind of walk would do him a lot of good. We accompanied him part of the way, and he walked without showing signs of fatigue. He stopped by his house, picked up a gift for the workers—dried raisins and things of this kind— then he went to see them, and he spent the day with them, conversing, joking, with great gentleness, as was his habit . . .

Oddly, among the family papers, and in the very envelope that contained the letter I am quoting from, there was a photo of Khalil in the fields, sitting on a stone, leaning on a stick, in a long black coat, wearing a hat with a scarf wound around it, and behind him, two jovial-looking workers. Had the photo been taken that day, or had it been put away there because it seemed to illustrate the contents of the letter?

That evening, he walked home with a firm stride, he dined with a hearty appetite, and then he stayed up until eight o'clock without complaining about any pain or fatigue. After that he went to bed, said his prayers, and fell asleep as usual. At around nine o'clock (of the evening of Monday, December 2, 1918) he summoned us. We rushed to his side and found that he was suffering from the usual symptom, namely the sensation of suffocation. Immediately we soaked his feet in warm water and treated him with reinvigorating medications and cataplasms. Alas, these remedies, which usually proved effective, were of no help this time. His condition deteriorated—a heart attack, according to Dr. Haddad—and after a few minutes the misfortune occurred. Our master fell silent, you could no longer feel his pulse, his princely soul departed, his pure body became immobile. And from all of us who were around him, whose eyes were upon him, there rose a wail of pain that could have melted a rock. The neighbors rushed over. At times they tried to calm us, at times they joined in our wails. It was both a luminous and painful hour, which the writer finds difficult to describe but the reader has no difficulty imagining.

When we regained a bit of serenity, we began to ask ourselves the questions that have to be asked in such circumstances: How were we going to organize a funeral worthy of such a man? How could we avoid having the present situation prevent us from paying tribute to him in the manner he deserved, as had been the case for many distinguished persons who passed away during the war years?

The first thing I thought of, and which I suggested to the other members of the family, was to call on physicians from Beirut to help us embalm the body so we would have time to distribute announcements in Beirut, Zahlé, the neighboring villages, and those of the Bekáa, and so that an impressive funeral could be organized in a few days. But after giving it thought, I realized that the people we would inform wouldn't be able to come, even if they wanted to, inasmuch as all means of transportation are still nonexistent, as everyone knows. Moreover, it is rainy weather, and there is a danger of storms and snow. Wanting the best, we would have had the worst. So we decided to send announcements only in the regions of Baskinta and Shoueir, and to organize the funeral at one in the afternoon, yesterday, Tuesday . . .

Botros's letter is much longer, since he describes the ceremony in detail and quotes excerpts from the speeches that were delivered and the poems that were read. It was recopied several times, so that it could be sent to all of Khalil's children, who all lived abroad—with the sole exception of Nazeera, the youngest—as I mentioned earlier. The fact that the family was scattered far and wide was present in everyone's mind during the funeral and in the condolences; all those who took the floor alluded to it, sometimes insistently. For example, when a procession of students from the Universal School sang a song composed for the occasion that supposedly reproduced the words of the deceased, some passages were pure piety . . .

> *The Lord has recalled me, may my nearest and dearest come bid me farewell,*
> *There is nothing here below that I could miss, it is in the heavens above that my aspirations will be fulfilled.*

Other passages contained undisguised reproaches leveled at the absent loved ones, such as Khalil's two oldest sons, the physician in Egypt and the pharmacist in Puerto Rico:

> *Shukri, where is that remedy I was waiting for? Nassib, where is the medicine you prepared for me?*
> *If the two of you are not here to heal me, no one will heal me.*

The next stanza mentioned the other son, the one who had left the village with Gebrayel in 1895 and had since been living in New York, but had never made peace with his father:

> *Tell Gerji that I am leaving; perhaps he will finally deign to write to me to bid me farewell . . .*

The discomfort aroused by these comments was bound to have created a strained atmosphere and intensified the pain of bereavement.

FORTY-ONE

Among the people to whom this very long announcement was sent, besides the persons already cited, was Khalil's son Alfred. By then he had been living in Havana for five years, working for Gebrayel, but his wife, Hada, had still not been able to join him, and she must have been present at the funeral. Another person was Anees, the deceased's youngest son, and his American wife, Phebe. I haven't mentioned them up to now and probably wouldn't have mentioned them at all—since I don't intend to list each and every member of my large family—if fate hadn't associated their names with the preacher's that year, in the cruelest way possible.

Anees had left for America very young and started a business in Pottsville, Pennsylvania—thereby doing exactly what the Anglo-Saxon missionaries advised the Levantines not to do. He married a local girl, and they had children.

There are several photos of the young couple in our

archives, taken in Texas and Utah. There is also a card bearing Anees's signature, mailed in Glasgow, Kentucky, on December 30, 1914, and received in Beirut on March 13, 1915. It is addressed to his father. It reads simply, "We're all very well, how are you?" On the back, a photo taken in front of a movie studio, under a huge sign:

Don't miss seeing
THE MOVIE PICTURES

A dozen people are smiling into the camera; under each one, there is a caption in ink, in Arabic: "Me," a frail young man with a shy gaze; "Phebe," a plumpish woman, possibly pregnant, in a long, light-colored dress, smiling broadly; "Louise," a niece; and the others referred to as "workers."

I am not surprised that this card was preserved, given the circumstances. What surprises me more is that it reached its destination in 1915. Judging by the archives I have in my possession, no other mail arrived from abroad during the war years. In fact, even in December 1918, when Botros drafted the announcement of Khalil's death, he found it necessary to add, in the last lines, that he was going to send all the letters to Cairo, to his brother-in-law Shukri, who would then forward them to the other destinations, "since only the mail to Egypt is reliable at present."

It was only in the first weeks of the following year that the mail service became reliable again, now run by the French, who had been victorious over the Ottomans and had just seized this portion of their Levantine possessions. Letters came flooding in from everywhere, bearing questions about next of kin—had they survived the war? the famine? the epidemics?—and bringing news, both good and bad, about those who had emigrated.

One letter in particular made a long-lasting impression on my relatives. It arrived in the village on February 1, 1919, and many people read it. I scoured the family documents for it, but try as I might, I couldn't find it. True, it wasn't expressly addressed to Botros or Nazeera, and these archives are theirs.

The shell may not be there, but its shrapnel is everywhere. First, in this letter written in English by my grandmother Nazeera, on February 2.

> *My dear Phebe,*
>> *I'm writing you these lines with the deepest sorrow and a broken heart. We were very anxious to hear from you these four years past, but all was in vain. Last week, I gathered your old letters and Anees's and read them all. I thought to write you soon to ask you how you are getting along these days and how are Anees and the children, etc. But Oh! yesterday, a dreadful day! We received a letter from Alfred which told us about the most terrible news, the death of our dears Anees and Gabriel; but he did not tell us what was the matter with Anees. I do not know how and what to do to comfort you, my mother, and myself.*
>> *We sent you a circular letter and a letter about the death of my father, which was on the first of December . . .*

Botros gave the date as December 2, but never mind. Nazeera was probably citing the date from memory. For this young woman of twenty-three, who was already the mother of three and had courageously faced the worst calamities of history over the last few years, the first weeks since the end of the conflict were taking on a nightmarish aspect: first her father, then her brother-in-law, and now her youngest brother, the closest to her in age, whom she held very dear, had died of unknown causes in America during the war years. Could he have been a victim of the Spanish flu, then at its height, which killed half a million people in the United States? I shall never know . . .

> *Peter—in other words, Botros—told me I must write and ask you if you would like to come over to Syria with your children and live with us. Mother said this would be a great comfort to her . . .*

Phebe never showed up. Nor did she send a reply. The letter in the archives, written by Nazeera, is not a first draft; it is the actual letter. I took it out of its original envelope in order to quote these few passages. Sent by registered mail from Beirut on March 1 to "Mrs. Anees M., Pottsville Pa., P.O. Box 165, USA," it was returned in June, riddled with postmarks. I count about fifteen, for each city the letter was forwarded to, along with the dates and a series of discouraging remarks: "Moved—Left no address, RETURNED TO WRITER," returned because the addressee had moved without leaving an address.

Among the older family members still alive, no one remembers the name Phebe. She probably remarried, her children probably took their stepfather's name. I didn't even try to find them . . . End of story.

But let me go back momentarily to my grandmother's letter and the invitation extended to her brother's young widow to come live "in Syria." Earlier, when I mentioned the card sent by Anees to his father, I almost reproduced the address in full, but withheld it until I had space to comment. The card was made out to "Professor Khalil M., Machrah, Beirut, Syria, Turkey."

Obviously this string of names calls for an explanation, and so do the variety of terms I have used from the beginning of this narrative to designate the land of my ancestors. We have a shifting geography, and I have often resorted to subterfuges—"the Mountains," "the old country," etc.—to avoid using a designation that would have been anachronistic at the time of my grandparents, or one that might be a source of confusion and bitter polemics in our day.

Though the Turkish state, as we now know it, was born after the First World War from the rubble of the Ottoman Empire, the latter had commonly been referred to as "Turkey" for some time. On Ellis Island, for instance, when Botros had to list his county of origin, he wrote "Turkey"; then under the heading "Race or People," he put down "Syrian." On the other hand, in his petition to the authorities requesting aid for the school, he had introduced himself as a "Lebanese Ottoman from the village of Machrah." In Cuba, his brother Gebrayel was the founding president of a cultural association called Syrian

Progress, but in Gebrayel's letters he referred to his compatriots as "the sons of Arabs" and expressed nostalgia for "the smell of the homeland" and "the bracing air of Lebanon."

In the minds of my grandparents, each of these various allegiances had its own "compartment": their state was Turkey, their language Arabic, their province Syria, and their homeland the Lebanon Mountains. Of course, in addition, they had their diverse religious denominations, which probably weighed on their lives more than the rest. These allegiances did not coexist in harmony, proof being the many massacres mentioned earlier; but there was a degree of fluidity about both names and frontiers, which vanished after the rise of nationalist movements.

Barely a hundred years ago, Lebanese Christians readily proclaimed themselves Syrian, Syrians looked to Mecca for a king, Jews in the Holy Land called themselves Palestinian . . . and my grandfather Botros liked to think of himself as an Ottoman citizen. None of the present-day Middle Eastern states existed, and even the term "Middle East" hadn't been invented. The commonly used term was "Asian Turkey."

Since then, scores of people have died for allegedly eternal homelands, and many more will die tomorrow.

FORTY-TWO

To return to another violent death, Gebrayel's death, it is clear from what my grandmother wrote to Phebe that the family learned of its circumstances from a letter sent from Cuba and received on February 1, 1919. I have good reason to believe that Alfred only mentioned an accident and did not allude to the possibility of an assassination.

To put my mind at rest, I rang up Léonore again and asked if, by chance, she had read the letter.

No, she hadn't. She was only eight or nine years old at the time and it never would have crossed anyone's mind to give it to her to read. But she had seen it in the hands of her grandmother Sofiya. She could still visualize her, sitting in an armchair in her bedroom, a large black shawl draped over her shoulders and knees, and the letter she was holding between her fingers resting against the shawl. She had a fixed stare and said nothing.

"I lingered for a moment looking at her; then I foolishly

asked her what was wrong. Someone instantly grabbed me by the arms and carried me out of the room. The house gradually became filled with people, like when my grandfather Khalil had died several weeks earlier.

"Later that day, Nazeera explained to me that the letter that caused such turmoil came from my uncle Alfred, who had written to tell us of the death of two of our relatives. He described Gebrayel's accident in detail, but said very little about Anees."

My grandmother could have told me exactly what was in her brother's letter, if only I had thought of asking her . . . She had read it over and over again; the words must have been permanently imprinted in her youthful memory. I am so mad at myself for my lack of curiosity. Elderly persons are a treasure that we squander in cajoleries and blandishments; then we remain forever unsatisfied. The roads leading up to us are hazy; they become distinct for a very brief moment, then vanish into the dust.

Some will think, so what? What is the purpose of knowing about our forebears? Let the dead bury the dead, as the hackneyed saying goes, and let's concentrate on our own lives.

True, there is no need for us to know about our origins. Nor is there any need for our grandchildren to know anything about our lives. We each live through the years assigned to us and then go to our eternal sleep in the grave. Why bother to think about those who came before us, for they mean nothing to us? Why bother to think about those who will come after us, for we shall mean nothing to them? But if everything is destined to sink into oblivion, why do we build anything, and why did our ancestors build anything? Why do we write anything, and why did they write anything? Why even bother to plant trees or have children? Why do we bother to fight for a cause, or speak of progress, change, humanity, and the future? By living exclusively for the present, we let ourselves be hemmed in by an ocean of death. Conversely, by reviving the past, we enlarge our living space.

For me, at any rate, the pursuit of origins is a way of rescuing territory from death and oblivion, a reconquest that ought to be patient, devoted, relentless, and faithful. When my grandfather courageously disobeyed his parents in the late 1880s and pursued his studies in a far-away school, he was opening the paths of knowledge for me. And if he left all these traces before dying, all these neatly recopied writings in verse and prose, along with commentary on the circumstances of their writing or oral delivery—if he left all these letters and dated note-books—didn't he expect someone someday to pay heed to them? Of course, he wasn't thinking precisely of me, for I came into the world a quarter of a century after his death; but he hoped someone would pay heed. And anyhow, it matters little what he personally may have hoped; now that the only traces of his life are in my hands, it is impossible for me to let him die in oblivion.

Not he nor anyone to whom I owe the smallest particle of identity—my names, my languages, my beliefs, my errors, my bouts of rage, my ink, my blood, and my exile. I am the son of each of my ancestors, and in exchange, I am destined to be their belated parent. My son Botros, who died suffocated, my son Gebrayel, whose bones were broken: I wish I could clasp you both tightly to my breast, but I can embrace only your shadows.

No doubt I should give up looking for Alfred's fateful letter. But the thick envelope he sent from Havana at the end of the Great War contained not just the death announcement but also photos that luckily weren't lost. I saw several when I rummaged through the family papers. I didn't pore over them all as attentively as I should have, because I was so fascinated by a sentence written in Arabic at the bottom of one photo:

> This picture is the last one we have of our late lamented Gebrayel.
> It was taken on June 16, 1918, in the Estrella de Oriente lodge. He
> is sitting in front of Alice; she is wearing the crown because she
> was the queen of the lodge.

The last picture? No doubt. But for me it was the first. I had never seen my Cuban great-uncle's features before. He looked different from his brother. In spite of all the care Botros took in the way he dressed, he always looked like a mountain man wearing his Sunday best, with his thick hair, his bushy mustache, and his way of looking into the lens with the gaze of someone who still marveled at the invention of photography. Gebrayel, on the other hand, looked urbane, trim, polished, well-groomed, and he seemed to be repressing his impatience as he posed for the photo. His wife, too, has the look of a wealthy city resident, a look her sister, my grandmother, never had—except perhaps in the photos of her as a young student in the American School for Girls.

In that "last picture" from Havana, taken in a luxurious residence, in a spacious drawing room with a checkered black-and-white tiled floor, I count thirty-seven other people gathered around the couple—men and women, some standing, others sitting—and at the back of the room an antique statue and a large Cuban flag draped over a mirror.

I discovered from my inquiries that the Estrella de Oriente mentioned in the photo caption is a Masonic-inspired order for women that is particularly widespread in the United States, with which Cuba had close cultural ties in 1918. Its lodges are called "chapters," and, predictably, its members are called "sisters." At present they must number close to three million. Though the majority are wives, widows, or daughters of Masons, their symbolic system differs from that of the "brothers." Masons, as the name implies, are supposed to build an ideal temple—that is to say, a better world—and they use the terms "apprentice," "companion," and "master." The sisters turn to prestigious female figures, particularly biblical ones; their ranks are named after Ruth, Jephthah's daughter, Martha, and Queen Esther—no doubt the rank Alice had attained the day the photo was taken, which explains her crown and scepter.

After this first, purely encyclopedic bit of research, I took a closer look at some of the other persons in the photo. At first I couldn't recognize any of them. I merely assumed that for a Masonic ceremony that was so important to them, Gebrayel and Alice would probably have invited their son's godfather, Fernando Figueredo Socarrás, a prominent figure in the Grand Lodge of Cuba. Having learned from earlier research that a postage stamp bearing his image had been issued in 1951, I consulted specialized catalogs. I found the man. On the stamp and in the photo. The same man, with the same bearing, easily recognizable with his black bow tie and goatee—the kind called "imperial," which he wore uncommonly long.

Encouraged by this discovery, which wasn't really unexpected, I tried to find another distinguished person in the photo, who had been mentioned by Gebrayel in his letters: Alfredo Zayas, former vice president of the Cuban Republic at the time, later elected president in 1920. In his letters, my great-uncle spoke about him as a friend, and I was curious to see if they were truly close. After finding the politician's portrait in a book on the history of the Cuba, I looked for his match in the photo and had no trouble recognizing him standing on the far left. After further research I was able to identify a few other men, a total of three former or future Cuban heads of state. But none of these men held my attention. It was Gebrayel's face that I wanted to look at again, his and Alice's, and then his once again. They had certainly come a long way from their tiny village in the Lebanese Mountains! As they posed for the photographer, they both must have been saying to themselves, Is this really me, or is this a dream? Am I really the center of attention, being feted and honored? Am I really enthroned in the midst of these noble señoras and famous men?

The Great War was so distant from them! The famine in the old country and the poverty of the Orient, so far away.

And yet this triumphant photo had arrived in an envelope with a black border. No one in the village, no one in the family could have looked at it without having their eyes darkened by the shadow of death. "This picture is the last one we have of our late lamented Gebrayel . . ." Given this fact, the photo is like a container with a false bottom: on the surface, incredible success; underneath, the curse. With one glance you could see the tragedy of our Cuban family in its entirety.

A tragedy, each stage of which is preserved in the family correspondence: 1899, move to Havana and opening of the La Verdad stores; 1910, marriage; 1911, first child; 1912, the General Gómez building; 1914, second child, a daughter; 1917, a son; 1918, death. Gebrayel had not even turned forty-two.

For all these events, documents remain. How many times have I lined them up before me: the hand-drawn christening announcements; the photos of the elder son in a carnival costume and the other photos of him with his mother on the stairs of a castle; the daughter in her crib; the children and their friends on a large terrace during a party; Gebrayel's thick letters and his triumphant telegram—TELL BOTROS BOUGHT GOMEZ BUILDING . . . Yes, everything was there spread out before me. At this point I should have known everything, but I knew very little.

At most, I had narrowed the time frame for my great-uncle's death. When I had had my nighttime conversation with my friend Luis Domingo in Paris, I had "wavered" between the turn of the century and the 1920s. Now, thanks to the family archives, I could state that he was still alive on June 16, 1918, and that he died sometime before the end of the same year. However, I sensed that I wouldn't learn much more from the archives.

It was high time for me to travel to Cuba—partly as a pilgrimage, partly to research locations. There were so many places I had to see for myself, but I knew which would be the first. This I knew very early on, when I was first groping in the dark and quizzed my father's cousin, the one whom I've been calling the Orator. I had asked him a few preliminary questions about his uncle Gebrayel, his prosperity, and his tragic death.

First, he confirmed what Léonore had told me: "Yes, it was an accident. He loved cars and drove like a maniac!"

Was he alone that day?

"He had a chauffeur who died too. But Gebrayel was at the wheel."

Was the chauffeur from the old country?

"No, but he wasn't from Cuba either. In fact, he was buried in the same grave as my uncle, because he had no family there."

When I expressed surprise that he knew all these details, he told me that he had been to Cuba in the late 1940s.

"I was a member of an Arab delegation that toured the countries of Latin America. When I arrived in Havana, I remembered all the things I had been told about Gebrayel when I was a child, and I asked the people from the Lebanese colony if they had ever heard of him. The older people still remembered him; they all said he had been an illustrious person, a generous man, a prince! And they took me to a huge cemetery in the center of the city and showed me his tomb. A real mausoleum, all in white marble."

Following this conversation, I hastened to consult a map of Havana in a recent guidebook to check if this vague piece of information matched an identifiable location in the city today. I found only one plausible spot: a large, ancient necropolis named after Christopher Columbus. If the ghostly Gebrayel still resided somewhere on the surface of our globe, it could only be there.

Worldly
Residences

FORTY-THREE

Here I am in Cuba to find Gebrayel; in my diary is his last known address: the Colón Cemetery in Havana. I know I'll recognize his residence among all the others and decipher its inscriptions easily. A name engraved on stone isn't much, I have to admit, but it is the name of my relatives and the missing proof of their transatlantic dream.

We nomadic souls have a cult for vestiges and pilgrimages. We may not build anything durable, but we leave traces. And a few persistent noises.

On the advice of all my friends who know this island, I resolved to stay far away from tourist routes and official channels, in order to move about, ferret around, and live as I please. I found accommodations in Vedado, a large neighborhood in the northwest of the city, at the home of a woman whose name is Betty. Her house is slightly less posh than some others in the area, but also markedly less dilapidated. On the colonnaded veranda are a welcoming table and plastic chairs. The legs of the chairs are attached to the legs of the table, so the chairs won't be tempted to run away with just any old petty thief. In the evening the smell of gasoline and jasmine hangs in the air. In the small courtyard, two bougainvilleas, a gardenia, and, under a sheet metal carport, a nice green car manufactured in the days of the Soviet Union.

Looking at the map of the city, I discover that the cemetery is just a few streets away. I had no idea I would be that close to my great-uncle—assuming his grave is really there. I shall go there tomorrow, first thing in the morning, on foot. "A ten-minute walk at most," my landlady assures me.

This pilgrimage to the cemetery was supposed to be first on my list, but I arrived in Havana more impatient than tired, and there is another place that beckons to me. I confess I never was able to dislodge from my memory the ever-so-prosaic sentence found in Gebrayel's letter:

> Soon I plan to buy the house that the government built eight years ago for General Máximo Gómez. It is located at the corner of Prado and Monte avenues . . .

These words had instantly aroused the longings for a treasure hunt that date back to my earliest childhood reading. Longings that I believe I share with many of my kind, but that adulthood, jealous of our childhood dreams, tries to stifle. I don't think I'll be able to fall asleep tonight without having set eyes on this house, which Gebrayel called "the Gómez palace" in some of his letters and which used to be ours.

According to the research I did on the day before leaving on this trip, the Monte Avenue mentioned by my great-uncle is now called Máximo Gómez, no less, while Prado Avenue bears the name of José Martí. As I write these names, now familiar and practically like family, I have gained the feeling of being among relatives in an America that my ancestors secretly rediscovered and reconquered.

It must be the euphoria of travel, the same euphoria that always makes me feel that my first hours and days overseas thicken like lava and flow at an infinitely slow pace.

Midnight

My nighttime exploration has been a sobering experience. I didn't see the Gómez house. Or if I saw it, I didn't recognize it. Yet I scrupulously followed the procedure I had set for myself in Paris.

At the beginning of the evening I took a short walk in the neighborhood to a main road I had located on the map. I hailed a taxi and self-confidently asked the driver to take me to the center of the city, "Avenida Máximo Gómez." First surprise, the man hesitates. Did I mispronounce? I repeat the words, articulating clearly. How can a Havana taxi driver not know one of the main thoroughfares in the city? I unfold the map and point to "Máximo." The man looks. Thinks. Pouts. Finally he smiles with relief. *"Claro, sí, sí! Avenida Monte!"* I should have suspected as much: as often happens, in all climes, it is the old name that the natives still use . . .

After starting up the car, the man asks me to tell him the exact spot where I wanted to be dropped off. I say, "At the corner of Prado and Monte." He says nothing, but I sense that we still don't understand each other. And as soon as he has to stop for a traffic light, he swivels around with his entire upper body and points at the map with all five fingers: "What corner? There is no corner!"

In fact, there is no real intersection between Prado and Monte. Not that the two avenues are parallel. One crosses the city from north to south and the other from west to east; it is therefore not "geometrically" absurd to speak of a corner. Except these are two huge thoroughfares that connect at one point, or rather merge, like two rivers flowing into the same lake, in this instance a square so vast and with such irregular contours that a person standing in the middle of it could never encompass its different sides simultaneously in one glance.

I had to face the facts: Gebrayel's aim in writing wasn't to provide an address; he just wanted to blow his own trumpet and let his relatives know that he had acquired a sumptuous building in the heart of the city. As for the exact location, he didn't give it to "us"; it was up to me to find it.

But not tonight. I didn't find anything tonight. I just wandered in the area and studied several old buildings that might originally have been conceived as residential palaces. I tried to convince myself that it might be the astonishing chalet with brown and bright red walls, which is now a hotel; or the white building there at the corner; or the one across the street, even though the initials engraved on it, J and E, don't match any of my relatives' names—they might have been added at a later date.

No, what was the point of speculating or coaxing the facts? When I looked around, it seemed to me that this part of the city hadn't undergone too many barbaric renovations. There are still, thank God, countless old buildings; though tonight I still don't know which one was Gebrayel's property, I'll know tomorrow or the next day. It was best not to dig my heels in.

I climbed back into my waiting taxi and finished my evening in front of a glass of rum on the terrace of my temporary residence. I can't help but be moved by the fact that—after my great-uncle and my grandfather—here I am, feeling very much at home in Havana too, if only for a transient moment in my life, my face inviting the caresses of the Caribbean breeze. All around me in the dark I hear all sorts of cries, especially the barking of thousands of dogs near and far, but also, from the neighboring building, every three minutes, a shrew's surly voice yelling the name "Lázaro!"

FORTY-FOUR

JANUA SUM PACIS, says an inscription at the top of the monumental entrance to the Colón necropolis: "I am the gateway to peace."

With a glance I assessed the immense size of the mortuary city, the endless rows of proud and flat tomb structures crisscrossed with paths, walks, and avenues as far as the eye can see. I also assessed the impact of the Havana sun beating down on my brow and immediately rejected the idea of strolling about. I walked straight over to the administrative buildings, where, in the most prosaic way possible, I asked for the information that had led me to cross the Atlantic Ocean: "A member of my family was buried here in 1918 . . ."

I am handed a notebook in which I write down Gebrayel's full name in block letters.

A good sign: they don't seem to be at all fazed by the remote date of death; nor does my initiative seem at all incongruous to them. The official at the reception desk opens a register, recopies the names and dates in the appropriate columns, then closes the register and invites me to take a seat.

I hardly wait. She appears almost instantaneously. She is my heroine of the day—I feel like calling her Black Angel. Not only because of the location, where everywhere you look there are stone angels; not only because of her African origins, which she shares with over half the Cuban population; not because of her name, María de los Angeles, but because of her wide, cunning, reassuring smile, which instantly convinces me that a miracle will occur.

A miracle? The word is probably too strong. In boarding the plane to come to this island and in visiting this necropolis, I suspected that I had a good chance of finding traces of Gebrayel, particularly his grave. But not necessarily today, on the very first day after my arrival!

I began by explaining to María in my labored Castilian Spanish that my great-uncle had died in Cuba.

"Su abuelo?"

I almost corrected her to clarify things and explain that he wasn't exactly my grandfather. But what was the point of going into detail? It was better to simplify matters. Yes, my grandfather . . . Gabriel M. . . . Yes, in 1918. No, I didn't know the month: no earlier than June 16, and no later than December. Maybe, at the very latest, in the very first days of the following year. Should we look in the 1919 register? No, actually, it seemed very improbable to me. Nineteen eighteen should suffice . . .

She asked me to follow her and wait outside the door of the archives office. I sat down on a window ledge. At times I watched the comings and goings of visitors in the cemetery paths; at times, through the half-open door, I watched the comings and goings of María and the two other archivists—elderly men in overalls who climbed up on stepladders and reached for tan leather registers.

This dance lasted only a quarter of an hour, after which my heroine returned, smiling like a huntress and holding one of the ancient registers I had seen. It was open at a specific page, and she put it right under my nose. Since I couldn't decipher the handwriting of the clerk of old, she read out loud while I took notes:

Book of burials number 96, page 397, registration number 1588.

On June 21, 1918, burial was given at this Cristóbal Colón Cemetery, in crypt number thirty-three, acquired by Alicia, Widow M., to the body of Gabriel M., native of Syria, 42 years of age, married, deceased as a result of the traumatism of crushing, according to the certificate delivered by Dr. P. Perdomo. He was sent to us by the parish of Jesús del Monte, with permission from the municipal judge of the San Miguel del Padrón district . . .

I listen reverently and then take the register in my moist hands to read it myself and get some abbreviations and opaque figures explained to me. I experience a filial emotion that brings tears to my eyes, but also, simultaneously, a researcher's joy hardly appropriate to the event recorded in the register, or to the place where I am, even if, for me, this sunny cemetery summons a mood of serenity rather than desolation, and permanence rather than death.

What particularly strikes me in this short, dry text is the date. If Gebrayel was buried on June 21, he must have died a day or two before, yet the last photo I have of him was taken during the great Masonic meeting for Alice's "coronation," which was held on the sixteenth. There was a four-day interval at most between the moment of triumph and the moment of death.

I ask María if I can see the tomb. She replies that there were actually two successive graves; the first, rented in haste, where *"su abuelo"* rested temporarily; the second acquired in September of the same year, a permanent burial plot located in the most expensive section of the cemetery, where national figures and wealthy Havana merchants are buried.

Actually, the first is an anonymous rectangular gray slab in the midst of dozens of other identical numbered slabs—its particular reference number is 333—whereas the second is a veritable mortuary residence, not quite the sumptuous mausoleum described by the Orator, but nevertheless a beautiful white marble structure.

The name engraved on it is not my great-uncle's name, but as soon as I bent down, I was able to read, as on a palimpsest:

GABRIEL M. M.

Apparently our vault at the Christopher Columbus Cemetery has been used for many other mortal remains throughout the last century. There are epitaphs for several individuals, some clearly of Levantine origin, others bearing Hispanic or Slavic family names. On the marble rooftop are funerary statuettes—seven or eight, that look like the Tables of the Law, or lecterns, or angels' wings.

Not far from the grave is a bush that I can't identify, with wine-colored flowers; it was either planted or grew there on its own. A bit farther away, there is a kind of midget cypress tree. Then, a few steps away, in the same section, there is a mausoleum, a real one, the sanctuary for the ashes of José Martí's parents—a proximity that would have flattered Gebrayel.

As we sat at the foot of the vault in the only triangle of shade, I took the time to tell María who Gebrayel was, what I had heard about him in my childhood, and what I knew about him now. She asked me whether he has descendants in Cuba, adding that she is a trained genealogist and would be glad to help me track them down. I gladly provided her with the few pieces of information and family rumors I have, and she jotted them down diligently. I mentioned Alfred's name, and also the puzzling name of Arnaldo, whom my friend Luis Domingo said was an influential person here. No reaction on her part . . .

Before I set off, she asked me if I would like to have a word-for-word transcription of the register entry, duly signed by the cemetery authorities. I said yes, of course. She promised to take care of it in the course of the day and told me I could have the document tomorrow if I stopped by to see her.

It wasn't quite noon when I left the cemetery. Giddy, I must admit. Giddy from having been able to commune at Gebrayel's grave less than twenty-four hours after landing on this island.

In the wake of this miracle, why not try to find General Gómez's house again, since I had been frustrated last night? I therefore set off for the city center, toward that elusive intersection of "Prado" and "Monte," and I started to wander, building up convenient theories. But this time no angel came from heaven to guide me, and I discovered nothing to justify adding more lines to this paragraph.

I returned to Vedado, to my landlady's house, to rest from the sun and take a few notes. But two hours later, egged on, as so often, solely by my impatience, I decided to set off again for the center of the old city with a completely different idea in mind. Instead of groping in the dark for a house whose exact address I didn't know, why not go to the one address that is explicitly mentioned in the family letters? Hadn't Gebrayel had "Egido 5 and 7" printed on his 1912 envelopes and stationery? This was where the La Verdad stores were located before he bought the Máximo Gómez residence and expanded his business. This is also where Alice and he had their Havana apartment, as proved by the christening announcement of their eldest son in 1911. It is even probable that it was at this address that my grandfather Botros had lived during his stay in Havana, when he had to sleep in an attic.

You might wonder why I didn't go there first thing, last night. There are two reasons why, though I am aware of them only now as I write these lines. The first is that I was eager to see the palace before anything else, for in my imaginative world it best represents the fulfillment of "our" Cuban dream. The second reason is that Luis Domingo had warned me that this address was going to be hard to find.

Before taking off for Cuba, I had had several exchanges, by phone and mail, with my diplomat friend—who, as I think I mentioned, had been posted to Cuba for a long period of time—and he had lavished advice on me. Among other things, I had mentioned Egido Street to him, and he had kindly asked one of his good friends in Havana, a historian, if he could go by that street one day and report to us what the facades of numbers 5 and 7 looked like—and possibly even take a photo.

I received no picture from him, just the e-mail message that I hereby reproduce and that merely added to my confusion, as might be imagined:

My Cuban friend tells me that small numbers don't exist on
Egido, for the simple reason that since the thirties, this street has

become an extension of Las Misiones Avenue, which runs from
the Malecón, the seafront, and of Monserrate, which runs to the
train terminal, facing the Martí house. By a town-planning quirk
that he can't explain—nor can I!—the Egido numbers take up
where the Monserrate numbers end, and the Monserrate numbers
take up where the Las Misiones numbers end—go figure! The
only possible hypothesis: the numbers 5 and 7 where your
grandfather lived are presently the 5 and 7 on Las Misiones
Avenue . . .

It is easy to see why I didn't feel encouraged by this muddle to rush
to that address first thing last night. However, I did go there today and
was very conscientious. First I went to Egido Street and found that
sure enough, the lowest number was 501. In the 400 range, the name of
the street changes to Avenida de Bélgica; then, at 200 and some odd, to
Monserrate; and finally, for the lowest numbers, to Avenida de las Misiones. Meanwhile, I had already walked for three-quarters of an hour.

There, a few steps away from the sea, I see a building bearing the
double number "5 y 7" on its front, as if to cut short any further hesitation. Watchmen are on patrol at the door, which discourages me from
lingering nearby. In any case, there is nothing to see. Instead of the old
building resembling the drawing on the 1912 letters, there now stands
a very recent building whose dominant color is electric blue, probably
one of the least aesthetic structures in this beautiful capital. It is the
headquarters of revolutionary youth, or some such thing. On the wall
there is a long quotation from the Great Leader: *"Eso es que lo queremos
de las futuras generaciones, que sepan ser consecuentes"*—"What we ask of future generations is that they know how to be consistent."

I should like to take advantage of the serenity of nighttime to clarify a
point I left unexplained in recording the events of the day. When I reproduced the tombstone inscription, I wrote only "Gabriel M. M."
These initials, which I've already used time and again instead of real
names, warrant an explanation.

No one will be surprised if I mention here that my family name, like the village of my origins and my country, is both identifiable and fluid. Identifiable because all of us who bear the name feel a kind of tribal solidarity at the mention of it that reaches beyond languages, continents, and generations. Contrary to most family names, it is not derived from a profession, a geographical location, a moral or bodily characteristic, or a first name; it is a clan name, which links us all, at least in theory, to a common trajectory, originating somewhere near Yemen and whose traces are lost in the night of legends.

An identifiable family name, therefore, and yet, as I said, fluid. First of all, because of the very structure of Semitic languages, in which only the consonants are stable and the vowels unstable. Though the M, the central *l*, and the final *f* are found in all the transcriptions, there are countless variants. I know of about thirty: double or single *a* in the first syllable, or *e* sometimes and more rarely *o*; *ou*, *o*, or *oo* in the second syllable; as well as some more unexpected permutations resulting in Slavic, Greek, or North African sounds. To be thorough, I should also mention an added difficulty: my family name includes another consonant, *ayn*, the secret consonant of Semitic languages, the one that is never transliterated into other languages. In Arabic, this consonant precedes the A in the word "Arabi" and the I in "Ibri"—"Hebrew"; it is an imperceptible guttural consonant that non-natives have difficulty pronouncing, let alone hearing. It was already present in my country's oldest name, between the two twin *a*'s in "Canaan," and it is also hidden between the two *a*'s in my family name, making all transcriptions approximate.

I hardly dare mention the added complication, which is that no one in my village ever called me by that family name. Neither I nor Botros nor Gebrayel, nor any of my relatives. I don this family name, so to speak, to go into town or out into the world, but I don't use it in Machrah, or in any of the neighboring villages, and no one uses it to refer to me. This is easy to understand: when most of the inhabitants of a village share the same family name, it is of no use. Some other, more specific name is needed. To refer to the different family branches, the term *"jebb"* is used, which has the literal meaning of "well," or, more simply, the term *"beit,"* which means "house." Thus, Botros and his brothers belonged to *beit Mokhtara*, a branch of the family whose name derives from a grandmother with that first name. Nowadays, when my grandfather is recalled in the village, he is never referred to by any other name than Botros Mokhtara.

People who never left the small world of the village had no reason to ever use another name. In our day, this is seldom true, but in the past this was most often the case. Sometimes, when they were asked to give their family name by an Ottoman, French, or Lebanese official, they spontaneously gave the name of their branch, and that name was recorded on their identity papers. Today, more often, the opposite occurs: the everyday name isn't included on official papers, only the name of the large "tribe." As might be expected, this can give rise to comical situations, such as the one of the elderly cousin waiting in line whose "official" name was called out ten times in a row without his realizing it referred to him. No one had ever called him by that name . . .

As for Botros and his brothers, they had become accustomed to using the two family names simultaneously. Especially when they were "in the American countries," where it is common to insert a middle initial between the first name and last—Mokhtara being transformed into a discreet, cryptic M.

After this lengthy digression, I can finally reproduce in full the inscription I read this morning on my great-uncle's tomb in the Havana cemetery:

GABRIEL M. MALUF

FORTY-FIVE

I returned, as promised, to the Colón Cemetery. But this time I didn't go on foot; I didn't have the courage to walk under the Caribbean sun, even for ten minutes. I called a taxi—actually, a neighbor of my landlady's who works without a permit. He was able to enter the grounds of the necropolis, drive up and down its pathways, and park the car on the grounds, all of which I would have thought forbidden.

María de los Angeles came to meet me as soon as I arrived, bringing me not one *transcripción literal*, but two almost identical ones from the same register, one regarding the remains of my great-uncle, the other that of a twenty-eight-year-old married man, originally from Spain, whose name is spelled in two different ways in the space of a few lines: José Cueto, then José Cuaeto, also deceased "by crushing," *por aplastamiento*, and buried in the same grave—most probably the "foreign" chauffeur the Orator had mentioned to me.

My valuable informant tells me that according to the cemetery registers, the "concession" where Gebrayel is resting still belongs to our family. It occurs to me that if I were to die on this trip, this is where I would be buried—a prospect that doesn't delight me, of course, but doesn't alarm me either. It also occurs to me that when I die, in some other country—France, for example—I have no idea where I'll be buried. Actually, I don't much care. After my death I'll be a nomadic ghost wandering everywhere in the world, or else I'll be inanimate matter. Isn't that the alternative human beings face: either being a kind of minor divinity or nothingness with no memory or suffering? In either case, being planted in a particular soil won't get me anywhere.

And yet, and yet, I crossed half the globe to gaze at this tomb! And this morning again, after having formally thanked María and paid for the transcription, I went and meditated again by the family vault, and my emotion was not feigned. A cloud had come to temper the scorching sun, and this enabled me to stand at the foot of the monument a few minutes longer, bareheaded, with images and nostalgia beating against my temples.

As soon as the shade left, I climbed back into the car to go to the National Library, which, in Havana, bears the omnipresent name of José Martí. I wanted to research something specific: since I had now narrowed down the date of the fatal accident to within a day or two, shouldn't I be able to find articles about it in the newspapers from that time?

In one of his letters, Gebrayel had included long quotations from *El Mundo*, a Havana daily that had published an article in 1912 referring to him as "the very well-known Sr. Gabriel Maluf." It is legitimate to assume that when that person is the victim of an accident, the same newspaper would report on it.

The person in charge tells me that *El Mundo*, alas, cannot be consulted. The collection is in the library, and according to the index cards, the year 1918 is complete, but it is in such a poor state that the pages could crumble in my fingers. And no, alas, it is not on microfilm.

Was there some other daily from that time? There is only one on microfilm, the *Diario de Cuba*, but it was a Santiago newspaper, not a Havana one. Never mind. If it's the only one, I'll consult it anyhow.

So I'm given the reel for the year 1918, and I insert it as best I can into the antique East German machines. I do my utmost to unroll it, page by page, day by day. The date approaches: April 27, May 3, May 12, May 31 . . . The front-page articles are about the war in Europe, pre-dictably, and about attempts to restore peace. June 14, 17, 18, 20. More war, more rumors of imminent peace, but also a report on the torren-tial rains on the island—bereft of the photos that, in our day, would have illustrated these calamities.

Suddenly, a big headline, right in the middle of the first page:

DOS MUERTOS A CONSECUENCIA
DE UN ACCIDENTE AUTOMOVILISTA

And right underneath, in slightly smaller characters:

One of the victims is the well-known Havana businessman, Señor Gabriel Maluf.

Then comes the text of the story:

Havana, June 21 (from our wire service)—
    Yesterday, on his way to the city by the road leading to Santa María del Rosario, the shop owner Señor Gabriel Maluf fell off the roadway in the car that was transporting him; this caused injuries from which he died a few minutes later. The car was being driven by the lawyer José Casto, who also died, almost instantaneously, as a result of the accident.

While I am recopying the text of the dispatch by hand, word for word, and wondering whether the unfortunate José's name was Casto, and not Cuaeto or Cueto, and whether he was a lawyer or a chauffeur, the woman in charge of the periodicals room comes and tells me that she has found another daily for the year 1918, the *Diario de la Marina*.

She'll make an exception and allow me to consult the original newspapers.

This newspaper must have been important, because it put out two editions a day, one in the morning and one in the afternoon. And it is on the first page of the late edition, *edición de la tarde*, dated June 20, 1918, that I am able to read, below exactly the same headline as the Santiago newspaper—"Two deaths from an automobile accident"—the following "introductory paragraph":

> The shop owner Gabriel Maluf and his chauffeur fell in an automobile, from a height of twenty meters, off the San Francisco de Paula Bridge.

Then this text:

> As we were about to put this edition to bed, we were informed of a regrettable automobile accident that occurred in the outskirts of the capital, one kilometer away from the village of San Francisco de Paula. The shopkeeper Señor Gabriel Maluf, owner of the La Verdad establishments, located at the corner of Monte and Cardenas, was heading for Havana by the Güines road and was at the wheel of his car when he drove off the bridge near San Francisco and landed in the river twenty meters below.
>
> The car was destroyed. The bodies of Señor Maluf and his chauffeur were removed from the car wreck completely crushed. The village authorities rushed to the spot to help, and the judge arrived on the scene and ordered the removal of the remains.
>
> We will give further details in our next edition.

In my haste to read the rest, I turn the page brusquely. The sound of ripping rings out in the silence of the library; nothing serious—a tear of less than centimeter on the edge of the sheet—but the woman in charge of the room is already standing in front of me and explaining that it is obviously too risky to let visitors handle fragile documents. Feeling embarrassed and at fault, I defend myself badly, and the collection is taken away from me. This trivial incident, which I am almost ashamed to relate, suddenly brings me back to childhood. Over a third of a century of adulthood, hundreds of white hairs, and here I am being punished like a schoolboy! I'm furious, but I also feel like laughing. Finally I stand up, assume an angry expression, and leave in a dignified manner.

I'll return. I'll stay away for a short time, the space of a weekend, then return as if nothing had happened. There is no point in my making a scene. I would be annoyed at myself if I did. After all, they have already done favors for me at the Martí Library. In the Paris reading rooms where I usually work, I would never have been allowed to consult an unavailable collection; I could never have gotten around a "no." Besides, to begin with, a person in my situation, a traveler out of the blue, a temporary city visitor, would never have been admitted to do research; he would have had to fill out a request, present various documents, and wait several days, with no assurance of being accepted. Here they did me a favor. It would be wrong to react with arrogance. It was wiser to let the storm blow over.

Anyhow, I have already gathered some valuable information. Not only the exact date and location of the accident that cost my great-uncle his life, but also, for the first time, the exact address of his shops—"at the corner of Monte and Cardenas."

Friday evening

When I finished lunch, without waiting for the cool period of the day, I called the gypsy cab to take me to that address. On the way, I glanced at the map and noticed that Cardenas Street runs from Monte Street to the train station Gebrayel mentions in his letter. Perfect. Everything fitted together. I was burning, as I used to say as a child . . .

Actually, I wasn't burning yet. As soon as I got there, I was perplexed again; the topography was muddled and the landmarks unclear. In theory, only the two corner buildings could have been, in a previous life, the residence built by the government for the hero Máximo Gómez and acquired by my great-uncle for his La Verdad shops. I walked back and forth from one sidewalk to the other, scrutinizing the first, then the second, then the first again, then the second. Neither of them convinced me; neither could have been a palace. One looked like a reconverted factory, the other like a residential rental property. I took notes, measured the height of the ceilings with my fingers spread apart, and leaned against a column. Being feverish, disappointed, preoccupied, I didn't notice that a growing number of people were clustering in the street or appearing at the windows, looking at me, intrigued or somewhat suspiciously.

I became aware of the commotion I was causing only when a woman, a *métisse* of about forty, called out to me from her balcony, her hands cupped around her mouth. I looked at her, mystified; she signaled to me to come closer, which I felt obliged to do. Then, standing right beneath her, hands cupped around my mouth, I started explaining my comings and goings to her.

I was sure she wouldn't understand a thing, but at least I wanted to show my goodwill by adopting an explanatory attitude. After that, I expected to wave goodbye and walk away quietly. But the lady turned out to be insistent, and since, not surprisingly, she couldn't understand a thing from my gesticulations, she did something that no one in any other country would ever have done: she pulled a bunch of keys out of her pocket and threw them down to me without saying anything. I caught them before they landed and looked up at her inquiringly and with amusement. She pointed to the entrance of her building and immediately disappeared inside so she could let me in. Did I have a choice? I went to the entrance.

Behind the metal door was a dark, steep staircase that instantly makes you forget that there is sunshine outside. Rather than grope for an unlikely light switch, I clung to the banister as if it were a mountain-climbing rope. For what might have been the hundredth time since I've been in Havana, I said to myself that this city is probably the most beautiful one I know, but also the ugliest. With every step I take as I walk around, I am tempted to stop in front of a potentially gorgeous building, pretend that I am an architect or decorator, and imagine how the facade would look if the revolution's "ravages of time" were fixed. Palaces here are chopped up into fourteen hovels, and I am constantly overcome by perverse dilemmas of conscience: Is it really necessary for the noble principle of equality to spread insalubrious conditions and ugliness?

Reaching the third-floor landing with questions like these in the back of my mind, I am almost ashamed to come face-to-face with the kind

woman who invited me into her home. In her one and only room, two adolescents are sprawled out on the floor in front of the flickering image of a
decrepit television set. As soon as they spot my foreign appearance, they
offer to sell me contraband cigars, but halfheartedly, without taking the
trouble to stand up, as if this were part of the normal social interchange
between their world and mine. I reply with a polite smile, but the mother
reprimands her sons and they go back to looking at the fascinating screen.

I try to explain to my hostess why I was in the street in front of her
building, and for the umpteenth time, of course, I mention my *abuelo*.
This immediately arouses a worried shudder in her and her sons; indeed, in a country where so many houses were confiscated and distributed to the present occupants, I could easily seem like a former owner
who has come to research locations and is planning to return some time
in the future with a bailiff to reclaim his property.

I go to great lengths to add reassuring details: the person who lived
in Cuba wasn't my grandfather, but my great-uncle; he didn't live in
this building, but in the one across the street; moreover, he died in
1918. I repeat the date two, three, four times, just to make it clear that
I'm a nostalgic oddball, not a vengeful émigré. Smiling once again, the
lady asks me to follow her down the hall to her neighbor Federico's.
More explanations, anxieties—*"el hermano de su abuelo?"*—details, dates,
et cetera. The man deliberates, scratches his head, and pronounces his
verdict: "Dolores is the only person who might know." His neighbor
agrees. Dolores is the only person who has been living in the building
long enough. She lives on the ground floor, if I want to see her . . .

The lady downstairs looked like a Spanish aristocrat whose ancestors
had come on Christopher Columbus's caravels and sailed back, leaving
her behind. Her apartment was as dark as a cellar, but a serene nocturnal
light emanated from her white hair. Her apartment opened directly out
onto the sidewalk; it may originally have been a store or a caretaker's
lodge. She had been living in the neighborhood for decades and had
worked, coincidentally, in the building across the street as a department
supervisor. However, she had never heard of the La Verdad shops, or of a
house that had once been built for Máximo Gómez. "In fact, see for your-

self, neither of these buildings could have been conceived as a residence for a national hero." She wasn't trying to discourage me; this was the absolute truth, as I myself had noticed. She said she was sorry and seemed sincere. From our first verbal exchange, her eyes had lit up with a glimmer of healthy curiosity. She questioned me about the shops, about Gebrayel, about how he had died; then she put forward some sensible hypotheses and a few suggestions. "You must consult the city historian; if you want, come pick me up one day, I'll take you there." She uttered *el historiador de la ciudad* with great pride, and I promised her—and myself—to call on her in the beginning of the week, for it was Friday afternoon and too late to approach an administrative office with a request.

Once again I didn't satisfy my curiosity as far as the famous Gómez house is concerned. I still don't know which house it was, or whether it still exists. Though I now have a more specific address than before, the mystery remains.

My day may have been punctuated by failure, but it leaves no bitter aftertaste. Though I don't know much more than yesterday, I have absorbed thousands of sensations, elusive and confused, but no less real. This country is winning me over, just as it had formerly captivated Gebrayel. Keys are thrown down to me from balconies, my reading matter is confiscated, people address me with the familiar *tu* in the street; they smile at me, woo me, help me, punish me. I am deeply shaken as a Levantine male and a Europeanized adult. My grandfather couldn't bear this, and I don't blame him for it. I am just a bit sad for him, and for us, that he chose not to stay on this island.

Yes, I know, this sort of reasoning is absurd. If Botros had opted for Cuba, he would have had a different life, different children, and different grandchildren. I wouldn't have been born in the Caribbean, the Levant, or anywhere. I was born from a succession of encounters, and had one of them been skipped, I wouldn't have been born, and no one would have missed me. All I wish to say is that this island fills me with deep affection; in another life I would have been glad for it to be mine, and I would have enjoyed loving it.

FORTY-SIX

Though I made no significant discovery yesterday, I did find out, from the newspaper I consulted in the National Library, the exact location of the car accident that cost Gebrayel his life and the life of the young man accompanying him. So today I went on a pilgrimage to the old bridge of San Francisco de Paula.

This small town, southeast of Havana, is mentioned in recent guidebooks only because it houses the Hemingway Museum. Though it is very close to the capital, it is not fully a part of it, at least not yet; the two towns haven't been completely connected by the growing number of constructions, and one has the feeling of not being in an urban area anymore, especially when one has driven beyond the few recent buildings in the center of the city and taken the road to Güines and Matanzas.

"One kilometer away from the village," it said in the

June 20, 1918, issue of the *Diario de la Marina*, there was—and still is—a bridge.

The taxi parked a bit farther down in a shady area, and I walked back to the spot where the accident must have occurred. The road going to Havana narrows abruptly at that point. If Gebrayel was speeding, he might have noticed this too late; he might have turned the steering wheel sharply, skidded on the muddy roadway, and dived into the ravine, which isn't "twenty meters below," as it said in the newspaper, but no more than six or seven—a sufficient distance, however, to kill passengers in a car plunging into it at top speed.

Had I been able to forget, for one instant, the tragedy that had taken place, the site would have seemed to me like a small tropical paradise: the stream of clear water dotted with white stones; the banana trees, the picture-postcard palm trees, the *yagruma* overrun all the way to the top by a climbing plant with gigantic leaves, and the carpet of unruly weeds. But on the day Gebrayel died, there must have been nothing but mud, spilled gasoline, and blood.

While the cabdriver and I were busily pacing around near the precipice, an older man came up and asked us if some misfortune had occurred. Wearing an orange hard hat, but only as protection from the sun, he struck me as a retired engineer. "I was gardening," he said, "and when I saw you looking down below, I was afraid there might have been another accident. There often are accidents right around here, you know. The road narrows too suddenly, so people who are speeding can't slow down quickly enough."

The man illustrated his explanations with gestures. I listened to him, nodding my head politely, not knowing whether to laugh or cry at this belated testimony. Spoken before a jury, his words would have brushed aside any lingering suspicion of an assassination. I still had doubts before I came here, but now, standing in this spot, I have none whatsoever. On that accursed June day in 1918, my great-uncle had had no enemy other than himself, and no killer other than his own lust for life and his desire to get ahead.

I may be wrong, but right now this is my deep conviction.

·   ·   ·

Since I have taken up residence in her house, Betty has quizzed me several times on my reasons for coming to Havana and on my comings and goings; I have been glad to oblige, and I speak to her willingly. As I have nothing to hide and am anyhow convinced that her neighbor with the gypsy cab would promptly inform her of all my trips, I am in the habit of describing my day to her in the evening on the terrace, sitting with a glass of rum, or in the morning, with a cup of coffee. Tea is nonexistent in Cuba this year; I didn't try to find out why.

So when I returned home tonight, my landlady told me that she had taken a document out of her old cupboard that she thought might be useful in my research: a very old map of Havana, drawn up in the days of Spanish rule, that her grandfather had acquired when he was an officer. Since it is hardly ever used, it is still in a good state, except that it tends to rip when it is unfolded. But it is still perfectly legible. Spread out on the dining-room table under a bright overhead light, it turned out to be full of information.

I start by looking for the main thoroughfares. Oddly, they are all practically the same as on modern maps, except that most of the names are different—at least at first sight. Thus the avenue now called Avenida Máximo Gómez used to be named after a Prince Alfonso in colonial times. Yet it seems that people already had the ingrained habit of calling it Monte, for that name is indicated in parentheses. Right nearby is the Isabel la Católica park, as well as "la calle de la Reina," now rebaptized Bolívar for part of its length. As for the "calle del Egido," to my astonishment, it hasn't moved an inch. I place the old map next to the present one; the street still starts at the same spot. I can even compare the numbers; where the modern plan has 517—an old Ursuline convent—in the days of the Spanish, the number was 17. This time, yes, I feel like crying "Eureka!"

I am eager for daybreak so I can go to that spot and see for myself.

I went inside to go to bed, but I was too impatient and couldn't fall asleep. I poured myself some rum, went outside, and sat on the veranda with my notebook.

The neighborhood may be slumbering, but not the sounds. The

dogs still bark, those in the neighborhood and those far away in the night. From time to time, the shrew next door yells her usual "Lázaro!"

I smile and shut my eyes. A gentle, warm breeze blows over my moist eyelids. I suddenly have the feeling of having been born in this city. Yes, in this city, too.

FORTY-SEVEN

Early this morning, when the seven or eight families living in 505 Egido Street began opening their blinds to let in the first rays of sunlight, they could see a corpulent foreigner with long gray hair posted across the street from their house, leaning against the strange rock, which had been planted, for some mysterious reason, on the little triangular square among the fan-shaped row of palm trees. He was holding an earth-colored spiral notebook and a letter written in that very house in 1912.

So long as I hadn't seen the building, I couldn't be sure of anything; I could only hypothesize, make suppositions, and hope. Now I had certitudes that I could confirm with my own eyes: the facade in front of me was identical to the one printed on Gebrayel's envelopes and on the letterhead of the La Verdad shops. Yes, absolutely identical, the same front columns, the same window frames, the same shape of roof, the same edges . . . Except that my great-uncle's stores occupied two adjacent buildings, the numbers 5 and 7. Today, only the first remains, the one on the left, rebaptized 505; the other has been torn down, and there is nothing in its place. It is a barren wasteland.

I looked at the drawing, the building, and the drawing again, measured with my fingers and compared . . . My great-uncle had had LA VERDAD DE G. M. MALUF written across the entire facade in white letters. On the building that is still standing, you used to be able to read LA VERDAD and the D of the DE, whereas the E straddled the two adjoining buildings. I got closer to the building. Is it an illusion, a hallucination, or a mirage? I could clearly see, right where I would expect, the lower half of the A from VERDAD and a bit of the final D. After so many years? My rational mind told me to keep quiet; it preferred to think that these are streaks of limestone or the remains of more recent paint. Later, I shall look at the photos under a magnifying glass or microscope. No. Why, what for? The house numbers and the drawings are right; why would I have to summon hallucinations? Why swap the pleasure of an unhoped-for discovery for a vulgar miracle?

I went up to the entrance of what is now dilapidated housing but whose door is that of an old store. The residents looked at me, intrigued; in my shaky Castilian Spanish I gave them the same explanation I've been giving since I arrived in Cuba. They didn't smile; they remained silent; they only nodded their heads, weary and resigned. Inside, everything was black from poverty and soot. I climbed upstairs on a ladder and looked around for the attic where my grandfather had slept during his short stay in the city, very likely a contributing factor in demoralizing him and dissuading him from extending his stay.

Like him, I felt ill at ease in that place. Still, I forced myself to stand there motionless, in the humid darkness, for one or two minutes, so that my spirit would imbibe some of the spirit of "our" former house. But I was eager to leave. I went and sat on the rock again, opposite the house, to look at it from afar, imagine times long past, and write these notes.

· · ·

I feel overcome by a feeling of pointlessness and oblivion. What had I come to look for, originally, in this city? The imprint of my relatives? Standing before me are their crumbling myths, and resting in the cemetery, their ashes.

FORTY-EIGHT

Return visit, this morning, to the José Martí Library. Locked doors were unlocked, as well as some others that I didn't know existed. The island's jovial divinities are watching over my trip, or perhaps it is the shades of our émigrés.

I walk in, sit down at a vacant table, and request the original paper version of the *Diario de la Marina* as if Friday's incident had not occurred. The woman in charge of the room brings the volume to my reading table herself and gives me a knowing wink to make it clear that she is not doing this against her will. Without thinking, I plant a kiss on her cheek; she is startled, but her smile broadens. Behind me, I hear her colleagues chuckling. God, how I love this country! And how sorry I am that my relatives ever turned their backs on it. Still, they might have left anyhow, for entirely different reasons, a few decades later. The roads of Cuban history are as slippery as the road in San Francisco de Paula . . .

I look through the June 21, 1918, issue for more details of the accident. In vain. But on page 4, I come across an announcement framed in black, topped with a cross and the letters "E.P.D." which stand for *en paz descanse*, "may he rest in peace." And the death announcement:

EL SEÑOR

GABRIEL M. MALUF

HA FALLECIDO

His funeral will take place today, Friday, at four o'clock in the afternoon. His widow, relatives, and persons close to him request that his friends attend the solemn transfer of the body from his residence at 53 Patrocinio Street, Loma de Mazo, to the Colón Necropolis.

Listed below are the names of Alicia and her children, Alfred, someone by the name of Salomón B. Maluf, and about a dozen close friends, including—I'm not really surprised—the omnipresent Fernando Figueredo Socarrás. I notice that the other intimates in mourning have diverse origins: José Cidre Fernández, Charles Berkowitz, Elias Felaifel, José Salaun, Milad Cremati, Pablo Yodú, Bernardo Argüelles, Alejandro E. Riveiro, Aurelio Miranda, Morris Heymann, as well as Carlos Martí, a well-known Cuban journalist and writer, of Catalonian origin like José Martí, but not related to him.

I note down all the names carefully, but I don't dwell on them. What most gives me pause is Gebrayel's home address, which I recopy in large letters on a separate sheet of paper: "Calle de Patrocinio num. 53, Loma del Mazo."

I vow to find this spot and go there. But before doing so, to put my mind at rest, I continue reading the *Diario de la Marina*, and on one of the following pages I find a second announcement, signed by the employees of the La Verdad stores, and a third signed by an association called the Syrian Progress.

In the next issue, dated June 22, there is a long description of the funeral, no doubt the best indication of the position Gebrayel occupied in the Cuban society of his day.

EL SEPELIO DEL SEÑOR MALUF

A moving demonstration of bereavement, a beautiful expression of sympathy, such was the burial ceremony of the very well-known and justifiably highly esteemed shop owner Mr. Gabriel Maluf, who met a horrible death from an automobile accident, as reported in our late Thursday edition.

The magnificent residence of the Maluf couple, number 53 Patrocinio Street, was turned into a temporary mortuary. The anguish of those close to him was very poignant. The corpses of Mr. Maluf and his chauffeur, Mr. Cueto, were in the same mortuary room, and we saw a wreath lying on the latter's coffin with the inscription "From the Maluf family to José Cueto." The hapless Spanish chauffeur having no family here in the Cuban Republic, this is an attitude deserving of mention.

The unfortunate shop owner's luxurious coffin was literally covered with beautiful wreaths and a large number of fresh flower crosses, sent by major businesses and many families in our city.

At exactly four o'clock, the funeral procession left La Víbora. The crowd was huge. Hundreds of carriages and automobiles followed the austere, luxurious hearse. Many people came and joined the procession at the entrance to the Colón Cemetery.

Those attending the funeral ceremony included, in the first row: the deceased's brother-in-law, Mr. Alfredo K. Maluf; Mr. Colonel Fernando Figueredo Socarrás, General Treasurer of the Republic; Mr. José Solaun; Mr. Aurelio Miranda; Mr. Charles Berkowitz; Drs. Bernardo Moas and Felix Pages; and our colleague Carlos Martí, as well as Mr. Elias Felaifel, Mr. Milad Cremati, Mr. Pablo Foch, Mr. Bernardo Argüelles, Mr. Alejandro E. Riveiro, and Mr. Morris Heymann. Behind were the delegations from the association of trade employees, of which the deceased was an honorary member, and from the Syrian Progress association, which he was president of, as well as representatives from the French, North American, Spanish, and Syrian communities and the major businesses established here in the capital.

He was buried in one of the bishopric vaults, after moving words were spoken in Spanish, English, French, and Arabic by the deceased's distinguished friends, praising his qualities, his character, his savoir faire, energy, enthusiasm, and decisiveness, which were apparent in each of his initiatives, in each of his daily obligations, in each of his infatuations. Among the close friends who said his farewells was Mr. Martí.

The deceased belonged to a distinguished Syrian family. One of his brothers, living in Mount Lebanon, is a high Church dignitary.

May he rest in peace, for he was a good husband, a good father, and a useful member of society.

We would like to address our heartfelt condolences to his inconsolable widow, the distinguished and cultured lady Alicia Maluf, as well as to Mr. Alfredo Maluf.

I had to recopy this long article by hand, since putting this large, fragile volume in a photocopying machine was out of the question. After that, I lacked the patience to continue searching through the old newspapers of the period. Above all, I was eager to go to the address where the author of the article said "the magnificent residence of the Maluf couple" was located.

I therefore looked on the map of Havana for the Mazo del Loma neighborhood mentioned in the article. In vain. I questioned the woman in charge of the library room. The name wasn't familiar to her. Evidently it was no longer used. She advised me to go check at the Mapoteca, the department of old maps. I could have waited until I returned home and consulted my landlady's old map, but since I was right on the spot . . .

The research was brief and fruitful; the name, in large letters, was spread across a map dating from the early twentieth century. It must have been the fashionable residential neighborhood for Havana's wealthy class, but the name Mazo del Loma, "Mallet Hill," was already competing with another, more commonplace one, which stuck. In fact, it was mentioned in the *Diario de la Marina*, for it said that the funeral procession left "La Víbora"; I had read the word while I was recopying the article, but in my haste, I hadn't made the connection.

Really, Cubans have no respect for the names imposed on them. It's not surprising that today's Great Leader hasn't given his name to any street, square, or building. A wise precaution; there is no monumental statue either, or postage stamp bearing his image. In the inevitable not-too-distant future, when his successors rebel against his posthumous fame, they will find no bronze beard to knock down and not much to rename.

Thus Mazo del Loma is forgotten, but not La Víbora, "the Viper." Nowadays this neighborhood, in the southeast part of the city, not too far from the San Francisco de Paula road, is known only by this name. Based on the approximate hour when the daily late edition of the *Diaro de la Marina* must have gone to press, we can reasonably assume that Gebrayel was rushing to get home for lunch when he lost control of his car.

When I left the library, I hailed a taxi—an antique red Dodge with a white roof, the kind of car that exists only in museums and the streets of Havana. I gave the chauffeur the address and became lost in contemplation. All around me, nothing but a brouhaha and fleeting images. I had the odd feeling that I had jumped inside a car that was going in reverse, back to the beginning of the twentieth century, and I dreaded the moment when I would wake up in my bed wondering what this dream meant. But when I opened my eyes, I was in front of the sign saying Patrocinio Street.

"What number did you say?"

"Fifty-three."

The taxi had to keep driving, the street being straight and endless. At a certain point, however, it seemed to come to an end; although the house numbers were still in 300 range, the road was suddenly blocked by a building. It turned out to be a false alarm. By deviating to the left and continuing in the same direction, we were back on Patrocinio again, and the numbers were getting smaller.

Then it became a mountain road. On both sides, right and left, there were long, steep stairways instead of sidewalks. The taxi lacked daring and stamina; the driver decided to make a U-turn and gather momentum in the plain. When he charged uphill again and reached the top in a final sputter, I was tempted to applaud, as passengers some-times do in Mediterranean countries after a plane lands.

The numbers kept getting smaller, 71, 65, and, on the left, 68. We were still going uphill, but the slope was gentler. Suddenly a commonly used Lebanese saying flashed through my mind; to say a man has suc-ceeded, we exclaim, "His house is way at the top of the village!" It isn't surprising that this son of the Mountains wished to make a point of his social success by making his home high up at the summit.

Fifty-three. Good heavens!

"Our house," I whisper, though it isn't mine at all—at best, it is the house of about a dozen distant cousins whom I've never met. But I whisper "our house" again, and foolishly, prosaically, I have tears in my eyes.

Then I look at it affectionately and notice that unlike most Havana houses, it isn't at all dilapidated. It even seems to have been repainted in the last year. Only the low outside wall, supporting the wrought-iron railing and giving directly onto the street, has recent mold stains, but the iron railing itself is intact, isn't missing a single spear, and is hardly rusty.

"Our house in Havana" is a solid bourgeois building with colon-nades, similar to many other houses in the residential neighborhoods of the capital, white and cream-colored, more elegant than showy, sug-gesting that in spite of having suddenly come into wealth, my great-uncle had known how to avoid vulgar ostentation. This was a pleasant surprise for me, and a comfort. The Levantine exuberance of his sta-tionery led me to have different expectations. This restraint can doubt-less be explained by the moderating influence of his Presbyterian wife, whose upbringing had made her uneasy with any form of ostentation. Having frequented the house of my grandmother, Alice's sister, for more than thirty years, I haven't the slightest doubt in my mind about this.

The railing was chained shut. Would I have to be content with this outside view and these reassuring observations, and leave with two or three photos of the facade? Normally, I would have abstained from entering the property, but ever since I've set foot in Cuba, I'm not averse to sometimes going against the grain. I decided to go in, trespassing if need be. I hadn't come such a great distance, both in time and space, to stand meekly outside the gate. I therefore started unwinding and unknotting the chain, which was fortunately fastened without a padlock. Then I climbed the steps to the tall, large carved wooden door; it too was extremely well maintained or possibly restored. It was slightly ajar, though I hadn't seen this from the street.

My fingers tightly bent into a fist, I knocked at the door, vigorously and closely enough to the edge for the knocking to cause the door to open a bit wider. When I was able to slip my head inside, I saw a man sitting behind a table that was cluttered with sheets of paper, pencils, and rubber stamps. Apparently, this wasn't a residence, but the offices of a business or administration.

So I opened the door boldly, with bated breath. And what was the first thing I saw? Earthenware tiles with Oriental motifs, like a signature, covering the walls of the entrance to about the height of a person. My great-uncle's arabesque signature on his faraway patch of American homeland. If that alone is what I crossed the ocean to see, I did not come for nothing.

The man at the reception desk, a tall, thin *métis* chewing on a cigar butt, smiles at me and shakes my hand. His name is Matteo. He listens to the now-polished story of my Cuban great-uncle, looks moved, then explains, in turn, that the house is now a cultural center, more specifically a "Centro de Superación para la Cultura de la Ciudad de La Habana," *superación* being a slightly more ambitious concept than "development," "promotion," or "advancement." Actually, the house is a music school.

Indeed, a few minutes after entering, I hear music. It comes from beyond the corridor, from a large room whose high ceiling and walls are covered with earthenware and stucco. The motifs and inscriptions are copied from the Alhambra, particularly the motto of the Nasrides, Grenada's last Muslim kings: *La ghaliba illa-llah*, "No victor but God." It would seem that in this room, which may have been the dining room, the influence of the austere parson's daughter failed to prevail—not that the room reveals an ostentatious overindulgence, but the show of wealth is, let's say, not timid.

It would be unfair, however, to see this as just a nouveau riche whim; it wasn't his affluence that Gebrayel displayed on these walls, but his original culture, his identity. He felt the need to proudly proclaim his allegiance to Andalusian civilization, symbol of his family's influence.

At that intense moment I recalled a Berlin synagogue I had recently visited, built in the second half of the nineteenth century and now a museum. When I expressed surprise at the amazing resemblance between its architecture and that of the Alhambra, an official explained that for the city's Jewish community at the time, adopting this style was a way of asserting its Oriental origins and a mark of self-confidence, though no doubt it was also a fashionable style to which they had wished to conform.

The very same thing could be said of my Havana great-uncle: assertion of identity, self-confidence, conformity to the decorative style of the moment. In fact, the Hotel Inglaterra, Havana's prestigious luxury hotel built in the same period, has the same motifs on its walls—including the motto of the last Nasrid King, Boabdil. With regard to Gebrayel, let me add that for a Levantine émigré in a Spanish-speaking country, this was also a symbol of his ancestors' contribution to the Iberian Peninsula.

As a way of further emphasizing his double allegiance, my great-uncle had ordered, doubtless from the most skillful artisans of the time, two earthenware pictures representing scenes from *Don Quixote*; these were hanging on the corridor wall, facing the large Moorish room, as decorative counterparts.

I didn't want to overstay my welcome in the large Andalusian room. A music teacher was there with three students, and they had interrupted their lesson out of consideration for my pilgrimage. Not wishing to abuse their kindness, I pursued my landlord's tour with Matteo as guide. His cigar butt still between his lips, with an impressive bunch of keys in his hands, he seemed as moved as I by my discoveries, and ready to give me as much of his time as needed.

The rest of the house, though by no means showy, was nonetheless plush, especially compared with the conditions of life at the time in our villages in Mount Lebanon and what Gebrayel's life had undoubtedly been like when he first settled in Cuba. "Thank God we now have a house where we will be able to live together like all respectable people instead of sleeping in the attic as we did before," he wrote to my grandfather, trying to coax him into returning. Indeed, there were seven bedrooms and three or four bathrooms in the main house, plus outbuildings where the numerous domestic servants were probably housed, including the unfortunate chauffeur.

I haven't forgotten the days when my grandmother Nazeera and sometimes my father used to take me to visit our house-school in Machrah. It had no bathroom or toilet; one relieved oneself in a small outhouse outside the walls, or simply went into the fields in an unobtrusive spot; one took a small flat stone, with which one wiped one's orifice and, standing up, hurled it as far away as possible.

The kitchen was outside the house as well, whereas on Patrocinio Street, Gebrayel had had a spacious kitchen built right next to the sumptuous dining room, with cupboards, a big sink, and a large work space.

The most moving aspect of "our" Cuban residence is not how it breaks with our origins, but how it recalls them. The Andalusian room, first, and on the roof, the huge paved terrace. The name of my family's original village, Machrah, probably means "open area," as I have mentioned, for the simple reason that when you are there, you have a panoramic view of the high mountains, the neighboring villages, and, on the right, the sea. It is true that the sea is far in the distance, but it is an integral part of our landscape, since we live at an altitude of twelve hundred meters and there is nothing blocking the view between the sea and us. In fact, this may be why the temptation to travel is never absent from our thoughts.

At the top of Viper Hill, from the roof of his house, leaning with his hands on the stone balustrade, Gebrayel could recapture the same sensations. Luxuriously tiled, his terrace was probably his main drawing room; this was probably where my great-uncle sat after work, surrounded by family and friends, until late in the evening. In the distance he could see the outline of Havana, and beyond, on the horizon, the sea. Not the sea he would one day be sailing away on, but the sea by which he had arrived. When he was on that terrace, he must have savored every minute of his life, every minute of his triumph over destiny. Alas, these minutes were allotted to him sparingly.

I can imagine Gebrayel's sentiments better than I can Alice's, who most certainly had mixed feelings. It is doubtful she had the same taste of victory in her mouth; she probably felt apprehensive before so much wealth so rapidly acquired and so proudly spent. In the letters that have been preserved, her husband mentions her only briefly: "Alice greets you," "Alice thanks you for the gift," "Alice requests that you ask our friend Baddour to send her a book of liturgical songs that includes the musical score." And then, once again, there is the photo taken during the Masonic ceremony, where we see her wearing a crown and holding a scepter. I've looked at it closely, very closely; nothing in my great-aunt's face reflects her moment of triumph. She seems worried, perhaps even frightened. Not that she has a premonition of imminent disaster, but everything in her upbringing advised her to distrust success and wealth; everything instilled a gnawing terror in her heart and gaze.

According to the memories of the older members of the family, after Gebrayel's death, Alice remained prostrate at home for months, crushed, disoriented, bitter, and slightly paranoid. Unlike her brother Alfred, she seems to have always believed that her husband had been the victim of a murder plot.

From the piece in the *Diario de la Marina* that I read this morning, and now that I know the house on Patrocinio Street, I can easily imagine the atmosphere on the day of the funeral. The widow dressed in black, slumped in an armchair, blinded by tears, surrounded by soft-spoken women who try to soothe her with words that she doesn't even hear; the children, seven years old, four, and the youngest barely one, kept in a room upstairs by friends or servants; the two oldest crying, the youngest babbling and occasionally asking for his father, causing tearful outbursts and wails among those present.

I am grateful to Matteo, who opened the doors for me with his heavy bunch of keys, one after the other, so I could stroll about and let my mind wander. Today the past is not so distant for me anymore; it is wrapped in the glow of the present, contemporary hubbub, and attentive walls. I roamed about, familiarizing myself, forgetting myself, imagining, taking possession. I went from room to room, harboring the obsession of a distracted mind: here, in the past, my relatives . . .

Severed Ties

FORTY-nine

I decided not to search out anything this morning. There is an accumulation of too many images one after the other, too many emotions in rapid succession. I have to let it sink in and see where I stand in my pilgrimage. I am beset by contradictory feelings: the feeling of having accomplished my mission and the feeling of having scarcely skimmed the surface of the past. So I shut myself up in my room for the day to re-immerse myself in the family papers I brought with me. These were supposed to guide my steps, but instead I let myself be guided by the everyday occurrence of miracles—not that I'm complaining. The papers were also supposed to remind me of how the events in Cuba affected the relatives who had remained in the old country. I brought with me only a minute fraction of the family documents, essentially those where the faces of our

Cuban émigrés come into focus or their names appear. I lined them all up on my bed so I could take them in simultaneously at a simple glance.

It wasn't until February 1919, seven and a half months after Gebrayel's death, that the first tears were shed for him in the village. A mass was celebrated by Theodoros—but I couldn't find out whether, in his elegy, he mentioned his premonition, the red ink trickling over the page in his diary, and his watch stopping mysteriously. Afterward, of course, "the houses were opened up," as they say, so that the people from the village and the surrounding area could come to offer their condolences.

As for Botros, he reacted to the tragedy, as he often did, by writing a poem. On this occasion he chose to address the mail service that had brought the news of his brother's death. Hadn't he himself written to Gebrayel and Alice in November 1918, rejoicing over the armistice and telling them that even though our family had endured hardships during the Great War, it had escaped unharmed, with no death to mourn among our nearest and dearest? He referred to this letter with sad irony several days later, when he had to write again announcing Khalil's death. But now the circumstance was even more cruel, for my grandfather had just learned that when he had written those reassuring words to his brother, his brother was already dead.

> Mail Service of the Orient, when you bear our message of peace to those
> we love,
> Don't tell them that we suffered in their absence, because, for them, absence
> was synonymous with death.
> Mail Service of the Orient, how could you tell them that for the past few
> years we were living as if in a tomb?
> It was they who had to go live in their tomb, while we were living like kings
> in palaces.

The comparison is cruel, no doubt unwittingly. To say of Gebrayel that our modest village houses are palaces compared with his tomb— isn't that a strange way of evoking the deceased brother? This isn't exactly what he says, but between the lines, it is hard not to hear the response to mockery, or an old quarrel: Should one emigrate or not? When you look at the sumptuous house on Patrocinio Street, you say to yourself that Gebrayel was right to leave; but as soon as you think of the slippery road in San Francisco de Paula and the wretched precipice into which his car plunged, you say to yourself that he would have been wiser not to leave the village.

I mentioned cruelty and mockery. It is actually fate that is cruel and mocking, devising things so that the brother who remains in the old country survives famine, war, and the collapse of the Ottoman Empire, while the brother who emigrates to an island spared the worldwide conflagration dies at the wheel of his costly, high-powered car, the victim of his own prosperity. Botros is merely seeing the incongruity of this, and though he congratulates himself again for having survived, he has a premonition that his brother's death will narrow his potential prospects and destroy a hope.

Destiny, which has hounded me so often, has never, to this day, succeeded in bringing me down!

Then he ends his poem with these ritual invocations:

May God grant consolation to those whom Gebrayel has left behind!
May God grant cool temperatures to the tomb where Gebrayel resides!

After the period of mourning was past, it seems that the family soon became alarmed. Word came from Cuba hinting that the fortune Gebrayel had amassed was in danger of being wiped out. Close relatives living in the outlying areas—the United States, Puerto Rico, the Dominican Republic—as well as in Havana itself, began to send messages, some of them allusive, some very explicit, mentioning debts, mortgages, and properties that would have to be sold. From afar, the reasons for these things were poorly understood, but the family was worried. For once a relative had prospered, wouldn't it be unfortunate to let it all go up in smoke? Some of the letters specifically accused Alfred of squandering Gebrayel's inheritance and went so far as to criticize Alice.

A family meeting was held, during which several people begged

Botros to go take things in hand, since he was already familiar with Cuba and Gebrayel's business enterprises. In addition, his close family ties with the two "defendants," the brother and sister of his own wife, would make his task easier. My grandfather flatly refused. It was unthinkable for him to leave the school he had founded and his home. He had just had his fourth child.

Someone then suggested Theodoros as the family emissary. Perhaps they had got wind of the articles about Gebrayel's death in the Cuban press, where it said, pompously, that the brother of the deceased was a high-level Church dignitary. If the prelate in person showed up on the island, doors would no doubt open, and he would be able to rectify the situation to the advantage of our family.

This was not the wisest decision. Alice and Alfred were both fiercely Protestant, and it was somewhat risky to send them a thickly bearded Catholic priest who would say, "Move out of the way, I'll take care of everything!"

As might have been expected, they reacted with mistrust, not to say hostility, as confirmed by a long, odd letter I found in the family archives. I brought a photocopy of it with me. It is dated Havana, December 23, 1920, and is signed by Theodoros. I have no idea if the letter relates the facts accurately and impartially, but it has the merit of being completely straightforward.

> To my beloved Botros, may God preserve him,
>
> After brotherly greetings and wishes expressed for you and yours, let me inform you that several letters preceded this one, mailed in Alexandria, Marseilles, and finally Havana, to tell you I had arrived safely. They were not addressed solely to you, but to all my brothers. This letter, on the other hand, is addressed solely to you. I wouldn't like anyone else to read it.
>
> I told you in the previous letters that when I arrived in the port, the widow of our late lamented Gebrayel, her brother Alfred, as well as our young nephew Taufic, came on board the ship to welcome me and invite me to stay with them—I told you previously that they now all live together.
>
> Two days later, Alfred came to talk to me very frankly and reproached me for having made the trip. He said, "When I learned that you were thinking of coming to see us, I didn't want to write to you directly to

dissuade you, so out of politeness, I preferred to write to various members of the family to ask them to make you change your mind if your plans were confirmed; apparently they did not do so. You should know that by coming here, you have caused us great harm." He began to speak with irritation. I answered calmly. I explained to him that I had made this trip to the Americas because of a spiritual mission assigned by my superiors and that I had made the detour to this island just to greet them, make sure they were well, and present my condolences on behalf of the family. I said this because he had just told me that not one among us had thought of writing a letter of condolence to the widow of the deceased, and that she and he were very angry about this and considered breaking off relations with the family; he even told me he had already broken them off . . .

After that, I met with my brother's widow in private and explained the reasons for my visit to her, telling her that the whole family thought about her constantly, and that everyone loved and respected her, and that I had been appointed as their delegate to come to Cuba and see her and make sure that everything was going well for her, etc. But her words were identical to her brother's; she even added that before my arrival, she was talking to a certain person with a view to remarrying, and that if this were to happen, my presence here would no longer have any meaning. Then she said that she and her brother could not give me accommodations indefinitely, since they all lived in one house. As soon as I heard this, I gathered my possessions and moved into this hotel; I am writing to you from there.

So the venerable Theodoros had been thrown out, in effect. Indeed, his letter was written on stationery from the Hotel Florida, 28 Obispo Street, Havana. When you know how spacious the Patrocinio Street house is, you can only smile at the excuse Alice used. This is assuming that her words and those of her brother were accurately reported. For between the lines you can hear the rumblings of a bitter quarrel. When Alfred criticized the family for not having written to his sister after her husband's death, the priest didn't contradict him. Yet by the time this conversation took place, Gebrayel had been dead for two and a half years, and the family had known about it for almost two years. That no one had thought of sending Gebrayel's widow a letter of condolence during all that time is very odd and very rude, to say the least.

Though these criticisms seemed to be addressed to the entire family, they were actually aimed at only some members of the family: the ones who had not looked kindly on the successive matches with Protestants—first and foremost Theodoros himself. While his brother Gebrayel was alive, he had maintained a close relationship with him, but he had always kept his distance from the Khalil household. How could he not see as a fiend the son of a Catholic priest metamorphosed into a Presbyterian parson?

The fact that Theodoros had no affection for these "heretics," and that they had no sympathy for him, a bearded, potbellied "papist," were feelings each party was entitled to. But there is no justification for the priest not sending his condolences to his brother's widow. And no matter how you look at it, sending a man like him on a goodwill mission was an incredible blunder. If Botros didn't want to make the trip, it would have been better not to send anyone. Theodoros continues:

> Once I had settled into the hotel, some of our late lamented brother's friends came to visit me, and I myself visited a few others, and most of them told me that they were displeased with Alfred's schemes but couldn't say anything to him openly, because he had become estranged from them all. The schemes they are referring to are the ones we are aware of, namely that Alice is the sole trustee of the deceased's inheritance and she has made her brother her proxy. He is very considerate of her and behaves with her children as if they were his own, but behind the scenes he is selling everything he can sell, mortgaging the rest, and with the money he obtains from this, he is buying land or other things that he registers in his own name, using certain legal subtleties that will eventually allow him to become the owner of the entire estate. And his sister doesn't worry about this, she trusts him blindly and doesn't want to listen to people who warn her against such schemes. Alfred, for his part, is bent on estranging her from our family; every gesture we make in their direction is presented as a threat. Actually, he is trying to maintain his influence on her until he has attained his objective. This is what many people here have told me, and all the evidence I've been able to gather proves to me that this is true—among other things the fact that he talked his sister and all the other members of

the family into not trusting me, not talking to me, and not listening to what I say.

In spite of this open hostility, I continued speaking gently, asking Alfred to tell me what each heir's share was, but he refused to answer, and he didn't want to explain to me the decisions he had made. I don't think it would be possible to put an end to his schemes other than by legal means, by starting a lawsuit, which I cannot do without the accord of the lawful tutelary, my brother's widow. I'll try again to bring her around to my views so that she'll understand the truth; if I succeed, all the better, but if I don't, a lawsuit will have to be started against both of them, to prove that they have joined forces against minors. But if things get to that point, you'll have to come over, Botros, because you'll be able to take over the stores and straighten things out. You're also the only one who can contact the American embassy here, without the need for an interpreter, to prove that the interests of minors are in jeopardy, and to safeguard what is left of their father's fortune—which obviously a man of religion like me couldn't do . . .

This last remark suggests that Gebrayel was a United States citizen, presumably having acquired citizenship in his youth, during his stay in New York; the fact that representatives from the Cuban North American colony attended his funeral seems to confirm this.

Theodoros then mentions the name of a person of Lebanese descent who could help Botros if he decided to come to Havana and start proceedings. He also suggests a "moratorium" aimed at "preventing Alfred from causing further harm." Then he vents his bitterness:

If my brother's widow continues not to listen to me, I shall soon leave Cuba, deeply affected by old and recent reminiscences, and will try not to think about all this anymore. Doesn't the folk proverb say, "If the whole house is lost, what's the point of crying over the chairs?" I prefer telling myself that my brother Gebrayel died as a poor émigré. I prefer telling myself that my being sent to this island is like others being exiled by the Ottoman Empire to the deserted expanses of Anatolia . . . I don't think I can ever tell you just how saddened I am by what I saw here. Oh, you should have advised me not to make this trip!

In spite of this, I send you all my warm greetings and hope to see you soon in excellent health. I pray that Heaven preserve you.

Below his signature, at the bottom of the page, Theodoros adds this:

When we last saw each other, I got the feeling that you hadn't ruled out coming here. If that is still a possibility, come quickly before everything is lost, for if you come and start a lawsuit, you could still rescue the small amount of the children's share that remains, and you could guarantee a better future for the whole family, as our late lamented Gebrayel's reputation is outstanding here. On the other hand, if you have ruled out coming here, then it would be best not to think about all this anymore and let things follow their course.

Botros did not go to Havana. Sailing halfway around the globe to sue his own wife's brother and sister, no thank you. He too preferred to think of Gebrayel as having died "a poor émigré." But it could well be that the priest's letter and the family discussions at the time were additional fodder for the legend of my grandfather leaving for Cuba to take legal action and to "rescue his brother." Legends, like dreams, mine memory and shape bits and pieces into a seemingly coherent whole . . .

When Theodoros returned to the old country, told his relatives that their Cuban fortune was gone, and named the culprit, they reacted with anger, even rage, but their mood soon changed to resignation tinged with bitterness. The dream had been too glorious anyhow; it couldn't have lasted forever; sooner or later one was bound to wake up.

But this didn't mean that Alfred was forgiven. He was banished overnight. Banished from memory forever. No invectives, no insults, no smear campaign, just oblivion and nothing else. His name disappears from the family correspondence after 1921. No one asks after him; he is never mentioned. He simply ceases to exist.

Cuba faded away as well. It had become a painful memory, so it was erased. Relations were broken off with the relatives who were still there. There was a reunion thirteen years later, but it was tragic. I'll come back to this again.

Evening

María de los Angeles called me from home. A conscientious genealogist, she scoured the public records office today to find all the children born in Cuba who had my last name in its various spellings. So far, she has a list of six; there are also a few marriages, but she didn't have time to look into them.

She read me the list of the children's first names, three or four for each, spelling those that seemed foreign to her: Nesbit Victor Abraham, Taufic Gabriel Martín Theodoro, Nelie Susana Margarit, William Jefferson Gabriel, Carlos Alberto Antonio, Henry Franklin Benjamin . . .

"No Arnaldo?"

"No, alas, no Arnaldo. Though I looked hard. But there are other registers, I'll keep looking."

My voice must have betrayed a slight disappointment, for María immediately asked me if I would "nevertheless" like to have *la certificación de nacimiento* for each one. Yes, of course! For all of them? Yes, all of them. And the *matrimonios* too, if possible.

What use could I possibly have for all these certificates? First of all, to keep a written record of names and dates. But also, for the time being, so my informant doesn't think I am less keenly enthusiastic than she. Anything she obtains for me will be welcome.

Another person whose enthusiasm I shouldn't dampen is Dolores, the woman who lives downstairs on Cardenas Street. Since she offered to take me to the city historian, it would be discourteous not to stop by to see her again. I shall go tomorrow, in the morning, without fail. I don't have much more time left in Cuba.

FIFTY

This morning, I returned to the center of Havana, where once again I looked at the buildings at the corner of Monte and Cardenas, and took a few location photos before knocking at Dolores's door. She had put on her best dress, as if she had been expecting me. We set off together, like a delegation, to the Plaza de Armas, where the museum of the city is located. This magnificent colonial building also houses, in the back, the office of the mysterious *historiador de la ciudad*, whose fine title is posted on every site under renovation. But alas, the man was absent. After listening to the explanation of what we were seeking, his secretary advised us to go to the photographic department to see if there wasn't some old photograph of the residence that had been built by the government for General Maxímo Gómez.

Dolores and I took seats in a small air-conditioned,

not to say freezing, room. We were told this temperature was necessary for the preservation of the archives. I became so engrossed in the old albums that I forgot the time. They were a delight, even if the harvest ended up being meager: only two panoramic photos taken in 1928, which show the entire neighborhood where the La Verdad stores were located. Since I couldn't immediately recognize "our" building, I asked for scanned copies on a disk in order to study them patiently at home in the weeks following my return. The woman in charge warned me, appalled, that this would be "very costly." I was too ashamed to tell her that the meaning of "costly" wasn't the same here as in Europe. I simply explained that the photograph had great sentimental value for me and that I couldn't possibly leave Cuba without looking at the prestigious residence once owned by my *abuelo*—which was the truth.

As we were leaving, Dolores suggested that we drop into the offices of the real estate archives. There is no better source, she said, for finding out what became of a particular building in Havana, what year it was built and by whom, what year it was sold and to whom. Why not? Let's go!

At first sight, the place looked promising: a huge room in which dozens of civil servants were bustling about and, in the back, a spacious rectangular courtyard resembling that of a convent and planted with trees. I inquired and found out that the building was indeed a former monastery. Dolores showed the bureaucrat a plastic-coated card, which earned her a respectful greeting; then she peremptorily asked where the archives could be consulted. Upstairs, the man replied, up that wide stairway there, all the way in the back.

We headed obediently for the large stairway in the back. We climbed to the second floor and looked around for someone in charge, or for someone to talk to. No one. The place was deserted. But it didn't look the way a place looks when the employees have gone out for lunch or to a meeting. No, it was empty, deserted, abandoned, vacated. There were three rooms with open doors, all three unfurnished: no tables, no chairs, no telephones, no office machines. Just bare walls that hadn't been painted in ages. Then there was another spacious room, equally empty, where all you saw, at the foot of one wall, was a heap of brownish, dusty files piled up as if for a book burning and, on another wall, still more files piled up on shelves and tied with frayed, blackish strings. Here lay the real estate archives.

I looked at Dolores and smiled; she smiled too, but with infinite sadness. I felt that she was hurt, wounded in her national pride. She stepped outside the room to look for someone to reprimand, then promptly returned, having found no one, her anger intact behind her smiling facade.

To console her, I decided to act as if this mess were a precious resource. I started to check the variously darkened brown-colored files on the floor and on the shelves, inside and out, for the dates. I thus established that the oldest files dated to the early 1950s and the most recent to the mid-1980s. There were none that could concern Gebrayel or La Verdad.

Frankly, this was just as well. Had I come across a file dating from 1912 or 1918, I would have felt compelled to plunge head and soul into the dust collector. My unsuccessful survey cleared me of any obligation and rescued my escort's honor. We could leave.

As we were stepping out of the room, I turned around for a last look. After all, these furrowed piles were touching, like ancient ruins; a talented photographer would have known how to immortalize them. I think I would even be disappointed if, on my next visit, I found these files prosaically put away in clean closets.

Dolores, on the other hand, didn't take matters so lightly. As we were leaving the old monastery, she couldn't help making a few scathing remarks to the civil servant who had directed us to the stairway, there, way in the back . . . The man couldn't understand what prompted her anger: The archives were upstairs, weren't they? I put his mind at rest as best I could in my broken Castilian Spanish. Yes, yes, the archives were upstairs, no problem, he didn't have to worry.

Then I hurried to catch up with Dolores. She had wandered straight out into the middle of the street and was blocking the way of a dumbfounded motorist. Her neck taut, she was limping slightly; this—combined with her anger—lent majesty to her gait.

Suddenly she stopped.

"Why don't we go see Teresita?"

Why not? Who is Teresita?

"My friend. Come along!"

I follow her. Ten minutes later we reach a corner building whose upper stories are old and whose two lower floors have been modernized. Obviously, another administrative office, with people in line in front of windows, a few civil servants engaged in work, and others pretending to work. Dolores asks to see Teresita. She emerges from an apple green elevator a few minutes later; slender, a cigarette in her mouth, and wearing thongs. They talk and talk, endlessly. A consultation from which I am kept at a distance. But when Teresita gets back in the elevator, Dolores comes up to me and informs me of their decision: "We have to go see Olguita!"

Who is Olguita?

"A friend. Come along!"

With time, many things from my Havana pilgrimage will fade from my memory, but not Olguita's kingdom. It is in the half-subterranean ground floor of an old residential building; you walk down a few steps and enter through an ordinary metal door. Once inside, anyone else in the world but Olguita holds his breath and stops dead in his tracks. In the shadowy light is a labyrinth of archives as far as the eye can see, and the gurgling sound of invisible, omnipresent water, as in a grotto. The archives on the second floor of the former monastery are nothing in comparison. This is where the city's memory is, neighborhood by neighborhood, street by street, building by building. For the visitor, once his eyes have accommodated to the darkness, these are just walls of undistinguishable files squeezed together so tightly that if you removed one, they would all come tumbling down and you would be buried under the landslide. Olguita is the sole person who can comfortably negotiate her way through this opaque memory.

"What streets did you say? Oh yes, Monte and Cardenas . . . And what numbers again?"

She heads straight in front of her, without hesitating, and comes back with an armful of files that she puts down on a metal table in the best lighted spot, under a skylight. I plunge right in with dread. Building licenses, demolition licenses, landlord disputes, inheritances, notarized deeds, court transcripts—do I really have to go through all this? From time to time, my eyes wander to the floor, where there are dozens of dead cockroaches, or to the wall in front of me, where there is a plastic yellow sticker with the slogan *"Viva el día del Constructor"*—"Long live the day of the Builder."

More documents, certified, stapled, stamped . . . But not one affords me the simple satisfaction of seeing Gabriel's name in writing, or that of La Verdad. I am overcome by weariness and would gladly throw in the towel. However Dolores's and Olguita's eyes are upon me, waiting for me to exclaim "Eureka." I don't want to disappoint them or hurt their feelings.

What I finally discovered in this administrative cavern, after an hour and a half of assiduous excavation, wasn't written black on white on any file or any document; I learned it by cross-checking various findings. The lackluster truth was this: the residence built by the government for General Máximo Gómez, bought by Gebrayel in 1912 and altered into large shops, was cold-bloodedly torn down in 1940; an ordinary residential building went up on that spot, slightly set back from the street. La Verdad—"our" Verdad—no longer existed.

As Dolores and I were getting ready to leave the premises, a comical scene took place. Olguita, who had carefully double-locked the metal door, couldn't unlock it. After the fourth fruitless attempt, with the key almost broken, our hostess gave up trying. Dolores and I exchanged glances, half amused, half worried. It was already dusk, and the prospect of spending the night in this dark, humid basement with no telephone, no contact with the outside world—in this den of cockroaches, most probably infested with rats, even if we hadn't actually seen one—didn't exactly delight any of us. So Olguita climbed up on a table and stuck her head out of the skylight in the hope of seeing a neighbor. As soon as she heard footfalls on the building staircase, she called out. A young boy walked over and bent toward the skylight to find out what we wanted: from the outside, the door would open without any problem. Our hostess handed him her entire set of keys. Our improvised savior became mirthful, and we were momentarily afraid that we wouldn't see him again, either because he would play a nasty prank on us or because the set of keys would excite his greed. But after what seemed like an endless stretch of seconds, we heard the click of the lock, and we were out in the open.

After escorting Dolores home through the poorly lighted maze of the Old City, where hundreds of youths sit around and chat on the stoops of their houses, I crossed a street named Obispo and found myself in front of the Hotel Florida, the very hotel Theodoros moved into when Alfred and Alice threw him out. When I saw its lit-up sign, I remembered reading in a guidebook that this mythical luxury hotel from a bygone era had recently reopened its doors after being closed for forty years.

Such as it is after restoration, and probably such as it was in the days when my great-uncle stayed there, the hotel has a definite Mediterranean look. The verdant vestibule is really a patio with a roof, the superimposed arches recall Córdoba, and upstairs, the doors to the rooms are surmounted with stained-glass half-moon windows identical to those in our house in the village. Though located in the West and called Florida, this establishment had a caravansary as its ancestor. I am not surprised that it reminded Theodoros of the deserted expanses of Anatolia.

In the evening

As I sit on the terrace of my temporary home, a glass of amber-colored rum within reach, I feel the need to take stock of what I've accomplished so far in my trip and what I still have to do in the small amount of time I have left—scarcely forty-eight hours. Before coming to Cuba, I made up a list on a bristol board of the places to visit and the things to be researched and verified. I look over the list to check things off, cross things out, and annotate it.

"Egido 5 and 7" . . .

Done. I even took many pictures.

"The Máximo Gómez house" . . .

No longer exists, alas, but I have an old photograph in my baggage where it should be visible.

"The newspapers of the period" . . .

Consulted. I could probably have unearthed thousands of other things—advertisements for the La Verdad stores, for example—but as is, I found more than I'd hoped for: news of my great-uncle's death, the funeral announcements, an article about the funeral, the location of the accident, the address of the family house.

"The Colón Cemetery" . . .

Visited and revisited, of course. But I'd gladly stop by one last time before taking the plane again, if I have the opportunity.

"The port and the quarantine" . . .

I now know where the quarantine was located at the time and how to get there; I doubt I would find out much else if I visited it. In any case, I don't have enough time left. As for the port, I roamed around the area, located all the old customs buildings and old quays, took a ferry to the suburb of Regla, and returned by the same route, hoping to see the same sight my grandfather had seen when he disembarked here in 1902. But I also studied the old photos I bought at the secondhand booksellers on Plaza de Armas showing the dusty crush of émigrés arriving at the port.

"The Presbyterian church where Alice went to pray" . . .

I didn't look for it. It doesn't matter.

"The Freemasons" . . .

Oh, yes, I almost forgot them. I should probably try to find out if they've kept some record of "brother" Gebrayel and "queen" Alice.

"The large photo of the Estrella de Oriente ceremony" . . .

I had promised myself that I would have a local historian identify the personalities around my great-uncle in the last picture we have of him. I didn't do anything about this. Actually, I began to wonder what the point of it would be. The illustrious Cubans of the past are unknown to us. Thanks to the newspapers and from what his house looked like, I am fully aware that Gebrayel succeeded in carving out a place for himself in the Havana bourgeoisie of the period. I need no further proof; I am not going to draw up a list of each and every one of his social acquaintances.

All of this, everything I gleaned here, remains fragmentary, I know. But it would be illusory to aspire to anything else. The past is bound to be fragmentary, bound to be reconstructed, bound to be reinvented. It serves only to collect the truths of today. If our present is the child of the past, our past is the child of the present. And the future will be the harvester of our bastard offspring.

FIFTY-ONE

In Cuba, Freemasonry isn't a secret fraternity at all; they even have an imposing building on the former Avenue Carlos III now named after "brother" Salvador Allende. I counted eleven stories, with the emblems of the Grand Lodge conspicuously adorning the facade. Which doesn't mean that they are open and transparent about everything.

I went there with Rubén, a Cuban writer who phoned me this morning on behalf of Luis Domingo, apologizing that he hadn't contacted me sooner. He used to work in the Spanish embassy, and he offered to help me in my research. He knew someone there, a cousin of his wife's, someone named Ambrosio.

However, this man didn't give him or me a warm welcome. He half smiled in annoyance and rose heavily from his chair as though he were extracting himself from a trapdoor. Then he shook my hand in a ritual way that is not unfamiliar to me, and I could easily have let him think I was one of their members. But out of respect for the memory of Botros, Gebrayel, Alice, and so many other ancestors, I didn't want to play the game; I greeted him like an uninitiated, and he instantly clammed up.

I should add in his defense that he obviously had no experience in public relations; his was a relatively subordinate administrative post, and he was probably afraid that a foreigner like me had come to wrest information out of him that he was not supposed to divulge. When I told him that my great-uncle had been a Freemason, he asked me how I knew. When I explained that his shop sold Masonic insignia, he shot back that this didn't prove anything. I then showed him the photo of Alice's enthronement ceremony, pointing to the distinguished persons present, the former heads of state, and, of course, Fernando Figueredo Socarrás, emblematic dignitary of the Grand Lodge. The man looked at all this and nodded politely, but he didn't show the slightest interest in what I was telling him. Though at this point he couldn't really call into question the fact that my *abuelo* had been a "brother," he asserted that he couldn't find out anything about him unless I could tell him what lodge he had belonged to. How would I know the name of his lodge? A discussion ensued in Spanish between the two Cubans, after which they suggested that I go have a look at the Masonic museum and library five floors below.

There, a surprise awaited me at the entrance: the museum is dedicated to the memory of Aurelio Miranda, one of the twelve intimate friends whose names were listed on the announcement published at Gebrayel's death, and whose presence was reported at the funeral. Surprise may not be the most suitable word, but it is a striking confirmation. According to the old guardian—this time, a very affable man—who showed us around the room, Miranda was the great historian of Cuban Freemasonry. Incidentally, another Miranda is known for having "initiated" one of the great liberators of Latin America: Simón Bolívar.

Another part of the museum space is devoted to a permanent exhibition around that other Masonic *libertador*, José Martí. On the old photos, I search for Fernando Figueredo's face—in vain. In a moment of distraction I catch myself searching for the face of the youthful Gebrayel in a crowd gathered around Martí, but they couldn't possibly be in the same picture. My great-uncle arrived in New York in December 1895; the revolutionary leader had left the city in February of the same year and died in combat in August. Gebrayel could have met only his legend, his growing legend, and some of the people who had gravitated around him.

Elsewhere in the museum, there were other pages of history, other heroes, handwritten letters, open books, ribbons, relics. Bending over a horizontal display case, I suddenly noticed two medals side by side, one belonging to the woman's order Estrella de Oriente, the other from a lodge named La Verdad. Emboldened by this discovery, Rubén and I ran back upstairs to see the incredulous Ambrosio, and I announced self-confidently, "I now know the name of my great-uncle's lodge."

To be honest, I couldn't be completely certain, but I felt it was a legitimate deduction: since Gebrayel had called his business La Verdad, since he must have belonged to a lodge, since there was a lodge by that very name in Cuba in his day, the connection was not far-fetched. Had I been dealing with an understanding person, I would have explained this rash inference, but since this person had systematically denigrated everything I had tried to explain to him, I was not going to invite criticism. I therefore pretended that I had just found the name of the lodge in my notes and that I didn't have the slightest doubt on that score anymore.

My self-confidence had the desired effect. The man appeared embarrassed. He said something in Spanish to Rubén in which I distinctly heard *"archivo"* and *"Estados Unidos."* My escort translated into English, "It seems the archives of that lodge have burned." I didn't pay much attention to this revolutionary white lie. It seemed very plausible to me that the Masonic archives had been taken to Florida by émigré "brothers." After all, Cuban Freemasonry must have included many more middle-class members than proletarians, and undoubtedly most of them had been exiled for many years. I assume that they must have a building taller than this one in Miami, and more abundant archives.

Before leaving empty-handed, I gave it a last shot: I took out of my pocket the text of the announcement published at the time of my great-uncle's death, and I underlined the name Aurelio Miranda in red ink. I handed my interlocutor the text, and he took it; he read it and reread it, and for the first time, he did not appear indifferent to what I told him. He gave Rubén the name and telephone number of a high-ranking official who would be there late in the morning on Friday and who could open doors for us.

I don't expect much from these archives. But I am told that there is at least an application file for each member, with information about his career, his origins, his convictions. If I could have access to Gebrayel's file, that would be one more veil lifted. We'll see . . .

Afternoon

When I returned to my house in Vedado with more questions than answers, inevitably disappointed and still unsatisfied, I was surprised to find María de los Angeles there. She had been waiting for an hour, she told me. She had brought the six birth certificates she promised me. "Three of them are Gabriel and Alicia's children, the others aren't."

I handle these documents with tenderness, even though they're just copies dating from today and cursorily handwritten by a registry-office employee.

Taufic Gabriel Martín Theodoro Maluf Maluf. Born in Havana, January 30, 1911. Of masculine sex, son of Gabriel Maluf Maluf, native of Monte Libano, Siria, Turquia, and of Alicia Maluf Barody, native of the same place. Paternal grandparents: Antonio and Susana. Maternal grandparents: Julián and Sofia. Registered by virtue of the father's declaration . . .

The rendering of the first names of my great-grandparents Tannous, Soussène, and Sofiya into Spanish as Antonio, Susana, and Sofia was unsurprising and conventional. But for my other great-grandfather,

Khalil, to have become Julián involved a train of thought that escapes me. Though the Arabic sound *kh* is probably the equivalent—and perhaps even the ancestor—of the Castilian *jota*, the metamorphosis is nevertheless astonishing . . .

"Taufic Gabriel Martín Theodoro" is mentioned several times in the family correspondence. There is his baptism announcement, which I already mentioned, with the name of the illustrious godfather, and there are also several photos of him at different ages. When I started to become interested in our Cuban family, he was the person I most hoped to meet, for he was the only one of Gebrayel's children to have been slightly acquainted with his father. Alas, he didn't wait for me, so to speak. When I sought to find out what had become of him, I learned that he had just died in the United States. I need not burden these pages with more dates; suffice it to say that his death occurred just as my mother, on summer vacation in Lebanon, found, in the wardrobe of our house, those first letters of Gebrayel's that she brought me in Paris.

When I think about what I might have learned from this faraway cousin, how could I not feel the burning sting of remorse? But this remorse is added to so much other, even more justified, remorse. There is no point in dwelling on it.

While I was pensively gazing at these certificates, María was watching me, silently and with a look of pride. I thank her once again, repeating how immensely grateful I am to her since the miraculous moment, before escorting me to my great-uncle's tomb, when she read out loud for me from the page in the cemetery register that concerned my relatives' fate. She laughs mischievously, like a little girl, and then whispers into my ear theatrically, using the familiar "*tu*" for the first time:

"This isn't everything. I have something else to tell you. I wouldn't have come all this way just for these few papers!"

Why else did she come?

"Because of him," she says, pointing to one of the birth certificates.

I wait. That's all she says. I seize the sheet and scan it. "William Jef-

ferson Gabriel . . . Born in Havana . . . 1922 . . . Masculine sex. Son of
Alfredo . . . and of Hada . . . Paternal grandparents: Julián and Sofía . . ."

I already knew from family letters that Hada had gone to rejoin her
husband in Cuba right after the war. After waiting six long years, they
could finally begin their life as a couple. The patient bride was escorted
across the Atlantic by her mother-in-law, Sofiya, who wanted to spend
some time with her bereaved daughter Alice. My great-grandmother
returned from Havana in 1920, shortly before Theodoros went there on
his fruitless mission.

I already knew that Alfred and Hada, finally reunited, had had a
first child, named Henry Franklin Benjamin, in 1921. I had found the
announcement of his birth. But this other son, William—I had never
heard his name mentioned before, nor had I read his name anywhere.
I'd like to point out in passing that it is significant that in this Spanish-
speaking country, these émigrés had decided to name their sons Henry
and William, not Enrique and Guillermo. And they had given them the
middle names Franklin and Jefferson! All the more significant in that
their ancestors, my ancestors, usually had the names Khattar, Aziz, As-
saad, Ghandour, or Nassif.

But my genealogist, who has been watching me during this time,
knows nothing, of course, of our Levantine incongruities. What made
her come all the way here today, late in the afternoon, and fills her eyes
with laughter and pride, is something else, something very different.

She points again at the certificate I am holding.

"He still lives here!"

Because she sees me suddenly freeze and not even bat an eyelash,
she repeats the sentence again, more slowly: "William. He still lives
here, in Playa."

My first thought is, Thank God, our family hasn't left Cuba. I
thought this chapter was over, but it isn't yet. The descendants of my
repudiated uncle are still here on Cuban soil! One son stayed here.

Not one of our relatives knows his name or suspects he exists.

"William Jefferson Gabriel . . ." I whisper audibly.

María puts her hand on my shoulder.

"I've just come from his house. He's expecting us!"

· · ·

Indeed, William was waiting for us in front of the door to his house. How many hours had he been waiting? How many years? With all the members of his present family gathered around him, he eyed all the cars passing by on Marrero Avenue, one of the widest and noisiest avenues in the suburb of Playa. He is eighty years old, and this is the first time in his life he is meeting a member of his ghostly family. Though he hesitated to admit it to me, he felt bitter about this. He never understood why their relatives had abandoned them—his father, mother, brother, and himself. His parents never spoke about it, and on this day of reunion, I didn't really feel like delving into this touchy question. Yes, of course, he knew that Gabriel, Aunt Alice's husband, owned the La Verdad stores and that Alfred, his father, worked in them. And he knew that they had to be sold after his uncle's death. The car accident: yes, of course, he had heard about it. His parents spoke about it occasionally.

"Apparently Gabriel used to go crazy whenever he heard the roar of his car motor," William told us. "He had a chauffeur, but his job was more like that of a stableboy: to wash the car, polish it, keep an eye on it during the day, and drive it into the garage at night. No one but the master did the driving. And he drove as fast as he could. That's how the three of them died."

The three of them?

"He, his chauffeur, and the little boy."

What little boy?

"Gabriel had neighbors whom he treated like his own family. People from a modest background. Their son, who was seven years old, always wanted to go for a ride in the car with him, and that day he had taken him along against his parents' wishes."

I turned toward María, and she confirmed this. A child had been buried the same day at the Colón Cemetery, and he had also died from being crushed. She had noticed it when she was recopying the register pages and was surprised by the coincidence, she said, but she had hesitated to connect it to "our" accident.

Why wasn't this tragedy mentioned anywhere, not even in the most detailed accounts of the accident or the funeral? I have no idea. I surmise that the child's parents were furious at Gebrayel and his family, and didn't want to be in any way a part of the same condolences. But the newspapers? Why didn't they mention it? To avoid tainting the image of the departed notable? I probably have to resign myself to never knowing.

I showed William various photos from the family archives that I had brought to Cuba with me. One of them gave him a start. It shows a young couple: the wife is tall and round-faced, her husband shorter and thinner; they are both smiling, but very faintly; her head is gently leaning against his in a gesture of maternal tenderness.

"My father and mother! As newlyweds!"

That was what it was. Well, not exactly: the photo, which bears the stamp of a Havana studio, dates from 1920. Perhaps it was the "official" wedding photo, but by then they had already been married for seven years.

"Where does it come from?" William asked me.

"From my grandmother's drawer," I said, watching his reaction closely: She was his aunt on his father's side, at one time his mother's best friend; her name was Nazeera. Obviously he had never heard the name, or if he had, from Hada, he didn't remember it. I seized the opportunity to add that she, at least, had not forgotten them completely, for she had kept their photos. This was my way of mitigating my family's wrongdoing, their years of neglect and never-ending aloofness.

In fact, it seems that my grandmother was the last one to maintain ties with the Cuban branch of the family for a while—but only for a while. The others had all broken off relations with Alfred by early 1921, after Father Theodoros returned from his disastrous Havana mission. At Nazeera's, I found letters dating from later. In a drawer, which she seldom opened, she had put away some letters, some announcements, and many photos taken on the other side of the Atlantic. The most interesting of these had been sent to her by her sister Alice, who had the fortunate habit of noting the date, circumstance, and identity of the persons on the back of the picture. On a photo dated February 1922, Gebrayel's children are dressed in carnival clothes on a paved terrace, possibly at their Patrocinio Street house. On another, dated 1923, we see the widow, still dressed entirely in black, sitting on a rattan armchair and turning on a Tiffany lamp. On the wall is a framed picture on which you can see, with a magnifying glass, the entire family, namely Gebrayel, Alice, and their three children; the youngest, no more than a few months old, is sitting on his father's lap.

I brought along some of these pictures, as well as the one of Alfred and Hada as newlyweds. It is not surprising that my newfound cousin reacted to that one. On the other hand, he didn't react to the photos of Gebrayel's family, or at least not much. I flashed the parents and children by him, reading off the inscription on the back whenever there was one. Yes, he was familiar with some of the names, but the faces meant nothing to him.

Suddenly he jumped and took a photo from my hands.

"*Soy yo!*"

He turned pale.

"*Soy yo!*"

The photo showed two young children, one a few months old, the other two years and some. The youngest had a conspicuous black birthmark on his right arm. William showed it to me on the photo, then lifted the sleeve of his shirt to show me the same mark.

"It's me!"

He had tears in his eyes, and so did I, and so did all those present at the scene, including María.

We looked at each other, he and I; we held each other by both hands, firmly, to seal the end of our separation, as it were. Yet in his eyes I read an anguished expression that had grown and become old with him: Why were they abandoned? Had he put the question to me, I would have told him what I knew by now, as painful as that might be. He didn't ask, so I didn't say anything. I couldn't see myself explaining to him the first time we met that the family accused his father of having squandered the fortune acquired in Cuba. And that a sanction was imposed, though it was probably never clearly stated, that led the family to behave as though Alfred, Hada, and their children didn't exist and had never existed. I was ashamed of what had happened, but since it was all a matter of impressions and conjectures, I didn't explain anything. Instead, I asked my own questions, to try to understand.

When did his father die?

In the late 1940s.

And what did he do after the La Verdad stores were shut?

He gave English lessons.

And his mother?

William rose, went to his bedroom, and brought back a box containing old papers. He took out a photo of Hada in the last years of her life; her eyes looked sad, but her face was still lit up by a youthful smile. Then the certificate of her death—in 1969, at seventy-four, in a Havana retirement home. In the same box there was a document in Arabic that the Cuban cousin had preserved carefully, though he couldn't read it. I unfolded it. It was his parents' marriage certificate, drawn up in the village in 1913. The witness: Botros.

And what had become of his older brother, Henry?

He left Cuba well before the revolution to go live in Utah and work in textiles with his uncles on their mother's side. From childhood, William told me, his brother had always been sad; he played very little and seldom smiled. "One day I was told that he had died." The fateful telegram was in the same box; it was dated January 1975 and signed by Henry's Norwegian wife: a heart attack, five months before his fifty-fourth birthday.

Had they always lived in this house?

Yes, since 1932. Before, they lived in an apartment in the center of the city, not far from the La Verdad stores. Then they moved to this outlying neighborhood, though in those days it must have been residential. Today their house is cramped, probably a fraction of its original size. Like so many others, it was split up. A wall crosses right through it.

William didn't talk about it. And I didn't mention it either, lest I embarass him. But we didn't have to talk about it; the dividing wall is an oppressive presence. Furthermore, apparently the people occupying the other half of the house were more influential, for the wall isn't at right angles; it was built diagonally, so much so that the house is more triangular than rectangular. As a result, the adjacent house must be a spacious trapezoid. Equality is often infinitely variable.

This despoliation didn't undermine my newfound cousin's unshakable good nature, a quality his wife, Amalia, described with tenderness. She met him when they were both working in the Ministry of Industry. They were both divorced. He had no children; she had a daughter and a son. Everyone in the office was very fond of William, for he was always jovial and lighthearted. One day his best friend died; he became so despondent, so disconsolate, that she decided to comfort him. They have never parted since.

At one point William started telling me, in a low voice, about the only trip he ever made. When he was a child, his mother had taken his brother and him to Utah to visit their uncles. They spent two years there. Their father had not come with them. His parents were probably having a serious marital crisis then; he became convinced of this many years later from listening to his mother's stories, but of course at the time he wasn't aware of anything. Nowadays, this kind of couple would certainly have divorced, he said, but in the twenties, that wasn't the case. Eventually Hada had had to resign herself to returning to Cuba and living with her husband. She never left the island again, nor did William. Nor did Alfred, for that matter.

Everything I heard about Alfred only confirmed what my cousin Léonore had said to me one day. The way she put it, he was simply "a difficult person to live with." Besides, the fact that the whole family in Lebanon no longer wanted to talk to him, that his sister Alice, after having trusted him blindly, eventually severed relations with him, that his own wife had felt the need to take her children and leave, means that I have no reason to call into question all the things that were said about him.

It remains to be seen whether he was dishonest or simply incompetent, pretentious, and grumpy. It seems to me that if Theodoros's accusations were true, and Alfred had embezzled funds, if he had registered land and various properties belonging to Gebrayel in his own name, he would not have had to give private lessons in order to support his small family.

I reexamine the photos of Alfred and Hada and Henry and William. Am I reading things into them? Things I've learned from other sources? Or do they really speak for themselves? For I now feel that they reveal everything essential. Alfred looking unself-confident, stiff, vulnerable, and Hada leaning toward him, affectionate, maternal, with a smile that both hides and reveals profound anxiety. And the two boys: one, already frowning, seems afraid of the photographer and afraid of moving, the other talking or babbling, paying no heed to the solemnity of the occasion. It is as if Alfred and Hada's home was divided in two. The father and the elder son were taciturn, irascible, melancholic, and constantly dissatisfied, while the mother and the younger son accepted life as it was and spread cheer around them rather than gloom.

This little boy dressed in a white lace dress is now an adored old man. He has a generous, smiling wife, a stepdaughter and son-in-law who idolize him, two little grandsons whom he bounces on his knee. It seems to me that his life is happy. But in his heart he still feels the wound of the separation.

After three hours, when I finally got up to leave, he asked me with unfeigned anxiety how much longer I planned to stay in Havana. Only until tomorrow, alas. At what time was I leaving? In the evening. Then why not come back to his house for lunch, just to catch up a bit on this lost century?

I was still thinking about him on my way home, and he will remain in my thoughts for a very long time to come. I'll tell his surviving cousins about him. I'll even urge some of them to write to him. But in what language? He spoke Arabic, he said, until the age of two; now he only knows one word—*laben*, the word for curdled milk as pronounced in our village. He still owns one book in Arabic—*The Tree*, in fact; he knows it is about the history of the family and that his father is mentioned in it, but he was never able to decipher the writing.

Later in life, he spoke some English. Up to age four, in Utah, it was his main language, and afterward he studied it a little with his father. But he has forgotten it; he is still able to grasp the general meaning of a sentence, but that's about it. He has only one language today, Spanish, and only one country, Cuba. Yes, of course, he knows his parents came from elsewhere. But this is the case for all Cubans, isn't it? Our family's behavior surely contributed to making him feel he had no ties anywhere else. As for me, I'll write to him. I promised him I would—in Spanish, if I can; otherwise in English. His son-in-law will translate for him. It is a promise, a definite promise. I won't drop him; I won't abandon him. Even after leaving here, when I'm far away, on my way back to my own adopted country.

This evening, I reimmersed myself in the documents I brought with me; I reread Theodoros's accusatory letter and some notes I had taken. In an attempt to understand . . .

If I am to believe the few survivors who still remember Alfred's name and story, he seems to have always been someone with problems. Whenever one of his brothers settled somewhere, he tried to wangle a job out of him in the same place. He would go there, not like it, and soon sink into depression. Unstable, touchy, introverted, he never managed to establish normal relationships with his colleagues or superiors, or with his own brothers for that matter. So he would set off again. This was how we find him in turn in Khartoum, in the service of the British army; in Cairo, as an Egyptian government employee; then, briefly, in 1913, in Alep, as an employee in the very recent Railroad Company; and finally in Havana . . .

At the time, Gebrayel had given up on persuading Botros to return and had given up on getting his nephews to work as he wanted them to. Alfred arrived at the opportune moment. His brother-in-law welcomed him with open arms, gave him a position of responsibility very soon, and included him in everything he did. The specific job Gebrayel put him in charge of was the professional correspondence, those dozens of letters that had to be written every day to suppliers, clients, and banks. This was drudgery for Gebrayel, who said it exhausted him. The newcomer wrote well, particularly in English; his boss merely had to skim through the letters and sign.

The two men were delighted, and Alice too, even more than they. The wandering brother had found stability and been put on a straight path, thanks to her!

Then the accident, the cataclysm. With Gebrayel gone, Alfred saw himself in charge of a small business empire—stores, workshops, dozens of employees, American, French, and German trademarks for which he was now the exclusive representative, though he had never had to deal with them before. Certainly he had been his brother-in-law's right-hand man for four years; certainly he had sometimes made helpful suggestions. But he had never run a business; he didn't realize how much energy had to be expended every day, in all sectors, just in order to survive. He didn't understand that the network of political, financial, and social connections Gebrayel had built up over the years was crucially important in enabling him to face up to his competitors, the envious, and nit-picking civil servants. It had all happened too suddenly. Alfred was still exhilarated by his rapid ascension; he probably thought he could move up to the highest rung as easily as he had moved up through the previous ones. Little did he suspect that the minute they heard of the accident, the competitors would contact the foreign suppliers and offer their services, and that as soon as he returned from the funeral at the Colón Cemetery, the banker would ask his secretary to give him the La Verdad file so he could see how to recover his investment.

Soon the business had lost its most distinctive products, lost the eye of the master who ensured its good operation on a daily basis, and lost the friendships that supported it. It began to lose money. In order to keep it afloat and calm the debtors, Alfred had no choice but to sell off property—in particular, land—that Gebrayel had acquired over his twenty years of activity in Cuba. Soon, in order to stem the hemorrhage, the stores were sold as well, and the prestigious Máximo Gómez house no longer belonged to "us"! Theodoros stated it very well in his letter. It was as if his brother had become poor again.

In the family, in the village, the anxiety expressed itself very early. Though Gebrayel was a symbol of success and cleverness, Alfred was close to the opposite. The knowledge that this young man with a chaotic career was now the custodian of a considerable fortune was far from reassuring to anyone. When Theodoros returned to the old country after failing in his mission, spoke of embezzlement, and announced that everything was lost or in the process of being lost, distrust turned into rage and hostility.

For Alfred, the final blow came from Alice herself, when she discovered the scope of the disaster and broke off with him too. Too late. Nothing, or almost nothing, was left of the fortune amassed by Gebrayel. Just enough for her to withdraw with dignity. She left Cuba with her three children and settled in the United States—in Chatham, Virginia. The most recent photo she sent to Nazeera dated from 1924; afterward there was a long, bitter silence. She was convinced that the family had dropped her too. It is true that she was considered partially responsible for the disaster, though she was granted extenuating circumstances and her brother was not.

Alfred vanishes from the archives at an early date. The photo of him as a "newlywed" with Hada is the last photo my grandmother kept of him. After that, there is the birth announcement telling us a boy was born to the couple on February 22, 1921—Henry Franklin Benjamin. I brought the tiny original envelope to Cuba with me; it is addressed solely to "Mrs. Nazeera Malouf . . . Mount Lebanon," though, logically, it should also have been addressed to her husband. My grandmother must have been the only person in the family with whom Alfred was still in touch. Unless it was Hada writing to her friend without her husband knowing it. No, it looks more like a man's handwriting. But what elegant calligraphy!

Then, finally, there is that other photo, the most poignant of all the ones I found in our archives. I must have looked at it dozens of times without knowing who was in it. It is only now that I can sense its meaning. Though there is no date or place listed on the back, I recognize Hada, sitting cross-legged on the grass and leaning against a tree. She is wearing a black dress, and the child lying on her knees is dressed entirely in white; he is at most three or four months old, but he has a surprisingly lively look in his eyes. As of this evening, I know that this infant is William. His mother, on the other hand, is looking out into space; she seems infinitely sad, like a pietà at the foot of the crucifix. To her right is another, older child, two or three years old.

The more I study this photo, the more I sense it is a call for help. As though the young woman in black was crying out across the ocean to her faraway friend, "Don't abandon me!"

Yet we did abandon them, her and her children. Today, as I faced the octogenarian child, I felt shame and guilt, though I am only a late descendant.

FIFTY-TWO

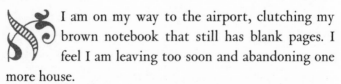 I am on my way to the airport, clutching my brown notebook that still has blank pages. I feel I am leaving too soon and abandoning one more house.

This last day in Cuba will have been like a perfunctory recapitulation. Another stop to take a final look at 5 Egido Street. Another fruitless attempt at the Grand Lodge building—"the person in charge is out of town." A rapid stop at the *historiador*'s to pick up the disk with the two 1928 photos. A pilgrimage to Máximo Gómez Avenue for another glance at the spot where his palace—our palace—used to be. I now can see which building was built in its place, and of course I find it ugly. A family luncheon at William's house, with our newfound connections, as though all the obstacles of space and time between us had suddenly evaporated, language being the only remaining obstacle. Lord, how I suffer from not understanding Spanish well enough. I've studied it off and on, but I haven't been sufficiently persevering, have too little patience for repetition and, to be honest, no willpower. Finally, to round off this last day, I made a new expedition this afternoon to the house on Patrocinio Street. I strolled from room to room, from the veranda to the bathroom, and meditated for a long time in the Andalusian room, this time without the presence of music, students, or teachers. Sitting on the floor, I gazed at the ceiling and imagined Gebrayel presiding over a holiday meal. I also strolled around the garden, picked up a few rusted fetishes dating from the period when "they" were here. A waking dream around a broken dream.

I looked at my watch. It was late, a century had come to an end, and my flight to Paris was not going to wait for me.

In flight

So ended my pilgrimage to the welcoming island that had been the ephemeral homeland of my relatives. From the day Luis Domingo first stirred up the slumbering dust in me, I knew I would eventually have to go to Havana. True, I found no trace of that Arnaldo whom my diplomat friend had mentioned. I am now resigned to regarding this ghostly cousin as a lure offered by destiny, an auspicious decoy. It hardly matters that he played a part in the last Cuban revolution, or whether he actually exists or not. It is thanks to him that I finally made up my mind and started on this patient trip back to my origins.

I look out the window and see nothing but a motionless bluish transparency. I wish I could see the expanse of the Atlantic Ocean spread out before my eyes; I can only sense its presence.

I glance at my watch so absentmindedly that when I look up, I don't remember the time. I have to check again and calculate; we must be halfway there, maybe a bit farther . . .

I wish I could doze a little, but my mind isn't on sleep. My obsessions are swirling around me like stinging insects . . .

Contrary to what I feared, this trip that is coming to an end did not interfere with what I had been told in my childhood about my ancestors' Cuban adventure. I wanted to be conscientious in my duties as a researcher and an amateur historian, so I combed through all the details one by one; however, at the end of the day, I feel I have by and large the same story to tell. In essence, the legend didn't lie, and the tragedy is there, climaxing—as so often happens since the world is the world—in a tragic sacrifice.

Gebrayel—the émigré Icarus who soared up to Heaven and then crashed to earth as by divine retribution. Prior to these last few months, I hadn't understood how ever-present this event was in the hidden recesses of my memory and my family's memory. A "founding" death, to be followed by a series of others, more tragic and more haunting still.

The history of my relatives could perfectly well be told thus: the ancestors die, and from their distant deaths, their descendants die in turn. Life engenders life? No, death engenders death. This has always been for me, for us, the silent law of origins.

Frustrations and Impasses

FÎFTY-THREE

On the evening I returned from Cuba, I sat on the floor on a cushion, unpacked the photos, notebooks, and envelopes, and spread them around me, convinced that I had established a new link with my family's past. Not that I had learned hundreds of new things, but I needed to get close to the legend, touch the stones of that country with my own hands, leaf through the newspapers of the period, and make my way, with thumping heart, into the house that had been ours, before I could, confidently and legitimately, reimmerse myself in the family archives.

Where was I again?

The last letter addressed by Botros to Gebrayel, in December 1918, had therefore arrived well after Gebrayel's death. On rereading it, you sense a kind of joyful mood emanating from it. Yet it announces Khalil's death and mentions tears, a coffin, embalmers, and condolences. But the sorrowful tone doesn't quite conceal the relief at having survived one of the greatest hardships human beings—those in Mount Lebanon included—had ever lived through in history. Seen from a certain angle, this death of a loved one was in itself a victory over war and bestiality: in the wake of the carnage, that the venerable pastor should have passed away from natural causes in his eighty-second year, his mind at peace, his soul resigned, a patriarch surrounded by those who revered him, wasn't this a triumph of decency and humanity?

It was only two months later that the tragic news reached the village, the untimely death of our émigrés, far away in the Americas, in the prime of life. Fortunately, Khalil had gone to his resting place without knowing of Anees's death. Fortunately, Soussène had passed away a few months before the war broke out, her mind at rest knowing that Gebrayel was radiant and prosperous. How sad for Sofiya, on the other hand. And for all the survivors.

For Botros, this was the beginning of a painful stage in his career, even if things didn't immediately appear in a somber light. The year 1919 even brought him some satisfactions, and his mood—judging from the letters that came down to us—remained confident and full of fighting spirit, for a time.

Of course, at the Universal School, problems persisted: parents who didn't have enough money to pay for their children's tuition; invariably tightfisted help from the Presbyterian missionaries; and countless other priorities of the government authorities. Nevertheless, the small village school continued to gain a good reputation for itself, so much so that the Greek Orthodox Church, regardless of the fact that Botros wasn't a member, asked him to open a series of similar institutions throughout the Levant. He received this offer in Beirut, where he had gone to settle some business.

But I'll let him tell it in his own way, in a letter dated October 1919, which he wrote to my grandmother Nazeera and her brother Shukri, who had come to stay in the old country for a while after the death of his father and was "helping out" at the school, though he was a physician and teaching wasn't his profession at all.

The letter was obviously written in great haste, since the two sheets Botros used were invoices from the "Al-Ahwal Bookstore, directed by Mr. Rahmet, Beirut (Syria). Stationery, office supplies, school materials, books in various languages, French and Arabic novels, etc., religious prints, novelties, photos blown up or reduced." All this information is printed in French on the left and in Arabic on the right, and on the lower half of each sheet there are columns for listing the type of article, the number sold, and the price.

I arrived in Beirut yesterday for some business concerning the house and the school, and I found myself swept up, so to speak, on this new wave that clamors for schools and quality teaching, and was introduced to His Holiness the Bishop of Alep, who had come here precisely to look for a person who could organize schools in his diocese. He held my hand and said, "It is Providence that led you to Beirut. You are the very man I was looking for!" I wanted to excuse myself, enumerating all the responsibilities I have toward our school and our family, but His Holiness "unleashed" a whole group of teacher friends against me who stood in the way of my making excuses. As a result I was forced into promising that I would go to the Alep diocese for a month to organize education there along the lines of our Universal School.

I shall therefore leave by the first train in order to return, God willing, at the beginning of next month. Hence I beg you to replace me in welcoming our dear students, in organizing the classes, and in giving practice in the three languages, with the help of our dear Theodoros especially for French, and with the help of our respected supervisors. Please tell each of them that I wouldn't have gone away for one minute if it weren't for the fact that we have a sacred duty to spread knowledge with a respect for religion and a love for one's country . . .

Botros felt exhilarated. Suddenly, as if by miracle, what he had always dreamed of but hadn't dared believe in was coming true: his pioneering experiment in a tiny village in the Mountains had become a model to be imitated. Alep in those days was the main Syrian metropolis; its Greek Orthodox population was probably the largest and most prosperous one in the Levant. That their modern schools should be modeled on Botros's school was bound to make him feel that he hadn't slaved away for naught.

It was not just one city or community. The entire country was entering a new era at the time, an era that seemed promising. The Ottoman Empire, defeated in 1918, had just crumbled after dominating the eastern Mediterranean for four centuries. Under a League of Nations mandate, France temporarily took over the present-day territories of Syria and Lebanon in order to prepare these countries for independence. And she immediately proclaimed her intention of developing education in order to stem the hemorrhage caused by emigration.

Botros rejoiced over this. Not that he was hostile to the Ottomans, far from it. When reforms were made during the last decades of the empire, he had applauded them. We saw him writing proudly "I, Botros M. . . . Ottoman citizen." But he had been disappointed by the revolution, disheartened by the blunders of the Young Turks, and he wasn't at all displeased to see the Great War upset the dusty, ancient order that weighed heavily on the people of the Orient.

His letter from Beirut—and the two following ones, sent from Alep—betray an enthusiasm that will rapidly be thwarted, alas. First, by the reaction of his relatives, because they didn't see things his way in the village, or even in his own household. They were wary of his growing ambitions, for he had a long-standing reputation for instability. Was he going to want to turn his family's life upside down and, on a sudden impulse, lead them into some new adventure?

Botros obviously feared this very reaction. He had tried to justify his trip by invoking the noblest principles, in the hope of avoiding blame from those who had remained in the village. In vain. The answer he received has been preserved in the archives, and it certainly didn't conform to what he hoped.

It is not signed by an adult, but by a six-year-old child, his own son, my eldest uncle. On reading it, I can't believe that this letter could be written in October 1919 by a boy born in July 1913. But I am the only person in the family to express such doubts. All the survivors, including its author, assure me that he had indeed written it and that his pre-cociousness was proverbial. I take note and translate:

To my dear respected father, may God keep you,

I kiss your hands fervently and devotedly, and ask the Lord to preserve you, as the support and pride of your family, for many long years to come. Then I notify you that I have already written to you two weeks ago, and once again four days ago, to inform you of the situation prevailing here, a situation that requires your returning as quickly as possible, for many pupils no longer attend school because of your absence, while others no longer want to pay tuition, as you will see from the list I have enclosed with this letter.

Some people fear that you won't return anymore, for Malatios told them that you had been taken to Alep manacled, for some mysterious reason. This news has discouraged some pupils from coming to school, especially those who live far away, in Baskinta, for example . . .

The students from the first class, namely Assad, Afifeh, and Khattar, maintain the discipline in school, with Mother's help, as much as her health permits. My uncle Shukri teaches English to the older boys. And they are all impatiently awaiting your return . . .

FIFTY-FOUR

Whether or not the letter was written by the "obedient son" who signed it, there is no doubt that the insistence on the necessity of Botros returning as soon as possible came from the adults as well, particularly from my grandmother, who was then in the fourth month of her fourth pregnancy—hence the allusion to her health.

The most effective argument for convincing my grandfather to shorten his stay in Alep was certainly the malicious rumor spread by his old rival, the parish priest Malatios, according to whom he had been "taken to Alep manacled" like a criminal. *Tsarkalt*, the Turkish verb for "manacled" used in the letter, smacks of the Ottoman Empire. On reading this passage, Botros's blood must have boiled, and he must have understood that he couldn't stay away from home much longer.

For the war of the schools, which had eased during the World War when the parish priest had to cease activities, had started up again even more intensely than before.

While the founder of the Universal School dreamed of extending his pioneering experiment to the four corners of the country, he was being threatened in his very own village, especially since his rival had just obtained support for his institution from the mandate authorities.

How was this possible? From France, the land of the Enlightenment? How could they grant subsidies to the bigots' school and turn down the one that promoted the ideals of the revolution? This sent my grandfather into a perpetual state of anger. On January 24, 1920, he wrote the following letter—a copy of which he carefully kept in his archives—to the cabinet of General Gouraud, the French high commissioner:

> *Sir,*
>
> *After presenting my respects and homage, I have the honor of bringing to your attention that seven years ago, in my native village, located in the neighborhood of Baskinta, I founded a school to which I assigned specific tasks, both in terms of the principles on which it is based, and in terms of language teaching and the teaching of all the other subjects. I have given the pupils freedom of religion, which displeased certain ignorant and fanatic people, and they have persecuted us. But their undertaking has failed, since our school's convincing results have attracted people to us rather than to them. During the war, when all the institutions in Syria had shut their doors, I made it a point to continue my activity in spite of food shortages and persecution, and I even used my own savings, with the thought that one day French aid would come . . .*

Actually, I very much doubt that Botros ever hoped for the arrival of the French, but this diplomatic white lie is only a slight stretching of the truth. As far as ideals were concerned, my grandfather always felt close to the country whose motto was Liberty, Equality, Fraternity. The fact that France now had the responsibility of determining his country's future path certainly didn't worry him. He saw it as a lesser evil, to say the least.

> *. . . with the thought that one day French aid would come and compensate these losses and put an end to the persecutions. Alas, I must say with great regret that when this French aid arrived, it was not for me, but for our*

*persecutors. They were given money, which they used to fight against us, and
we were given nothing.*

*When I questioned some civil servants, I heard answers that can't
possibly reflect the opinions of a universalist reformer like Monsieur
Gouraud. They said, "We don't give aid to two schools in the same
district." I asked, "If that's the case, why don't you help a school that
exists instead of financing the reopening of a school that closed down?"
They replied, "Your building is too small!" I said, "First of all,
what difference does it make whether the building is small, if everyone
acknowledges that the education is good. Secondly, help us, and we
will build bigger buildings!" They replied, "You receive aid from the
Americans." I said, "If foreigners felt it was worth it to help us, that is
an even greater reason for our government to do so, for its mandate is
to ensure our well-being . . ."*

Botros dug in his heels, rose up in arms, argued endlessly, compared
his school with the other one: "We have sixty students, they have fewer
than twenty, for the most part fictitious enrollments . . ." He brandished lofty principles, the struggle against sectarianism, fanaticism,
and ignorance, and demanded that an impartial inspector be sent. All
to no avail. The fact that the Universal School had received aid from
the Anglo-Saxon missions made it suspect to the French. The founder
of the school became nothing more than a tiny, pathetic pawn in the
power play of the great powers; his revolutionary ideals were of no use
to him. Not only did he not receive aid, but the war waged against him
was much fiercer than in the past. It was enough to make him miss the
good old days of the Ottoman Empire, the Great War, the famine, and
the swarm of locusts that had swooped down over the green wheat fields.

But Botros didn't give up right away. When, on August 31, 1920,
General Gouraud proclaimed the creation of the country that would
briefly be called Greater Lebanon—which is actually present-day
Lebanon, the joining of the Mountains, Beirut, Tripoli, Sidon, Tyr, and
the Bekáa plain—and the French governor of the new state, Georges
Trabaud, made an inaugural tour that brought him all the way to the
town of Baskinta, an hour away on foot from our village, my grand-

father went to meet him and laboriously prepared a speech for the occasion. I take the liberty of saying "laboriously" because this text, which is in the archives, seems somewhat muddled. Usually, Botros's writings are clear, legible, and neat-looking; the corrections, when there are any, are decipherable and carefully written in the margin, or added in small letters between two lines. This is not true of the speech he made in front of Trabaud: crude, with barbed deletions, ink splotches, and an agitated, indistinct handwriting, it all reflects the tormented mind of someone who didn't know whether to bow to adversity or rebel.

If I have come to interfere this way amid . . .

No, the line is crossed out.

If I may be so bold as to address you . . .

No again. Why this contrite tone? A more direct, firm phrasing would be better:

Sir, I am addressing you in my capacity of founder of the Universal School, and on behalf of a large number of men in that region . . .

This phrasing shows greater pride; my grandfather keeps it. A few conventional sentences come next, expressing welcome and praise, then, very quickly, reproaches:

Our complaint to Your Excellency is the pernicious "specialization" that is practiced with regard to us: when there are unpleasant obligations, we are included, but when advantages are allotted, we are excluded. No doubt we are too far away from the decision-making centers, where there are clever people who carry off all the advantages and pass along the obligations to those who are farther away. Thus it has been years since the government imposed a tax for road repairs. When it is a matter of collecting the tax, the people from this region are required to pay twice as much as the others, but as soon as these funds are allocated for the repair of a road, our region is never considered, our roads are never the ones that get repaired, so that they are still in the state you see, and dangerous for those who use them. If one day we were to create a museum of roads, ours would have to be put in them as antiques . . .

Similarly, France—may God sustain her!—has allocated millions for the improvement of education in this country, but did not think it necessary to make us benefit from this. Some of our schools haven't received a cent yet, although it is perfectly well known that ignorance alone is at the origin of fanaticism and divisiveness, ignorance alone prevents us from devoting ourselves efficiently to vital works such as agriculture and industry, and ignorance alone leads people to emigrate. If we don't succeed in reducing ignorance, we will have neither progress, nor civil concord, nor future. Knowledge is life, but we will not be able to attain knowledge without the help of the government. And the government is you, Monsieur Trabaud . . .

The speech ends with a few verses that start like this:

May France be protected, mother of Virtues, courageous pioneer . . .

Ultimately, the appeal turned out to be useless. The "courageous pioneer" continued to ignore her pioneering son and, with each passing day, the son became a little more distraught, incensed, and bitter.

FIFTY-FIVE

Having said this, let's be fair. Botros was not persecuted by the new rulers of the country; his school was not banned. But he never succeeded in getting his voice heard, while his "ignorant and fanatic" opponents received significant subsidies from the French and used these to hound him in a hundred different ways, with the aim of exhausting, demoralizing, and destroying him.

The spiteful rumor spread by the parish priest Malatios during my grandfather's trip to Alep is a typical example of such harassment. Other episodes in this endless little war have come down to us in the family correspondence.

For instance, this one, which I went to great lengths to piece together by patiently sorting out the relevant yellowed sheets of paper. There was an abandoned plot of land near the Universal School, belonging to a widow who had emigrated to Australia; the students, who didn't have much space where they could play between classes, were accustomed to using it as a schoolyard. One day

Botros received an official notification enjoining him to evacuate the field immediately and to forbid his students to trespass, lest they be prosecuted. A two-year trial ensued, traces of which remain in our archives. For instance, this letter addressed by my grandfather to one of his friends, asking him to intervene with the owner.

Your relative Mariam, widow of the late lamented Milad, sent power of attorney to the parish priest Malatios for him to start a lawsuit against me. The priest in question harbors feelings of hostility toward me that everyone here is aware of, and he immediately created a situation of conflict that perturbed the students, something your relative, who is an honest and sincere lady, certainly didn't intend . . .

I would therefore be immensely grateful to you if you could write and explain to her what this person who sports the title of priest is like, and who I am, and tell her she can address her complaints directly to me, or through another representative, and I promise you I shall satisfy all her demands. I don't seek to deprive her of her due; I simply wish to avoid having this person use your relative as an instrument against me and against the school . . .

The mediation of the friend to whom this letter was addressed seems to have borne fruit, since another letter added to the same envelope states that the conflict was resolved a few months later. Written in Malatios's handwriting, it states that by virtue of the power of attorney certified by the French consulate in Australia, the priest is entitled to rent the aforementioned plot of land to my grandfather for a period of five years at the price of one Syrian pound a year, payable in advance. Along with this letter, an extremely polite but dry and pompous calling card enjoins "Botros effendi" to send a written money order with the mule driver Aziz so that the above-mentioned deed can be delivered to him. You would think it was a treaty between two chancelleries, when all you had to do was step over a little wall and two bushes to walk from one school to the other . . .

Various other documents are in the family archives, dating back to the end of the war or the immediate postwar period, and they mention trials, complaints, summonses, and testimonies. There is even a copy of the *Official Newspaper of Greater Lebanon*, where two court decisions in favor of Botros were published, one against someone called Mansour, the other against a woman whose first name is Hanneh.

I am inevitably tempted to side with my grandfather and see things from his point of view, but I won't conceal the fact that I find this profusion of lawsuits disturbing. Although I don't for a minute doubt his moral integrity, my own integrity requires that I ask all sorts of questions, even the most improper and painful ones, questions he would not have liked me to ask. Was he really the purehearted being steeped in ideals, whose sole preoccupation was spreading knowledge and contributing to the progress of the nations of the Orient? Essentially, yes, and far more so than most people of his time or mine. But he also had his failings. Not just his "redresser of wrongs" side, which is ultimately charming, even if it didn't simplify his life or the lives of his relatives. Not just his moralizing side, irritating but respectable, and anyhow inseparable from his educator's temperament. He also had—from all indications—a strong craving for material possessions and recognition. The kind of craving that is felt only by those who have never been gratified. This is not, in itself, dishonorably reprehensible—or if it is, it also applies to me, my compatriots, and most of our fellow men—but it seems to me that in some circumstances, in particular during the war, this "craving" led my grandfather to serious errors in judgment.

The following letter, signed by someone whose first name is Sabeh, illustrates what I mean. It concerns a plot of land that was being offered to my grandfather for purchase during the Great War. The property belonged to two young heirs, and the author of the letter was a go-between introducing himself as a cousin—though in our villages we are all cousins in some way or other.

The aforementioned cousin, therefore, had set a price, and Botros answered that he found it too high. Which caused him to receive this scathing, insidious reply:

To our respected cousin khweja* *Botros,*
    After the greetings I owe you, I would like you to know that your letter arrived, that I understood your explanation, that I was happy to

khweja = Mr.

learn that you were in good health, but that I wasn't happy to read your answer concerning the inheritance of our uncle Ghandour, seeing as I had explained the reality of our situation, making it clear that we didn't have time for drawn-out discussions. This is why your reply should have been clear; either you buy or you don't buy. I don't want to believe that you wish to argue over the price of what these unfortunate children own, being convinced that you are a magnanimous man. So for pity's sake, tell us clearly how much you want to pay! If the price suits us, one of us will come with power of attorney to close the sale; otherwise we will have to find another solution for these children.

This is why you must answer very quickly concerning this matter, while setting our minds at rest, of course, concerning your precious health . . .

Did my grandfather appreciate the writer's caustic sense of humor? It is very unlikely. But the fact remains that he had the elegance to preserve this letter as well as another one, written by the same person six months later, on November 12, 1918. In the interval, it had not been possible to make the sale, and an expert had come who evaluated the property at one-fourth the price at which it was offered to Botros. In his second letter Sabeh accuses my grandfather of having influenced the expert, depreciated the property, and thereby prevented the heirs from selling to anyone but him.

If it is true that you seek to make a profit at the expense of these unfortunate souls, you should know that they are weak, poverty-stricken individuals who don't deserve to enter into conflict with persons of your stature. It would be shameful for people to say that you lowered yourself to attack such paltry opponents. For that reason, I beg the great teacher and famous scholar, so respected in the literary and learned world, to think of the prophet David and not covet the poor man's flock. Better you pit yourself against opponents who are able to defend themselves . . .

The letter contains a thousand other sarcasms that must have stabbed the recipient to the quick.

· · ·

Was Botros right or wrong in this affair? As far as the specifics go, I don't have all the facts at hand that would allow me to say. The thing I am deeply convinced of, on the other hand, is that he was wrong, a thousand times wrong, to get involved in this kind of quagmire. Of course, here I am passing judgment from my armchair in the tranquillity of my adopted country, while he, in the village during the Great War, must have been convinced every minute of the day that he was fighting for his survival, for his school, for his place in the sun—something he ultimately never obtained.

But I wouldn't want to give in to leniency or compassion with regard to him. Nor would I want to pass over his failings in silence because of my own feelings of guilt. I also owe his memory the truth. Not as a way of inflicting a sanction on him, but in homage to his complexity, and because truth is the ordeal by fire facing a man like him who wanted to escape darkness and longed for full light.

During the war years, when famine was rife, when there were already thousands of dead, my grandfather, thanks to his foresight, found himself safe from need, with more grain than was necessary to feed his children, with a bit of money too, enough to wait for better days and to keep the school open. Not a very enviable position, paradoxically, as I've already had occasion to point out. People were reluctant to believe that Botros was avoiding disaster because he had had more foresight than they; they were reluctant to believe that he had slightly more money than they because he had administered the family properties very competently for twenty years, that he had taken good care of the grain and the harvest. He had even studied accounting and obtained a diploma in order to better manage the small, not to say meager, family fortune. In a time of famine, people were reluctant to believe that Botros had simply been a better manager. They saw him as nothing more than a man of affluence and privilege, and therefore, necessarily, a profiteer.

When, during the war, he was offered a plot of land for purchase, said the price was too high, and requested an expert appraisal, he was looked at disapprovingly, mocked behind his back, and called a vulture. For him, however, this was normal procedure, and without having to be influenced or corrupted, the expert proved him right. How could it have been otherwise? The entire country was up for sale, and no one wanted to buy, or could buy. Every day people died of hunger because they were unable to convert their property into cash; so, inevitably, prices dropped very low, and if you could find a buyer, he could easily obtain the most attractive rates. Botros must have even felt that he was doing a good turn by parting with some of his emergency funds in order to acquire a plot of land that no one else wanted and was also useless to him. But seen from the other side, the transaction must surely have seemed one-sided, abusive, and sordid—if not right away, at least after the war, when prices went back up and people started regretting that they had undersold.

There is no doubt that Botros lacked judgment. He should certainly have abstained and not purchased anything during the war years. But perhaps he couldn't overcome the temptation of owning a terrace of fig trees in one spot, a forest of pine trees in another, or, better yet, an entire hillside. Perhaps, too, somewhere in the recesses of his mind he had the desire to equal, in the old country, Gebrayel's material success in the Americas. Having said this, since he was a man of integrity and feeling, the most honorable possibility of all shouldn't be excluded, namely that he sincerely wanted to help families in need who, if they didn't sell their plots of land, would die of hunger. And he simply failed to see that his gesture could be interpreted as dishonorable.

He committed another error of judgment in the same period: he lent people money. It was never said that he did so at usurious rates of interest; he even sometimes lent money at no interest at all. But there is an unstoppable logic in this area; it is hard for a debtor to maintain pure human relationships with his creditors. In perusing the letters from those years, I discovered that during the war many people in the village had lived on Botros's money: his brothers; his nephews; his father-in-law, Khalil; and several others. At a time when everyone was ruined and penniless, my grandfather found himself inopportunely in a privileged position, which earned him, I imagine, nothing but rancor and enmity.

Here again, a dilemma arises. What should he have done? Had he had an enormous fortune, I would have liked to hear that he had distributed money to everyone who was in need, that our entire large family and our entire village had survived thanks to his generosity. But this was obviously not his dilemma, since he had only a modest sum at his disposal, large solely in the eyes of the villagers, but not enough to make him a rich man. To realize this, one need only see his house and how his children were dressed. No, he really wasn't wealthy; all he had was a small nest egg, and he might have been wiser concealing it. He opted not to, and did what seemed to him both more moral and more judicious; he decided to lend money to those who didn't have any, and to get reimbursed when the war was over.

Where was the dividing line, in those calamitous years, between honorable actions and abusive transactions? This is a subject for endless discussion. The only thing that is certain is that Botros's image was tarnished, and it wounded him. He felt all the more wounded in that he honestly didn't see what he had done wrong.

As if to capture this painful period on paper, there is a picture in the family archives of Botros, Nazeera, and their first four children. Judging from what seems to be the age of the youngest child, the photo must date from the spring or summer of 1921. My grandfather is only fifty-three, but he looks like an old man, his smile forced and disillusioned, his mind engrossed in worries that are reflected even in the eyes of the children—like black olives that hardly dare to dream. They are all dressed in the same checked fabric, like orphans, though they weren't orphans at the time; in the background is an old stone wall and the bare trunk of an unidentified tree. They don't know what the future holds for them, even as I do, today, though I deserve no special credit. Who died first? Who emigrated? Who stayed?

Only one among them is still alive, and in the photo he is the only one who looks joyful: the eldest of my uncles still living far away in his long-term retreat in New England.

My grandmother was pregnant at the time. In the picture, this can't really be seen, but I know from the dates. She gave birth in early December 1921, and my grandfather had already chosen the child's first name. It was going to be Kamal in honor of Atatürk.

FIFTY-SIX

Why did my grandfather develop a passion for Kemal Atatürk that year? He doesn't explain this anywhere in his writings, but I can easily guess. For Botros was a person who had always dreamed of seeing the Orient shaken up, who had spent his life battling against backwardness and the stifling weight of tradition, who was strongly in favor of modernity even in his sartorial habits. How could he possibly have been impervious to the developments taking place in postwar Turkey: an Ottoman officer, born in Salonika and educated in its schools, brought up on Enlightenment values, proclaiming his intention to dismantle the old order and, one way or the other, bring what was left of the empire into the new century.

I don't think Atatürk's strong-arm tactics displeased my grandfather. I recall verses in dialect that my father recited to me often, written by his own father and clearly aimed at religious men—first among them, I suppose, the priest Malatios. I would translate them as follows:

If only a cobbler's scissors could shear them
Shear them from head to foot!

I quote this epigram here because it reminds me of the way Atatürk ordered religious Muslims to cut their beards—just as Peter the Great had ordered the popes to cut theirs two centuries earlier. In 1921, none of this had taken place yet, but the secular and modernist convictions of Turkey's leader had already been established, and I am not surprised by Botros's infatuation. He must have felt a deep affinity for this man, for his ideas and his temperament. I am even certain that he must have regretted that his Mountains were no longer Turkish territory. For at least Kemal was secular consistently, not like those Frenchmen who separated church and state at home and financed the priest's school in our village!

There may well have been, here and there, certain differences in attitude between the admirer and his hero—I actually pointed one of them out when it came to headgear. Whereas Atatürk wanted to replace the fez and the turban with the European hat, which he himself readily wore, Botros preferred to go around bareheaded, to distance himself from both groups—men who still complied with Oriental tradition and men who mimicked Western ways. But this was more of a surface difference than a real difference. My grandfather wanted Orientals to take the West as a model; his criticism was chiefly aimed at people who aped the West without seeking to understand the deep reasons for its advancement. As for Atatürk, even though he was an admirer of westerners, he also knew how to stand up to them.

Indeed, in that year of 1921 he had had a series of successes against the European armies occupying Turkey. And in October he had got France to recognize his government and withdraw her troops from his country. This was the liberator of lands and minds whom my grandfather wanted to pay homage to by naming his child after him, using the Arabic pronunciation: Kamal.

Botros had not been shy about announcing his decision ahead of time. This was obviously an act of bravado against the advocates of obscurantism and traditionalism, the opponents of his Universal School, General Gouraud and Monsieur Trabaud, and all those who feuded with him, slandered him, or failed to give him aid.

The child was born on December 9, 1921. Botros was in Beirut that day. When he returned to the village a few days later, people whispered, sniggered, and jeered. And his close relatives, starting with Nazeera, were embarrassed. Alas, he wouldn't be able to keep his promise; Providence had decided otherwise. The child could not be given Atatürk's first name, for it was a girl!

My grandfather frowned and said nothing. He went and sat at his desk in a corner of the bedroom, very close to the bed where his wife was lying. She signaled with her hand for everyone to leave the room, the older children leading the younger ones. The mother, father, and newborn baby remained alone in the room, all three silent.

After meditating for a long time, Botros looked at Nazeera and said, "So what? So we have a daughter. I can still call her Kamal! Who cares if it's a boy's name? What difference does that make? Why should that make me change my mind?"

History doesn't say whether my grandmother tried to dissuade him. I imagine she did. I imagine she courageously tried to explain to him that it would be difficult for a girl to have this name. But he dug in his heels, as he always did, and she eventually gave in, as she always did.

In the days that followed, other members of the family, I imagine, tried to talk him out of it. But to no avail. My grandfather's nature was such that if you tried to show him the road to reason and common sense, this became a powerful incentive for him not to take that road. His daughter, my aunt on my father's side, was given Atatürk's first name.

Kamal—I was waiting for this moment to talk about her. I have quoted her several times in the previous chapters, with and without quotation marks, but was careful not to mention her name until I reached the point in my narrative when I could explain it. Yet her name and her husband's appear in the very first pages of this book, since it is mainly dedicated to her.

As soon as I had the idea for this research project about my grandfather, my great-uncle Gebrayel, our family, and our origins, it is to her that I turned, letting her in on the secret. What I lacked for this sensitive journey was an intimate guide, someone close to me and to that period who could give me discriminating and accurate descriptions of the people and the feelings of the moment and tell me what was plausible in interpreting the past and what was not. A guide by my side to replace all those who were gone. I speak about her with emotion and gratitude as well as sadness, because she too has passed away, too soon, in the course of this journey.

Recently we were both stimulated by the convenience and speed of electronic mail. We often wrote long letters to each other, I in French, she in an elegant and precise English. Whenever I quizzed her about a story someone told me, or one that I might have inferred from documents I dissected, I knew I could completely trust her opinion. "This version of events seems doubtful to me," "This account matches what I've heard before, and I think it's closer to the truth," or "I have another version of this story, which I got from the person involved," or better yet, "When I was thirteen, I overheard Alice whisper into your grandmother's ear that Gebrayel's death wasn't accidental." Her scrupulous appraisals didn't stop her from sometimes relating gossip when she thought it might be instructive, but then she added "hearsay" in parentheses to avoid confusion.

The stories about her birth and name belong partly to this category, the hearsay category. But only partly. Everything concerning Atatürk, my grandfather's infatuation with him and his unbending resolution to name his child after him, is strictly authentic. On the other hand, my grandfather's words in the bedroom are not from firsthand accounts. The only witness, his wife, Nazeera, certainly didn't relate them word for word. Why not? Because my grandmother never talked about such confidential matters; this was not the kind of thing she indulged in. Not with her daughter or anyone else. In fact, no one would have dared question her. The daughter of the Presbyterian parson and the austere Sofiya didn't inspire the least familiarity in those who approached her; if anything, she aroused caution and even fear. Not in us, her grandchildren, who knew her as elderly, mellowed, and affectionate, but persons who had known her in earlier years treated her with great respect, and her own children behaved with deference toward her. Doubtless they also loved her, but above all they feared her; there was no idle chatter between her and them. And no great outpourings of feeling. I have already told the story of the little girl who asked her mother why she never kissed her, the way other mothers kissed their children, and whose mother answered, with embarrassment, that she did kiss her, but only when she was asleep. That little girl was Kamal.

I have a specific reason for bringing up my grandmother here and discussing her at greater length. But I approach the subject with infinite caution. I am made of the same clay as my grandparents, and I have the same sense of propriety, the same cult of silence and dignity. I therefore find it difficult to tackle the question that has been plaguing me for a while, about which the survivors have spoken only with reticence: How could Nazeera, steeped in common sense, having a strong, demanding, domineering personality, cohabit with such a capricious, unstable, provocative husband? The conclusion I have finally come to was that they didn't often live under the same roof.

The first clue came to me years ago, from my father, but I hadn't paid attention to it. I was terrified, in my childhood, at the possibility of losing my parents one day, particularly my father, for ever since I found out that he had lost his father when he was a child, I saw him as fragile, vulnerable, and threatened. At the time, of course, I wasn't engaged in any research; I wasn't thinking of writing; I just wanted to allay my fears. I had therefore asked a series of questions about "*jeddo* Botros" that my father patiently answered before adding, "I'm telling you these things as they were told to me, because I didn't know your grandfather very well. He worked in Beirut, and we lived in the village."

"Didn't he come home in the evening?"

"In those days, you know, there were no roads, and very few cars . . ."

At the time, I didn't see anything abnormal about this. When I was a child, we used to spend every summer in the village—my mother, my sisters, and I. My father too, though he never stopped working. He "went down" to Beirut, to the newspaper, every morning, and "came back up" to the village in the late afternoon. As soon as he reached the other side of the Mountains, he would toot his horn in a characteristic manner and we would run down the road to meet him, to the place called the Tannery. It was a daily ritual. But this was only during the three summer months. During the nine other months of the year, the whole family lived in the capital.

Today I find it very odd that I never asked my father how my grandfather could possibly have worked in Beirut when everyone always told me that he was the headmaster of "our" village school, whose abandoned premises I had visited so often.

Many years later I came across another clue. From my father again, but this time in a piece he had written about his own father—the only such piece he wrote, to my knowledge. It was written for the fiftieth anniversary of his death. Not that Botros was an illustrious person whose anniversaries are celebrated, but precisely because my father wished to seize the occasion to rescue him from obscurity. The piece, covering half a page in the literary supplement of a major daily newspaper, began with a preamble in which my father apologized for not being able to describe his father adequately, since he had only hazy memories of him.

> He died when I was still very young, and in the last years of his life,
> I saw him only rarely, since he worked in Beirut . . .

I came across this article by accident, lost among thousands of other papers, in a drawer under my father's bookcase. My father was no longer alive, nor was my grandmother, but I could still question some invaluable survivors—in particular Kamal. After a few days she sent me the following answer:

> *In your last letter, you wondered whether my father had a regular activity in Beirut in the latter years of his life, which kept him away from home. I questioned three or four people who might still remember, and here is the gist of what I learned. After the school in Machrah was well established and he had able senior students who could manage it during his absence, my*

father opened an office in Beirut, where he gave private lessons, which he named "the office of knowledge and work."

Though Kamal didn't express any doubts about this version of events, she distanced herself from it by attributing it to her informers (she mentioned each one in another part of the letter). Indeed, the explanation was a bit elliptical. When you are aware of Botros's many scruples during his extended stay in Alep, when you know of his school's difficulties in surviving the priest Malatios's incessant attacks, you can only smile on reading that he felt he could embark on a new enterprise, far from the village, safe in the knowledge that the ten-year-old pupils were taking charge of the six-year-olds! And this at a time when his wife had to cope with five children and was expecting a sixth.

Kamal, who knew how to read my thoughts, was careful to add in her letter:

In Beirut your grandfather boarded with the Abou Samra family. This explains the close relation we had with them. The first time I accompanied my mother to Beirut, I remember sleeping at their house . . . In fact their son eventually married Sarah, the head teacher in our school . . .

I got the message: my grandfather didn't leave his family in order to lead a double life. But he clearly wanted to get away. Perhaps not from his home or his school—though maybe a little bit—but certainly from the village and the villagers. All the quarrels about plots of land, money, loans, and his refusal to baptize his children; all those diatribes; all the lawsuits against neighbors and cousins; and let's not even bring up the priest again . . .

Botros was obviously exhausted and disgusted. He needed a breather, a new outlook and a change of scene. His bachelor instincts had gotten the upper hand again.

FÍFTY-SEVEN

The year 1922 brought nothing that might have assuaged my grandfather's rage. France appointed a new high commissioner for its new possessions in the Levant: Maxime Weygand, an already famous general and fervent Catholic. Botros didn't even go to the trouble of writing to him. With Gouraud, he could try to point out that his actions weren't consistent with his humanist convictions; with his successor, sadly for my grandfather, there was no inconsistency. As soon as he took up his post, Weygand made it clear he would favor parochial education.

In the family archives, the verses written that year intensify in violence against men of religion.

> *They are demons in the clothes of decent men*
> *Or, if you prefer, Satans without tails,*
> *Except that tails grow on their faces*
> *As beards, may God set them on fire!*

Let's hope that Theodoros, who wore an imposing prelate's beard all his life until he breathed his last, never got wind of these words written by his brother.

Nor of these:

> *Who will tell the Jesuits that they are now*
> *Like wolves who have been entrusted with sheep?*
> *Evil, all evil, is concealed in the word "love,"*
> *A word that is frequently heard in brothels.*

I'll never know what specific events incited Botros to this assault on the Society of Jesus. What I do know is that this religious order played a major role in the field of education under the French mandate in Lebanon, a role that wasn't to my grandfather's liking, of course. But I suspect that he had been directly affected by some specific incident. For instance, the Jesuits may have somehow supported the priest Malatios's school; they may have lent him their educational backing in some way or other . . . I have no tangible proof, but it seems plausible, and it would explain Botros's acrimony.

Do I dare further irritate my grandfather by quickly mentioning here, between two sections, that years later, several of his "sheep" descendants found themselves under the iron rule of the Jesuit "wolves"? Fortunately for him, he left this world without having seen this; may he rest in peace!

After this brief digression, let me embark on another one that is slightly longer but which I feel is essential in order to dissipate a misunderstanding.

I've just quoted, in rapid succession, several of Botros's violently anticlerical statements. I felt that it was important to do so, for I was chagrined at seeing his image in the family toned down, tempered, blurred. He was a rebel, and it is in the ruins of his rebellion that I search for my origins, for I claim to be a follower of his rebellion, to have descended from it. On the other hand, I don't want to replace one inaccuracy with another one. This would be the case if I passed over in silence the fact that though there is this handful of angry anticlerical verses, there are hundreds—yes, several hundred—that imply otherwise.

Thus, in the very first pages of the oldest notebooks preserved by Botros we find an 1893 hymn to the glory of the Greek Catholic patriarch Gregory I, and an even earlier poem, in 1892, in honor of this same prelate—dating to when my grandfather was still at the American mission school. In 1898 a book was published in Beirut to pay homage to the newly elected Greek Catholic patriarch, Botros IV; it contains a poem by Theodoros that is one and a half pages long, as well as a poem by Botros that is just as laudatory and three pages long.

Wherever we look in my grandfather's notebooks, we come across patriarchs, bishops, archimandrites, *ekonomous*, convent superiors, holinesses, beatitudes, reverends . . . Some of them Greek Catholic, others Greek Orthodox, Maronite, or Protestant.

Does this mean that Botros used the same double language that he so lambasted in his compatriots? I think it would be unfair to say so. A man who refused to baptize his children, and thus took the risk of turning his entire community and his entire family against him, can't reasonably be accused of duplicity. He had a coherent, conscientious line of conduct, full of nuances, for which he was prepared to suffer and which therefore deserves to be respected. When he declared that children shouldn't be assigned a religion that they haven't chosen of their own free will, but should be allowed to decide on their own when they come of age, he really meant what he said, and he proved it. When he added that he wasn't in the least hostile to Christianity—or to religion in general—and intended to inculcate the true precepts of the faith in his students while avoiding sectarian quarrels, once again he meant what he said.

His anticlericalism had a circumscribed target: the persons who fought his Universal School out of obscurantism or fanaticism, such as the priest Malatios, and those who came to their aid. That was it. His dream was not to abolish religion or churches; his dream was to live in a free country one day, surrounded by free women and men and even free children—a country governed by the rule of law and not by arbitrary power, controlled by enlightened, uncorrupt leaders who guaranteed its citizens education, prosperity, freedom of belief, and equal opportunity, regardless of people's denominational allegiances, so that people would no longer think of emigrating. A legitimate but unattainable dream that he pursued doggedly to his dying day. And which often led him to bitterness, rage, and despair.

I think back with bitterness on all those years I lost between notebooks and inkwells in a country of futility and superficiality!

I cite once again this passage from a letter addressed to his brother-in-law Shukri, for it reveals a sense of failure that Botros felt often but which he usually silenced out of pride and a certain feeling of responsibility. Actually, he had constant doubts—doubts about everything he did, and doubts about the future of the "Oriental lands," even when the situation seemed conducive to hope. For instance, during the great Ottoman revolution:

If time goes by without our having caught up with the advanced peoples, the latter won't even regard us as human beings anymore!

Then a bit later:

One sultan has abdicated, another has mounted the throne, but power is still exercised in the same way.
We are a fickle nation, blown this way and that by the winds of passions . . .

I also quoted these last words earlier on, but not the following ones, scribbled in pencil on a loose sheet of paper, titled, simply: "Beirut, 1923."

I am weary
Weary of describing

The state of our countries of the Orient,
Replace "country" by "calamity"
Replace "Orient" by "malediction."
You will have an idea of what I am trying to say.

These disillusioned words can't be explained solely by the ordinary calamities he constantly had to face. A tremor of a completely different magnitude had occurred. A tragedy that was both brutal and emblematic, from which he never recovered.

FIFTY-EIGHT

In 1923, one of Botros's nephews—an unusually intelligent boy whom everyone compared to his uncle and who had been one of the top students at the Universal School—told his parents that he didn't intend to work in the family business; he was going to register at the university to study literature. He even added, perhaps out of simple bravado but maybe also out of conviction, that he had decided to dedicate his life to poetry.

His mother—Botros's sister—and his father were hardly delighted by these plans. They would have preferred to see him have less fanciful ambitions. However, I am told that they might have been more conciliatory if the father's elder brother, who, as custom has it, was the real head in that branch of the family, had given his consent. But he refused obstinately. When his nephew dared to argue with him, he said, "You won't go anywhere! You'll work right here with us, like us! You're a man now and it's time you started earning your daily bread." To which the young man replied, "I'll stop eating bread!"

In one of my books I related a village legend about a boy named Tanios who went on a hunger strike in order to get the right to pursue his studies. When he was on the brink of death, his parents capitulated and put him in the care of an English pastor. He then started eating again. I was inspired by a story that had taken place in my family, of course, but I changed it to suit me.

In the real story, the young man died. On July 28, 1923, to be precise.

When he started fasting, his parents proved to be inflexible, convinced that he would eventually give up. When they saw that he really wasn't eating anything and was becoming increasingly thin and weak, their attitude changed, and they promised him that they wouldn't interfere with his plans anymore. But he had already crossed the invisible divide between the desire to live and the desire to die.

My father, who was born in October 1914 and was therefore a little under nine at the time, talked to me about the tragedy on several occasions: "I remember it as if it were yesterday. The whole family filed in front of my cousin to beg him to start eating again. They brought him food he liked, hoping to tempt him and stimulate his appetite. They made oaths and promises . . . There was a crowd around his bed, and his mother kept crying. But he wouldn't listen to anyone."

"He fasted until he died?"

"He didn't go out slowly like a candle. One day, though they still hadn't given up hope of making him change his mind, his heart gave out."

Botros was in Beirut when this crisis erupted. At first the boy's parents didn't want to notify him; they felt that he was a bit responsible for their son's whims, and they were afraid he would arrive and bolster their son's stubbornness, his own stubbornness being proverbial in the family. They appealed to him only when the situation had deteriorated dangerously. By then it was too late. The hunger striker no longer wanted to listen to anyone.

. . .

The whole family was shaken by this tragedy, and it haunted them for years. Coming so soon after the great famine, which had traumatized all the inhabitants of the Mountains and left a lasting mark, this self-imposed voluntary starvation, based purely on principle, had disturbing nobility. Botros's nephew had emigrated to death as others emigrated to America, and for the same reasons: he felt that the world around him was narrow—the communities, their ideas, beliefs, schemes, and servile bustling. The families too were constricting, narrow, and stifling. One had to escape.

My grandfather recorded in one of his notebooks the elegy he delivered on this occasion, part prose, part verse. In the introductory sentences he doesn't mention the hunger strike, only the "sudden death . . ."

His every word shows how affected and outraged he was. At the same time, he couldn't further torment his sister, who was living through a nightmare, or his brother-in-law, or the other members of their clan, regardless of how blameworthy they were. Funerals aren't appropriate times for arguments, settling scores, and denouncing people's obtuseness. Nor are they occasions for telling the whole truth. They serve to console, comfort, and soothe people's sorrow.

Botros's first words remained within this framework. After saying that some human beings, after staying among us all too briefly, left a trace that many others who lived much longer failed to leave, he addressed words to himself, in the style of ancient elegies:

I have already seen you cry, but never before tears of blood . . .

He praised the deceased, occasionally using conventional images, "his age will have been the age of roses," and occasionally less conventional ones. Then he approached the unmentionable on tiptoe:

Life had offered us a gem, but, struck with remorse, took it away from us.

Until the moment, very near the end, when he said:

We made you hate our existence and its vexations
So you left it, you left us, of your own free will . . .

The words had been said. The mask of decorum removed: the young man had left of his own free will, and it was "our" fault.

May this other life you desired be beautiful
Up there, above us, in the Lord's palace.
As for us, we will stay here, near your grave
And sprinkle it with tears so that the grass stays green.

In the audience that day, countless whisperings were heard mingled with the sobs, as well as the following story, which is still told in the village: the young deceased's parents had had a first child who was sickly and died in early childhood. To ward off ill fortune, the father decided that from then on, he would give his sons the names of ferocious carnivorous animals. Three sons were born to him and he gave them the Arabic names for Wildcat, Lion, and Cheetah.

I knew the youngest very well, Fahd—"Cheetah." I used to visit him occasionally with my father. He was a reserved, affable, somewhat bashful man. Nothing about him suggested ferociousness. I imagine that his two older brothers, "Wildcat" and "Lion," weren't very different. No doubt the father who had pinned those artificially fated first names on them must have felt swindled. They all three wrote delicate, well-turned verses; a few poems by each, in their handwriting, have been preserved among the family papers.

The one who let himself die of hunger was the middle brother, Assad, or "Lion." "The lion is king, and you were the king, but the king of purity and knowledge," Botros said in his elegy. One part of the audience certainly grasped the underlying meaning of these words.

This tragedy had an immediate repercussion that my father once talked about in front of me, and at the time, I felt it was a satisfying epilogue: "When Assad died, his older brother, who was inseparable from him, decided to leave the country that day, without waiting for the funeral. He sneaked out of the village by night and set out on foot for the coast, by small pathways, all the way to the port of Beirut, where he boarded the first ship leaving for Brazil. He was never seen again."

For decades, this was the story I remembered. While going through the family archives, I found mention of a different epilogue. In a letter to my grandmother Nazeera, one of her brothers, an émigré in the United States, asked her to convey his condolescences to her sister-in-law and her husband, "who just lost their two sons, one after the other."

Their *two* sons? I immediately sent a question to Kamal, and four days later, she answered as follows:

> In my childhood I heard that the older brother left for Brazil and that we never heard from him again. Later, I was told that he had joined a radical political movement and was killed in a shoot-out. But I've just had a long conversation with his niece Aïda, who gave me another version of this event. According to her, in Brazil, her uncle had an affair with the wife of a governor. It seems the governor found out about it and asked one of his guards to kill him. Apparently the murder took place on the steps of the monumental palace stairway. They claimed he was an anarchist who had come to kill the governor. I don't know if the story is true . . .

I don't know either, but it is probably the original version, the one reported to the parents in the letter they received from Brazil at the time. The parents may have found it unseemly for the family's respectability and for the memory of their deceased son, and they may have decided to expunge the romantic part and keep only the political explanation—the very explanation put forward by the killers. "Wildcat" had joined a militant movement, and that is why he was killed.

Whatever its exact circumstances, the tragedy of the eldest son didn't leave traces in people's memories—the facts were too hazy and too distant. The middle son's tragedy, like a naked blade gleaming close by, lacerated souls for a long time to come.

For Botros, no event could have been more painful. It was worse than a bereavement; it was a defeat, the defeat of everything he believed in and everything he had sought to build. What was the point of his staying in his native country and dedicating himself to teaching if his most brilliant, most talented, most purehearted, and dearest disciples ended like this? My grandfather was now far beyond bitterness; he was on the edge of despair.

Oh, if only he could still take his wife and children and leave, yes, go far away, to Havana, and become his brother's partner, become prosperous like him, build a beautiful house in the hills like his . . .

But this dream too was now ruled out. Gebrayel was dead, his fortune lost, his only remaining residence a pompous and pathetic tombstone in the Cristobal Colón Cemetery.

Cuba will never be ours again, Grandfather, nor will the Levant! We are, and will always be, wanderers who have lost their way.

FÌFTY-NÌNE

In 1924, Botros had some promising news—
news from a world far away from his, but likely
to affect his personal battles. In May, elections
in France brought victory to the Cartel des Gauches,
"Left-Wing Coalition," which had the strict enforcement
of secularism at the top of its agenda, especially in education. In the Levant, the consequences were immediate:
the ultra-Catholic Maxime Weygand was forced to hand
over his position of high commissioner to Maurice Sarrail, also a general and also a hero of the Great War, but
a Freemason and violently anticlerical. If this radical
change in political orientation and men was to become
official at the end of the year, it was known as early as
July, and the Beirut newspapers, relaying the Paris press,
spread the news. They even quoted the incredible words
of the new French representative: at work he didn't want
to hear a word about communities, bishops, patriarchs,
muftis, or ulemas! The country's religious dignitaries
were stunned by this, and outraged.

For Botros, by contrast, these statements brought great hopes. This time he, and not his rivals, would receive "French aid." His Universal School would finally benefit from the support of the mandate authorities; it would be able to recover, expand, and disseminate knowledge. Malatios and his protectors wouldn't know what saint to turn to!

But this is not what came to pass. Sarrail, an upright man, was also tactless, and he was insensitive to the local political subtleties. He aroused so much mistrust and hostility and caused such unrest—among other things, a bloody rebellion in the Druzean region—that he was recalled to Paris after only a few months.

My grandfather never knew how the reign of this Freemason "brother" ended. Botros lived only through the initial secular euphoria and died hoping for good news. It was August 17, 1924, a Sunday. He was in his room, sitting at his desk and writing. My grandmother was preparing the midday meal when she heard him call her in a strange voice.

He was in the habit of jotting down things in the course of the week on scraps of paper, cardboard, the backs of cigarette packs; and on Sundays, while the other villagers were at mass, he used to take this jumble of papers out of his pocket and recopy whatever deserved to be recopied into virgin notebooks.

If this is what he was doing on that Sunday, I think I know which notebook he was writing in for the last time. I have found a total of thirteen notebooks, including the small New York savings booklet that he used as a notebook when he was crossing the Atlantic Ocean, probably because he had no other paper handy.

Only one notebook contains writings from 1924. It has a marbled ivory and burgundy cover and a pasted label with the following words:

First draft of a few improvised words
in unexpected circumstances,
between the year 1917 and the year

My grandfather was in the habit of leaving the last date blank until the notebook was filled up; then he would start a new notebook, labeling it in similar fashion. This time the notebook wasn't filled up. Two double pages are left blank.

Leafing through it, I can't help anxiously looking for the date on which his pen stopped. I've sometimes had a similar feeling on reading a writer's diary, when I knew his date of death and saw him approaching it blindfolded. Except that in this case, there is an added dimension for me, which is not just due to the family relationship but also to the nature of the document in my possession. Not a printed book, but a unique specimen, it is written in the very hand of the man who will die, written with his own ink. I could even find fingerprints on these sheets and minute traces of sweat and blood.

At the beginning of this final notebook are verses that probably weren't conceived as an epigraph, but become one:

> *You begin to shed tears over your youth*
> *As soon as your first white hair appears,*
> *Tiny flowers in the midst of brambles.*
> *But you are wrong to squander this mature age on lamentations,*
> *For it too will not last.*

The same idea recurs, or almost, at the bottom of the same page:

> *It is useless to mourn one's youth,*
> *Or to curse old age,*
> *Or to fear death,*
> *Your life is the day you are living now,*
> *Nothing more. So enjoy yourself, be happy,*
> *And be ready to leave.*

And two pages later, still another attempt to reconcile himself with the end that he must have vaguely felt was near:

> *Whoever observes the world with a wizened eye*
> *Is bound to notice that life*
> *Is a perishable commodity,*
> *Only a free mind knows how to turn away*
> *From pastures where you graze only on poverty,*
> *And inhale the fragrance of eternity.*

This notebook contains poems and speeches delivered in various places—among them, Alep, Zahlé, Baalbek. And the funeral oration, already quoted, for "Lion," his nephew, in 1923. Then some verses written in 1924 for a ceremony at the American University of Beirut—the month isn't specified.

On the same page, I find a folded sheet of paper. It is a medical prescription, written in French on June 4, for "Professor Pierre Malouf." It bears no resemblance to present-day prescriptions, on which doctors merely scribble a list of foreign words in illegible handwriting; it contains precise dosages intended for the pharmacist who had to prepare the drugs. It is also typed in full to avoid mistakes.

SODHII ARSENIATIS	*00.05 grams*
YOHIMBINES SPIEGLES	*00.20 grams*
EXT. NUCIS VOMICAE	*2.00 grams*

It is useless to continue; this jargon is completely abstruse as far as I'm concerned. But I have no cause to worry, because I have a close relative who is a scientist and can compensate for my ignorance. Yes, among the scores of literary persons in the family, there is one genuine scientist, and he happens to be a walking encyclopedia of medical chemistry. I hastened to send him a copy of the prescription by mail. His detailed explanations came a few days later.

You will find below a few notes in answer to your query concerning drugs prescribed to your grandfather. It seems he was feeling weak and needed something to boost his energy and give him a feeling of well-being. Even the food prescribed (in Arabic writing) on the back of the prescription points in the same direction.

For your interest, I am including below brief notes about the prescribed drugs. Most of these are no longer prescribed. They are of the age before the advent of synthetics and modern pharmacology.

The first drug is an old polypharmacal prescription:
a. Sodium arsenate. Arsenic could produce a general toning effect, like what the professional Alpine climbers used to take to give them

"*power*" *to climb and be able to withstand the harsh weather and very low temperatures.*

b. *Yohimbine is an alkaloid from an African plant, which is a sexual stimulant, an aphrodisiac.*

c. *Ext. Nucis Vomicae is an extract of an Indian seed containing strychnine, believed to be a nerve tonic, and a bitter tonic (stimulates the appetite).*

d. *Zinc phosphide—used formerly as a source of phosphorus, a tonic (now used as a rat poison).*

e. *Ext. Damianae—is an extract of a leaf, damiana, from the American and African tropics, which contains a number of constituents having different actions, so that the leaf is described as aphrodisiac, tonic, stomachic, and antidepressant.*

f. *Ext. Kolae—is an extract of an African seed cola nuts (cola), which is very rich in caffeine, a nerve stimulant.*

g. *Ext. Cocae—is an extract of coca leaf from South America (Peru, Bolivia, etc.). It is the source of cocaine, a central nervous system stimulant and a local anesthetic. The natives of South America chew the leaves to help them climb their mountains and withstand fatigue. It enables them also to go without food even for a few days.*

a, c, and d mentioned above, are poisonous beyond certain minimal doses.

Another remedy prescribed to my grandfather was plaster, Alcock's American porous plaster, No. 1. There were instructions in French on the prescription: "To apply to the lumbar region until it comes off on its own."

This "band aid," known here as "lazka amerikaniyyeh," is still in use today. It stimulates blood flow to a painful organ of the body. The pain may be of rheumatic origin or caused by a draft of air or some other cause. It may be applied to any part of the back, shoulder, neck, etc. It is effective when needed.

Now, concerning the food the doctor recommended to your grandfather, it is interesting to note that the nutritious foods listed are supposed to foster

the energy of the body, a supplement to the drugs. Thus soft-boiled eggs,
testes of sheep, fish, chicken, pigeon, or other bird meat . . .

So my grandfather wasn't treated specifically for a heart condition.
Which doesn't mean he didn't have one. At any rate, this was what
Nazeera believed at the time. Later in life, she confided the following to
her daughter Kamal, who in turn confided it to me:

Regarding Father's death, I remember Mother mentioning that
shortly before he passed away, he began to inform her about
various affairs, to know how to manage alone. She was under the
impression that he had gotten warnings from his doctors about a
heart weakness.

SIXTY

 While we're on the subject of the heart, I found some verses that intrigued me in Botros's last notebook.

> *If my lady persecutor had some of*
> *the same feelings for me*
> *As I have for her,*
> *She would exhibit toward me*
> *A bit of what I exhibit toward her.*
> *She would not have sought to wreck my heart.*
> *How can a person be so determined*
> *To wreck the house that shelters her?*

It is true that the use of the word "heart" in romantic metaphors is one of the most common among all peoples, not just among poets. But I can't help thinking that in the quote above, Botros is also alluding to the heart as an organ. Particularly when he adds the following lines two pages later:

Be more conciliatory, more loving,
Relieve my sufferings
My heart is not made of steel!

And then, right afterward, as though he were still pursuing the same reproachful conversation:

You ask for news of my heart
After what struck it? You should know
That no creature made it suffer more than you—
Now you have your answer!
My heart didn't want to unbind
What is bound . . .

Though I don't want to indulge in simpleminded psychoanalysis, it doesn't seem insignificant to me that he has this tendency to mention the heart on every page, usually in connection with suffering, a short time before the heart attack that caused his death. Anxiety and pain may have elicited the words, and then they may have taken on the vestments of fateful muses.

Though Botros's last writings show he had intimations that the end was near, he didn't give up his professional activities or social obligations, and he fulfilled them with apparent good humor. Hence, when he left Beirut just after his doctor's appointment, he went to Souk-el-Gharb to attend a wedding. It was a town he knew well, since he had attended the American mission school there for part of his schooling. In fact, he took the time to visit the place and write some verses, as he usually did, in honor of the teaching and administrative staff, saluting their dedication and competence. He cited the institution's founder, Pastor Calhoun, as well as the man who was then headmaster, Pastor Shearer.

This was his mother-in-law Sofiya's native village and, as it happens, the young man getting married that summer was one of her nephews and therefore one of my grandmother's first cousins. I knew him well many years later, in the 1960s—a pudgy, courteous old man whom my father affectionately called Uncle Émile, who used to send Nazeera a basket of flowers every spring for Mother's Day.

On June 21, 1924, Botros wrote the following letter from Souk-el-Gharb; it was addressed to his eldest child but intended for all those who had remained in the village.

> I wish I were already with you today, but I haven't found a suitable means of transport, and I'll probably have to stay here until next week.
>
> Émile is getting married on Saturday in church; then he and his wife will leave for a few days' honeymoon, on their own. Those attending the wedding will go their separate ways after leaving the church, except for the intimates of course, who will wait for the newlyweds at home (no one knows that they'll be going back there, but Émile told me so in secret).
>
> So tell me, who among you wants to come, and when? Discuss this among yourselves, make the decision that seems reasonable to you, and tell me your plans on Monday so that I'll know and be on the lookout for you should you decide to come.
>
> As for the leaves of the mulberry trees, definitely don't pull them off now, not yet . . .
>
> The wife of your uncle Sleymenn told me she wanted a can of halvah; I don't know if she was able to order it from the mule driver; if she hasn't yet, let me know.
>
> Apply yourselves to reviewing your schoolwork, and if you have any questions, save them for when I return.
>
> I met Pastor Friedenger at Souk-el-Gharb; he told me that he might come to visit you on the twenty-second or twenty-third of the month. Mrs. Shearer asked me to greet your mom . . .

This is the last letter Botros wrote. It shows his propensity to organize everything from afar, down to the tiniest details, his strong sense of responsibility, but also his acute respect for other people's freedom. Few fathers, in his day, would have said to their children, "Confer among yourselves, make a decision, and inform me."

The eldest wasn't even eleven years old. His birthday was celebrated on July 19. It was the last occasion on which the entire family was together.

SIXTY-ONE

It was during the Sundays of July and August 1924 that Botros, now back in the village, took the time to recopy, on that notebook with the marbled cover, the various speeches and poems he had delivered in the course of his last trips—the trip to Souk-el-Gharb, for instance. At the very end is his account of the wedding ceremony, along with his rather conventional encomium of Émile and his young bride, as well as of the entire family and the officiating pastor.

Suddenly the text breaks off. For no apparent reason. At the bottom of a page written in rather messy handwriting.

The last verses say:

> *Don't you see those streams of light*
> *And those angels from Heaven walking among us,*
> *Messengers who have come to say to us: rejoice . . .*

The pages that follow this are blank.

It would be tempting to interpret these last lines as a premonition of his imminent departure for the hereafter. That's what I believed when I first read them. But on rereading them now, with greater composure and taking the context into account, I have to admit that this isn't the case. These verses are simply the concluding lines of the speech he delivered at the wedding; the "angels from Heaven" are the children dressed in white who were walking among the guests.

When death seized him by the shoulder, my grandfather wrote no poem. But he may have had sufficient time to realize that the end had come. His nephew the Orator told me the following:

> I wasn't in the village that day. I had left with my mother to visit cousins in Rayfoun, when they came to tell us the news. They said that my uncle had just taken his bath . . .

I imagine that when he rubbed his body and moved his arms, my grandfather felt an ache, stiffness, a shooting pain, and discomfort on the left side. But I also imagine that he had had similar sensations for a long time and had become used to them. In any case, he said nothing to his wife, dried himself, and dressed, no doubt in one of those fancy shirts that no one else in the village wore. Then he sat at his desk and opened the notebook in front of him, the same notebook that I in turn just opened in front of me, at the same page . . .

When she heard him call out in a strange voice, my grandmother ran to him. Kamal, then two and a half, scurried behind her. She recalled the event in her book of memoirs three-quarters of a century later.

> I could only remember the moment my mother ran to their bedroom, with me following her, and found he had passed away. I knew later that it was a heart attack. I have no recollection of his funeral. I assume we, the little children, were instantly shoved away to one of my uncles' houses to be spared the pain and not be in the way. This was the typical practice under such tragic circumstances, and I often regretted that it had to be so.

In my childhood, I used to hear about my grandfather's funeral from time to time. I never heard a detailed description, but occasional allusions all implied that large crowds had converged on our village, on our house-school, from the four corners of the country. To be truthful, I should point out that among us, when someone beloved dies, it is customary to use hyperboles in describing his funeral, as though the size of the crowd and the intensity of the lamentations were an infallible barometer of the deceased's distinction and fame. I have heard the same adjectives and exclamations used so often that I don't attribute much credibility to them anymore. That said, I do believe that Botros inspired admiration, gratitude, and exasperation—as well as, quite simply, curiosity—in his compatriots. People probably did come out in large numbers to accompany him to his last abode—even those who didn't hold him dear. I am convinced, for example, that Father Malatios was ostentatiously present in the procession.

In any case, the priest was duly informed of his old enemy's death. I know this because it is confirmed by one of the documents in the family archives—the kind of document that no other family but mine would have kept: a very long list, with dozens of columns, on such large sheets that they had to be folded in eight to be fitted into an envelope. Names and more names, often followed by an honorary title or position, and sometimes a place of residence: "our" villages and the neighboring towns, as well as Zahlé, Beirut, Baalbek, Alep, Damascus, and even Baghdad, Jerusalem, and Cairo. "People to inform of the misfortune that has occurred" is the sentence scribbled in pencil on the envelope.

This endless list of names was not drawn up by one person. Some of the names are in Botros's handwriting, others in Nazeera's, and there are four or five other handwritings I can't recognize. It took me a while to realize that this list was used over a long period of time as a "database," so to speak. It was first used at the death of my great-grandfather, Khalil, in December 1918. The first names on the list are those of his friends and acquaintances, many of them educated Levantine men who were converts, like him, to the Protestant faith, as well as fellow pastors, some of them "national," others Anglo-Saxon: Reverend Arden, Reverend Shearer, Reverend Friedenger . . .

Initially, I think my grandmother kept this list out of filial devotion. But when her husband suddenly died six years later, she used it again to spare herself the trouble of drawing up another list, since both men had countless common acquaintances, including the reverends who were still providing aid to the Universal School, our entire extended family, and the people in the neighboring villages. Then she added names in her own hand or asked relatives and friends to add them.

The list also includes the newspapers that had to be notified, starting with *Sawt el-Ahrar*, "The Voice of Free Men"; *al Barq*, "The Lightning Bolt"; *al-Watan*, "The Homeland"; *al-Aalam al-Israïli*, "The Israelite World"; *al-Chaab*, "The People"; *al-Dabbour*, "The Hornet," a satirical magazine . . . I stop in puzzlement. I examine the handwriting more closely and compare it with other documents. The handwriting is clearly Botros's. Therefore this part of the list dates back to Khalil's funeral in 1918. Why did they want to publish an announcement of my great-grandfather's death in a Jewish journal? I don't know, but what I've just read brings back my recurrent nostalgia for the blessed period when there was no war between Jews and Arabs, no enmity, no particular hostility.

As soon as Botros's death became known, from announcements or simple word of mouth, condolence letters and telegrams began pouring in. Nazeera kept them all, out of fidelity, pride, and also habit. More than eighty messages from Zahlé, Beirut, Alep, Cairo, New York, El Paso (Texas), São Paulo, and the Mountain villages—but none from Havana. She kept them all carefully, and each one has a pencil inscription, learned from Botros, "He has been answered."

In the midst of this flood tide, one letter arrived that wasn't a condolence letter, but was kept in the same spot. This one remained unanswered. It had been mailed from rue de Cléry, in Paris, on August 23 at 19:15. The heading on the envelope is "Hôtel du Conservatoire, 51 rue de L'Échiquier, Près des Grands Boulevards . . ." The recipient's address is written in two languages. First in Arabic: "To His Excellency the Erudite Venerable Professor Botros M. . . ." Then in French, more soberly: "Monsieur Botros M. . . ."

My grandfather had been dead for six days; clearly the sender didn't know yet. He was obviously a former student and now a friend. He was stopping in France on his way to a more distant country of emigration, a prospect that apparently didn't delight him but to which he was resigned with sad humor. However, this is not why the letter was saved.

Paris, August 23, 1924

Dear Professor,

I took up my pencil to write, but my pencil refused to listen. I put it aside and lit a cigarette in the hope that it would wake my slumbering inspiration—with no result. So I began pacing up and down the room as though I had to solve a serious political problem, or like Napoleon when he was held in captivity. (Here I am comparing myself to Napoleon! Excuse this lapse, Professor, I wrote it without thinking . . .)

I came back to my desk, I took up an iron pen, dipped it into the inkwell, but the sheet remained blank . . . So I decided to take a walk. I went out, I walked, and I saw people gathered in front of a black door. I waited around with them to see what was going on, and I saw them take off their hats; then I saw a coffin come out of the door, carried on the shoulders of four men and taken to a car draped in black. Having nothing else to do, I decided to walk to the cemetery with them. The deceased was buried; then the people returned, me among them. They weren't at all reverential; they chattered freely about politics and business . . .

I suspect that Nazeera's fingers must have trembled on reading these lines. God knows if she kept on reading or immediately put the letter away, keeping it as evidence of a disconcerting coincidence.

I am leaving Paris in three days for Boulogne, and shall sail from there on the thirtieth of this month. My misery and worries will be going with me; they are so heavy that I am afraid they might sink the ship. Ah yes, I am finally going to that faraway country, Mexico, which could either fulfill my dreams or shatter them. I might stay there forever and be buried in its soil, or I might leave in a month. I have no idea; right now I feel like the whole earth is narrow.

I must seem arrogant saying this, though I am not. All I say to myself is that I didn't deserve so much suffering. I dreamed of fighting for what is right and for God under your banner, my dearest professor, but the circumstances that everyone knows compelled me to leave the country and abandon the ambitions I had nurtured in my homeland.

The ship of despair has dropped anchor on the shore of misery, and I don't know if it will remain there forever or leave one day. You must write to me, dear Professor, for your letters will be the only light in the dark night of my life. I hope you won't forget the young man who found in you his spiritual confessor.

Write to me at Sr. Praxedes Rodriguez, San Martin Chachicuhatha, Mexico, requesting that they forward the mail

to the sad young man
your spiritual son
Ali Mohammed el-Hage

N.B. In any case, I would like you to salute the land of Lebanon, and say goodbye to her on my behalf, for I don't think I shall ever see her again.

SIXTY-TWO

When Khalil died, Botros had wondered how he could organize a funeral worthy of him. He had contemplated embalmment, in order to organize things on a grand scale and give people who didn't live in the vicinity enough time to receive the news and make travel plans. But my grandfather eventually gave up this risky plan, for reasons he himself explained in a letter I quoted at length when I recounted the episode. "Wanting the best, we would have had the worst," he concluded, before embracing more realistic aims.

When Botros himself died, six years later, a similar dilemma arose. Once again there was talk of summoning embalmers, but this pompous idea was quickly dismissed in favor of another, more ingenious one, which was also more in keeping with my grandfather's personality. For the moment, they would have an ordinary funeral for the people from the surrounding villages, the students of the Universal School, and their parents; then they would open the house for three days for condolences, and afterward they would take the time to quietly organize a grand ceremony for the first anniversary of his death. Kamal wrote about it in her memoirs:

> I . . . remember the memorial gathering . . . There was a great deal of fussing about this important function several weeks prior to it, and we were clearly told that we were expected to attend. This gathering was held on one exceptionally wide *jal*, or terrace, with fig trees and vines at its border. It was close to the house and was a part of my father's favorite garden.
>
> I cannot explain how they managed to spread large sheets above the whole area to ward off the sun, as he had passed away in mid-August. Also, enough chairs were borrowed to have everybody seated. All I can remember is that there were many people, and I sat in front with my brothers and sister. I couldn't recall other details. But I was later told that relatives and friends of the family came from near and far to honor my father's memory. A number of prominent persons spoke that day, and a touching eulogy was also delivered by my cousin Nasri, who was then thirteen years old . . .

I adopted the rule of not giving out the real identity of persons who were still alive by the time I had completed this book, but I have just changed my mind. I see no reason to camouflage a first name that Kamal cited openly in her memoirs. All the more so since this cousin, who had a way with words, is one of the people from whom I learned the most about my grandfather and our entire family—from the day I started researching this book. His name is Nasri. Up to now, I have called him the Orator—a nickname inspired by the episode I just mentioned, namely the fact that he delivered a speech at the first anniversary of his uncle Botros's death, though he was still only an adolescent.

After adding ellipses to Kamal's description and writing this explanatory paragraph, I stood up. Right now I am near the Atlantic Ocean, on the island where I retire to write; it is eight in the morning, June 6,

2003. I step out into the hallway, pick up the telephone, and call Nasri's house in Beirut. He and I plan to meet in Lebanon, in the family village, at the end of the month, but I can't resist the temptation to call him right now, to ask him, with no forewarning and in a deliberately neutral tone of voice, if he still remembers what he said on that August day in 1925—seventy-eight years ago.

"I couldn't recite entire sentences to you, but in broad outline, yes, I remember what I said. I was asked to speak on behalf of the students from the Universal School. So I mostly spoke about your grandfather's contribution as an educator, the fact that he let the older children teach the younger ones, the fact that he was the first person to found a coeducational school, the fact that it was a secular school, yes, staunchly secular, of the kind that didn't exist yet in that part of the world . . . You can't imagine what education was like in the Mountains before him! There was only one reading textbook for generations of students: *al-Ghosn al-Nadhir min Kitab al-Rabb al-Qadir* . . ."

The loose translation is *The Verdant Branch of the Book of Our All-Powerful Lord*. Botros's nephew bursts out laughing. His uncle Botros also used to make fun of this reader, a simplistic anthology of stories drawn from the Scriptures, all intended to inculcate a narrowly pious, timid morality.

"Your grandfather opened our minds to the world at large. In fact, that's what all the people who spoke that day kept saying. The most prominent persons made the trip for the ceremony . . ."

He cites names, one after the other, without making much of an effort to recall them, as if he were reading off a list. Poets, editors of newspapers, judges, notables, among them several of my grandfather's former students, either from the village school or from the Oriental Secondary School in Zahlé. My contemporaries have never heard of most of these people, but I have heard of some of them—among others, the politician and known man of letters, cousin and friend of my grandfather's, who was a high-ranking Freemason dignitary at the time.

Some of the speakers recalled Botros's poetry, his erudition, his sense of repartee, his proverbial intelligence, the fact that he learned

Spanish in forty days aboard the ship on the way to Cuba to visit his brother . . . Others spoke of his convictions, his dedication, his character, and sometimes of his stubbornness as well.

Nasri even remembered some of the words that rang out in the village sky on that day of commemoration:

I knew you as a free man, refusing to fraternize with two-faced persons, refusing to recognize any creator other than God.

People follow so many roads, in the belief that they will reach Him, but they end up forgetting Him, and worshipping the road itself.

Everyone, in any case, stressed the fact that Botros had brought enlightenment to that corner of the Mountains and that because of this, he would never fade from people's memory.

At the end of the ceremony, the white sheets were put away, the chairs were returned to their owners, and the papers and cigarette butts littering the grass were picked up. The guests went home.

And my grandfather's face faded from memory.

Repercussions
and Denouements

SIXTY-THREE

I grew up struggling with my memory to bring to
mind a true image of my father, some specific situation where I could visualize him in person. But I
couldn't . . .

No real-life photographs of him were shown to
me at an early age.

Some time after his death, a large hand-painted
portrait supposed to be of him was put up on a wall
in the house. A new word came to dominate the
household, *"Al Marhoom,"* as my father came to be
mentioned, meaning "the one to whom mercy was
shown." This implied being deceased.

Many years later, while sorting family papers, Kamal
came across a photo of her father, her mother, and her
eldest brother, taken during a picnic in 1914. She was
surprised to discover that there was no resemblance
between the man in the photograph and the man in the
portrait.

The portrait showed him with a serious, severe look, and bore little resemblance to him. The painter had been told what my father looked like and did this portrait as a mere approximation of reality.

I remember the day when Kamal gave me and all the other close members of the family that photograph of Botros. I was twenty-three then, and she was fifty. Yes, she was fifty years old when she saw her father's real face for the first time. It was the first time I was seeing it too, of course. Until then I had seen only "the other"—"the usurper." As a child, whenever I went to see my grandmother, I stopped in front of the portrait for a few minutes; it was hanging in the drawing room, next to Theodoros's, with his majestic beard.

In one of our e-mail exchanges, I asked my aunt if she remembered what had happened to the "official" portrait. I received her answer the very next day:

> During the troubles in Lebanon, a family entered the flat as refugees. One day your uncle stopped by and spoke with the squatters. They let him take a few personal items, including the portrait of our father. It was damaged with a knife, God knows why. Your uncle took it away. He thinks it is still in the attic of their country house. He promised to check.

One week later:

> I have good news for you. The painted portrait of my father was found. According to your uncle, it is not in the best shape, but is still recognizable and is there for you to take a look at. Let's hope that will be in the near future! In the meanwhile, we'll send you photos.

As I write these lines, I have before me, on my desk, copies of the two pictures of my grandfather, the one from the 1914 picnic and the one painted after his death. The contrast is striking. The spurious

Botros is wearing the local fez, the *tarbouche*; you see a touch of gray hair, smoothly combed, on his temples and just above his forehead; he is wearing a tightly knotted necktie and a white shirt with a stiff collar, fastened with two nail-like pins; under the impeccably trimmed mustache are the strict lips of a headmaster about to scold a student. The real Botros, on the other hand, is bareheaded and wearing a fancy bouffant open-collared shirt; he is in a rural setting, his wife sitting in front of him, leaning against his knees. It is he who is holding their son's baby bottle, and he is laughing happily and mischievously under his bushy mustache. Studying his face closely, I see that he may have been slightly cross-eyed, but not in the official portrait, of course.

I have placed a third picture on my desk next to the other two; it is neither real nor false, or perhaps I should say it is both. It is a drawing my father made in his early youth. When his father died, he wasn't ten years old yet, and like the young Kamal, he never saw any other picture of Botros but the one hanging high up on the wall. Except that, unlike his sister, he recalled his father's real face—only vaguely, but sufficiently to sense that the portrait on the wall was a misrepresentation. He didn't know it had been commissioned from an artist who had never seen his late father; he assumed it did represent his father, but in an unusual pose and with distorted features. In an attempt to recapture the face he remembered, he made a sketch, in lead pencil, on the back of a French postcard, the kind of postcard that was common in those days—blank on both sides with the warning "Not all foreign countries accept the correspondence on the other side (enquire at the post office)." Evidently my father based his drawing on the only portrait still around. The pose is the same. But he removed Botros's hat and necktie, opened his collar, thickened his mustache, changed his hair, and, in addition, made his eyes dissimilar. The result is a hybrid individual, resembling neither the father on the wall nor the father anchored in his memory.

Dissatisfied with his drawing, my father tore it up. Yet it is still here in the archives. Either he felt guilty and decided not to throw it away, or his mother retrieved it from the wastepaper basket behind his back; the fact is, the hesitant witness remains, tear included.

Ever since I reconstructed the story of this child's drawing, I never tire of looking at it. I have had many copies made, both large and small, to make sure the draft is never lost again. Having found no less than five forgotten photos of my grandfather since I began my research, I have to admit that the pencil sketch of Botros by his son isn't a better likeness than the official painter's portrait. But they don't have the same importance for me; one is inspired by an ardent desire for truth, whereas the other seeks to fit a rebellious soul into the deathly strait-jacket of convention.

SIXTY-FOUR

It is no accident that the Botros with laughing eyes was exchanged very soon after his death for a Botros with a stern gaze. My grandmother felt the need to put up on the wall a picture that aroused fear of the father, not a picture of a bareheaded rebel or a dandy in a flowing shirt, or of a doting father who cuddles his daughter or gives the bottle to his son. Nazeera had become a widow at twenty-nine; she had to run a school and bring up six orphans. "The oldest was eleven years old, the youngest eleven months," she kept saying to the end of her life, possibly to be forgiven for having subjected her little brood to her stringent rule of law. She felt she had to govern her household as if it were a kingdom that had been plunged in anarchy for many years and had just recently been hit by a natural disaster.

It is also true, however, that in this she was following her family tendency, so to speak. My grandparents' marriage was an improbable meeting of two opposing traditions, one of austerity, the other of imagination.

Two streams that intertwined but never merged. At Botros's untimely death, one of the two springs suddenly dried up. Or rather, it became subterranean. It took me years to understand this family duality: under an inflexible facade, ferment that often verges on madness.

The atmosphere in the house-school of Machrah changed very rapidly after the tragic loss, but not only because of bereavement, though this was bound to weigh heavily on the six orphans and the young widow. One of the first consequences of Botros's passing was the arrival of my great-grandmother Sofiya in the house, with her black dress, her black Bible, and her unsmiling face. She moved into the master bedroom, next to her daughter, in the place now left empty by the husband's death. From one day to the next, peals of laughter became rare, voices were lowered, and effusiveness was banned.

My great-grandmother's severity was already proverbial in the village; before long, my grandmother's became so as well. Everyone knew that Nazeera had a magic word and she merely had to pronounce it for her children to instantly stop moving: *"Smah!"* meaning "Listen!" She herself explained to me what its purpose was, not without pride.

"As you know, we were living in a village where there are precipices, badly covered wells, and vipers' nests everywhere, and I was responsible for a bunch of turbulent kids—my own children and my pupils. If I cried out to one of them 'Stop!' and he continued to run for one second more, his life could be in danger. So I had accustomed them all to obey without even catching their breath. I just had to shout *'Smah!'* and they froze instantly on the spot. How many times did I rescue a child from death just with that word!"

One of my grandmother's principles was that authority should not be exercised with chatter, but in silence, or at least with very few words.

This is what my father used to tell me: "When I asked your grandmother something and she continued to go on about her business as if I hadn't said anything, I was not to assume she hadn't heard me. It simply meant her answer was no. If I had the bad idea of asking the question a second time, she would turn toward me with a frown, and I would bitterly regret having been insistent."

The worst thing you could do was resort to shaky arguments.

"One day I planned to go for a long walk in the mountains with some cousins my age, and I went to ask my mother for permission. She didn't seem too unwilling, but she said, 'Let me think about it!' I left her alone and came back an hour later. She said, 'I'm still weighing the pros and cons. I wonder if it's reasonable for a group of young people to go into the mountains for hours, far from everything, without any accompanying adult . . . Tell me again who'll be going.' So I enumerated the walkers, starting with the oldest ones, who were probably around fourteen or fifteen. Then I thought it would be clever to add, 'All the other parents said yes!' Your grandmother stiffened, her face hardened, and she looked me straight in the eye and said, 'In this house, when we make a decision, we follow our own good judgment; we don't go by what others do or don't do. You can tell your friends you're not allowed to go with them. And don't ever use that sort of argument with me again.'"

On another occasion the children had found an almond tree loaded with velvety-skinned green almonds. A cousin explained to them that the owners were in America, so they need not have qualms about helping themselves. Nazeera's children listened to the argument and stuffed their pockets with almonds, but they didn't eat any until they had consulted their mother.

My father went on: "She listened to our justification without saying a word, but frowned slightly. 'Is this almond tree ours?' she asked. 'The owners are in America,' we replied. She frowned more noticeably. 'It doesn't matter to me where the owners are,' she said. 'What matters is that we are not the owners. Go empty your pockets in the garbage bin.' My mother had no need to repeat an order. For sure, I never got to taste those appetizing almonds."

What I find unusual about this story, which I heard from my father on more than one occasion, is that Nazeera's children were reluctant to disobey her even when they were far from home. I know this tendency to internalize maternal authority has something extreme about it, and I think it may even have had castrating effects. But all things considered, I don't disown this exacting heritage. From having lived in a society that lacks a strict moral code, I have come to feel pride and gratitude for this Presbyterian tradition. No doubt, in the end, I have unconsciously made mine the family axiom whose substance, though never explicitly formulated, is this: little does it matter that our education has made it difficult for us to adapt to the prevailing milieu; our pride resides expressly in refusing to be contaminated by the established decline—better to suffer, withdraw, or go into exile!

It is clear, in any event, that it was never my grandmother's aim to prepare her children to live in Levantine society as it was. In this she was in complete harmony with her rebellious husband. But unlike him, she never wanted to define her objectives in abstract terms; she never spoke about the struggle against obscurantism, the need to reform society, or the advancement of the peoples of the Orient. On the two or three occasions when I questioned her about the Universal School—which she headed after my grandfather's death—and the ideals that were its driving force, she avoided delving into these matters.

"I just wanted my children to reach adulthood in good physical and mental health, and for all six to attend university," she said. "I had set these goals for myself a long time ago, and I never diverted my gaze from them. That's all I wanted for myself and my children."

In those days, most families lost a child in infancy or adolescence; it was a common misfortune to which all mothers were resigned. Not Nazeera. She had vowed to herself that she wouldn't lose any of her children. And this being her aim, she didn't just pray, light candles, and make wishes. To avoid being helpless when faced with the sicknesses of those she held dear, she proceeded to study all the medical textbooks she could find. Eventually she developed such competence in the area that people came to consult her from all the neighboring villages and she prescribed remedies with complete confidence. I found a textbook in the archives that she apparently used often. Its author— why be surprised?—is a Scottish Orientalist missionary, and its title is *What Laymen Should Know, or How to Remain Healthy and Fight Disease in the Absence of a Physician*. It is worn and practically dismembered from having been consulted so often; it is also extensively annotated by Nazeera, and also by her mother, Sofiya, who seems to have been even more competent in this field.

The six orphans survived the difficult years without any of those unfortunately common diseases that caused the death of children at the time or debilitated them for life—typhoid fever, polio, diphtheria . . . Nor did they have any accidents causing serious bodily harm.

Another of their mother's nagging preoccupations was feeding and clothing them properly. This required enormous sacrifices. Botros had left them enough to live comfortably, and by the modest criteria of the village, he was even regarded as wealthy, but as soon as he died, they found themselves poor.

My grandmother herself told me how this turn of events came about.

"Your grandfather was the only member of the family to have a bit of money, and everyone, or nearly everyone, used to come and ask him for money. A short time before his death, when he sensed the end was near, he told me what each person owed him and gave me all the signed papers. There was a small fortune, my mind was at rest.

"After the funeral, Theodoros was appointed guardian of his brother's children. So he came to see me and said, 'I know my brothers and cousins borrowed a lot of money from Botros. I assume they all signed IOUs.' 'Yes, of course,' I said, '*al-marhoum* gave me everything.' 'That's good. Could you show them to me?' I went to the bedroom to fetch them. He started reading them one by one, very attentively; then, without warning, he started tearing them up, each and every one of them. I cried out! These were our entire savings he was busily destroying! But he silenced me. 'We don't want to make enemies in the family!' In a matter of seconds, we had lost everything and become poor again. 'And how do you expect me to feed my orphans?' 'The Lord giveth and the Lord giveth again,' Theodoros replied. Then he stood up and left."

Each time my grandmother told me this story—which she did six or seven times, if not more—she relived the same gamut of emotions: rage, tears, resignation, and then the vow not to let it get her down. When I was a child, I always identified with her rage, but now that I have immersed myself in the family papers for three years, I am inclined to be less harsh with Theodoros. Though his method was unquestionably brutal, the reasons for his action were not absurd. Hadn't my grandfather spoiled the last years of his life with lawsuits and quarrels about money and plots of land? It would have been unsound for his children to waste their youthful years, and possibly their entire lives, in arguments about debts. Their uncle's decisive action probably spared them that quagmire.

That said, I can well understand that Nazeera saw Theodoros's magnanimous gesture as a betrayal. From then on, and for many years to come, she would have to slave away without ever feeling free from financial worries, particularly since her sole source of income was constantly threatened.

By this I mean the Universal School and, more specifically, the subsidies granted to "our" school by the Anglo-Saxon missionaries. Immediately after Botros's death, they considered cutting off funding. Most of them were wary of the idea that a widow could replace her husband and become headmistress. My grandmother had to prove to them, with supporting evidence, that during the last years, her husband had spent most of his time in Beirut and she had actually been running the school. They finally gave her the benefit of the doubt, provided that she show her ability. Inspectors came by several times a year to check that the institution was running properly and the students performing well.

Yet she was able to obtain only a fraction of what had been allocated to her husband. This sum, added to the meager tuition fees paid by her pupils' parents, just about allowed her to cover the school's operating expenses and feed her household. It wasn't enough to cover anything else, any extra expense, or any nonessentials. Buying clothes for the children was ruled out, for example; she had to sew their smocks, dresses, trousers, and shirts, with her mother's help.

In order to earn a bit of extra money, Nazeera spent her nights embroidering place mats and knitting sweaters and woolen shawls that she sold to foreign ladies on her trips to Beirut. Later, in her old age, she continued to knit several hours a day, not so she could sell the things she made, but so she could give them away, particularly to her grandchildren. From time to time I still wear a winter scarf she gave me; it is pristine white and so long that I have to wrap it around my shoulders several times so it won't drag on the floor.

SIXTY-FIVE

Much as my grandmother was unprepared for Theodoros's "magnanimous" gesture, his other brazen act was no surprise—in fact she had been expecting it with resignation from the moment her husband breathed his last.

I am referring to the issue of baptism. Botros had succeeded in imposing his views on this subject, namely that his children be allowed to choose their religion freely when they reached adulthood and that nothing be forced on them before then. This stance—should I remind the reader again?—was completely unacceptable, completely unthinkable in those days in that milieu. My grandfather had had to summon all his stubbornness to maintain this position against the whole world.

As long as he was there, his wife and children could take refuge behind the towering walls of his wisdom and madness. With him gone, they were defenseless, exposed, assailed. They couldn't take up his struggles, his stubborn convictions, or even his appearance—so much so that they had seen fit to put up a doctored portrait of him on the wall.

The struggle against baptism was a lost cause. If Theodoros didn't bring the family to heel immediately, it was only because he respected his brother too much to flout his wishes right after his death. So he waited a year, and a second and third year, and decided to take action only in 1927. He arrived in the village without warning on a day when he knew Nazeera was away, and he gathered his nephews and nieces in order to baptize them right then and there. My eldest uncle, then age fourteen, courageously reminded the priest of his late father's wishes on this issue and announced that he refused to disobey his father; the five others, my father and his young siblings, allowed themselves to be baptized without turning a hair.

Obviously this Catholic baptism wasn't to the liking of the Protestant branch of the family. Nazeera and Sofiya were greatly offended by it. But my grandmother's eldest brother, Dr. Shukri, is the one who reacted most angrily. He considered himself personally disparaged, insulted, and attacked by this brazen act. He had very harsh words for the priest, his bishop, his patriarch, and his pope, and vowed that the matter would not rest there.

And indeed it didn't. In 1932, a census was conducted of the Lebanese population under the aegis of the French authorities. It was the first census, and it was going to be the last, oddly enough, for the very fragile denominational equilibrium made any new population count into an explosive issue. The distribution of power among the Lebanese communities would be based, for many years to come, on the numbers obtained that year: fifty-five percent Christian and forty-five percent Muslim; within each group, a smaller breakdown of Maronite, Greek Orthodox, Greek Catholic, Sunni, Shiite, Druze, etc. In my family, however, the 1932 census would have specific consequences.

French and Lebanese civil servants showed up in the village and made the rounds of the houses, asking people, among other things, to which religious community they belonged. When they knocked at our door, Shukri was the person who welcomed them. Being a medical doctor, he spoke to them authoritatively, served them coffee and refreshments, and offered his help. He carefully spelled the first names of his nephews, gave their dates of birth, and, to the question of religious affiliation, without batting an eyelid, answered that they were all Protestant. And this was duly recorded.

Thus was Theodoros's Catholic baptism annulled, at least as far as the public authorities were concerned. The Protestant branch of the family had just been avenged. The score was even, so to speak. But the match wasn't over yet.

My father and his siblings no longer knew to which community they belonged. From time to time they introduced themselves as Catholic, from time to time as Protestant.

Three among them eventually requested that their civil status be officially listed as Greek Catholic. It took years for the change to be made, and it remained incomplete. Even today, when I ask the Lebanese authorities for my birth certificate, it is duly specified that I am "of Greek Catholic denomination" but "listed on the Protestant registry."

SIXTY-SIX

In the spring of 1934 Nazeera and her mother received a piece of news from the United States that they had resigned themselves to never getting: after years of estrangement, silence, and discord, Alice wrote them a letter announcing that she intended to come and spend some time in her native country. She sailed into the port of Beirut on June 18 with her daughter Nelie, twenty, and the youngest of her two sons, whose name was now Carl though he had been baptized Carlos at his birth, seventeen years earlier, in Cuba. The families of Botros and Gebrayel were reunited for the first time: eight young people who had never met before, and their mothers—simultaneously sisters and sisters-in-law—who had been adolescent girls the last time they had been together. They had lived on two different continents, as wives of two impatient and exuberant brothers, both now deceased. They had so much to talk about.

· · ·

There are a great many pictures in the archives from this period, some of the entire family, others of the young people on excursions to Baalbek or Mount Sannine. I assume that the American cousins had come with the latest cameras. There is also a short piece by my father, written ten years later, where he says that the summer of 1934 was the most joyous period in his life. Indeed, there is an impression of intense happiness in the photos of the period; even my great-grandmother Sofiya had traded her eternal black dress for a light gray one. Looking closely at her face, you think you see the ghost of a smile.

This joyousness clearly came from across the Atlantic. Nelie's face is lit up by such an authentic smile that it is mirrored in the faces around her; as for Carl, he has had the boldness to casually throw his long arms around Nazeera's shoulders. She is perceptibly startled and has an amazing expression—an amused smile in the lower half of her face and a frown in the upper half, like the last holdover of severity.

When the end of the summer drew near, Alice was so happy, she didn't want to leave. When she shared her feelings with her children, they were upset. Naturally, the family reunions had made them just as happy as she, and so had all the things they had discovered and the trips and banquets . . . but not to the point of giving up their America. "I don't want to force your hand," she said. "When you want to leave, we'll leave, I promise. But remember we'll probably never make a second trip; we won't see the people here again—particularly not your grandmother, who is getting old. So if we could stay a bit longer . . ."

The stay was therefore extended beyond the summer, through October and November. Alice felt happier and happier, and more and more at home, but her son and daughter were growing impatient. After another discussion with them, she promised them halfheartedly that she would reserve return tickets, but for after the holidays. They would spend Christmas and New Year in the village, and sail on January 15.

The holidays that year had a magical quality for both families. Usually they seldom freed themselves of their perpetual worries, which meant that the holidays were never a perfect separate moment, like a bubble. Usually they never forgot their material discomfort or bereavements. The sudden, untimely deaths of Gebrayel and Botros, though both in the distant past, were ever present, for the grief and upheaval caused by these losses were still vivid. Yet during these particular holidays, a haze of happiness enveloped the guests, young and old.

Immediately after the first of the year, preparations began for the return trip. But on the twenty-fourth, my great-grandmother Sofiya became sick. True, she was not young, but she seemed, even the day before, in good health. She woke up in the morning with chest pains; during the day she coughed a lot and had difficulty breathing. In the evening she died.

In his funeral oration, the pastor made a point of mentioning the return of her daughter and grandchildren, and how happy she had been to spend time with them. It was as though the Lord, in His kindness and wisdom, had not wanted her to depart without having this last joy, which someone with her irreproachable life so fully deserved. Then Sofiya was buried alongside her husband, Khalil, in the grave built for him sixteen years earlier in the middle of the vineyards, a few steps away from the house that had been his and which is mine today.

After the period of condolences, Alice tried to convince her children that she should spend a bit more time with Nazeera. But their grandmother's death had had the opposite effect on them; they now felt they had stayed too long and should have left at the end of the summer as initially planned. They were more eager than ever to return to America. Their mother prevailed on them to delay the departure by two short weeks, to January 28.

But on the twenty-fourth—it was a Thursday—Alice woke up with a pain in her chest. During the day, she coughed a lot and had difficulty breathing. In the evening, she died . . .

The return of the émigrés, which had started like a drawn-out wedding feast, was ending like a macabre farce. In his eulogy, the pastor pointed out that clearly the deceased had not wanted to depart from her native land and that the Lord in His unfathomable wisdom had allowed her to make it her permanent abode.

Alice was buried in the family vault, freshly unsealed and resealed, next to her father and mother, but thousands of miles away from that other vault she herself had built years back for Gebrayel, where she thought she too would rest when her hour would come—the grave over there, in the Americas, in Havana, in the necropolis named after Christopher Columbus.

SIXTY-SEVEN

On more than one account, 1935, which had begun with these successive bereavements, was a
pivotal year for my family. Chiefly because our
Universal School shut down for good that year after
twenty-two years of operation, eleven years while Botros
was alive and eleven years thereafter, and our family left
the village and settled in the city.

As my grandmother told me repeatedly in her last
years, she wasn't at all lured by the bright lights of the
capital; she just wanted to bring her children closer to
the university. University, for her, meant AUB, the
American University of Beirut, originally founded by
missionaries as the Syrian Protestant College. Khalil, her
father, my great-grandfather, had been one of its very
first students. The apartment she rented was a short distance away from the gates of the spacious campus, on a
street that the mandate government had named after
Joan of Arc.

The house-school of Machrah was relegated to the

status of summer residence. The family still went there for a few more years, but only in the last days of June, to get away from the hot summer days on the coast. Winters were spent in Beirut in a rented apartment on the top floor of an old building dating from the Ottoman period. Now Botros's fake portrait hung there, in the drawing room from which all the bedrooms radiated.

My grandmother didn't make the transition from one kind of life to another on an impulse. To avoid upsetting the running of the school or the stability of her household, she kept the decision secret and announced it only in the last semester—first to her own children, then to the pupils and parents. But she had planned everything out years earlier, down to the last detail. When her two older sons reached high-school age, she would find boarding schools for them; when they were ready to enter the university, she would rent a student room for them; and as soon as her oldest daughter was of university age, the entire family would move to Beirut.

First, my grandmother had found schools for her eldest children. For the sake of balance, or perhaps because of the opposing pressures of Shukri and Theodoros, she sometimes placed them in Catholic schools—such as the Beirut Patriarchate School or the Zahlé Oriental Secondary School—and at other times in institutions connected with the American Presbyterian Mission, for instance a certain Gerard Institute, near Sidon, in the south of the country, from which I found in our archives a graduation certificate awarded to my father. In any case, whatever the school's affiliation, Nazeera managed to pay only a fraction of her children's tuition and board. It was difficult for her to cope with these expenses. She even had trouble getting the appropriate schoolbooks for the boys, as can be seen from this letter my father wrote her in February 1930.

Respected Mother,

Yesterday I received the Arab literature reader you sent me, and at first glance I was worried. It seemed so old that I was afraid you had sent me my grandfather's book, which I studied from when I was in the village, and on which he had written the acquisition date: "January 18, 1850." Most

*fortunately, I was wrong; the reader you sent me is much more recent, since
the inscription on the flyleaf is "This book belongs to Botros Mokhtara
Maalouf, who bought it on December 14, 1885." So this worthy manual
has been devoting itself to the cause of literature for a mere 45 years.
Being a man of great compassion, I immediately made it take its
retirement. For the day when I decide to open an antique store—in Paris,
for example!—I'm sure these kinds of books will be very valuable. But for
my studies, it is not of much use. So, enough joking, if you could get me a
recent reader, I would be infinitely grateful to you.*

*Here, at school, everything is fine. Except that the headmaster seems
very worried today. Probably because there was a big fight among the
students yesterday and one of them was seriously hurt. Which won't help
the school's reputation, I suppose. Aside from that, everything's going very
well. Be well and send news of yourself regularly*

To your obedient son
Rushdi

My father was fifteen years old; humor was both his shield and his
sword. This was because he was under constant pressure, as was the
eldest of his brothers. Their mother made it clear every day that she
was waiting impatiently for them to grow up and finally lighten her
burden. She was willing to make huge sacrifices so they could study,
provided they would take care of financing the studies of the younger
children as soon as possible. She also made it clear that they had to be
first in the class in every subject. Hadn't they benefited from the best
education? Weren't they the children of the renowned *moallem* Botros
and the grandchildren of the no-less-renowned *moallem* Khalil? Didn't
they live in an educated environment? Even their elderly grandmother
was educated and owned a library. Why wouldn't they be outstanding
students? What excuse did they have for not being always first in the
class?

At twenty, the eldest of my uncles was indeed as brilliant as his
mother wished. His intelligence was already as proverbial as Botros's—
also in Beirut, not just in the village. His younger brother, my father, was
a good student, but his grades were more uneven. This sometimes irri-

tated his mother, as can be seen from the following story found in one of his school notebooks.

One day, when I was home for Easter vacation, my mother received my report card in the mail, sent by my school. She unsealed the envelope and asked me to sit on the stool opposite her while she went over my grades.

Knowledge of the Bible, A, in other words, excellent. French, C, in other words, average. English, B, in other words, good. Arabic, B as well. Geometry, C. Biology, B. Geology, B. History, B. Discipline, A. Concentration, A.

"Bravo," she said. "You're doing well. I'm pleased."

Then she turned the page, frowned, and cried out, "What? You're only tenth in the class?"

"But Mom, you just said bravo to me!"

"Tenth! You should be ashamed of yourself!"

"What does it matter if I'm tenth as long as my grades are good?"

"There's no excuse. Never again do I want to read that my son is tenth!"

I returned to school with my mother's words still ringing in my ears: "Never again do I want to read that my son is tenth!" I kept wondering, what can I do? How can I satisfy her?

I couldn't study much harder; I had already studied as hard as I could up until then. On the other hand, I could try to do something so my fellow students' grades wouldn't be as good. Yes, that was the solution. I would try to change my behavior and move up a few notches at their expense. For example, if the student who is ranked ninth comes and asks me to help him with a geometry problem, I'll refuse. He might put pressure on me and say we're friends and that it would be natural for me to help him. To cut matters short, I'll get into an argument with him at the first opportunity, so he won't ask me anything anymore, and I won't have to help him.

Also, if I notice, in one of the subjects, that the teacher stressed one question more than the others and that he'll probably quiz us on it, I'll avoid telling everyone, as I always did up until now. On the contrary, I'll keep this information to myself, and when the students come out of the exam bemoaning the fact that they hadn't prepared that question, I'll feel joy in my heart rather than sorrow.

That's it; I must learn to change my entire behavior. For example, if one of the students gets sick, instead of going to his bedside as I do now and explaining to him what was discussed in class so he won't fall behind, I'll rejoice over his sickness and hope deep down that it lasts a long time so he'll be out of the competition and I can be ranked above him.

You'll see, Mom, I'll change in every way, I promise. In the next report card, your son won't be tenth anymore!

My father hadn't simply written this darkly humorous piece for his own amusement, as a secret revenge. He arranged to speak on behalf of the students at the year-end ceremony, and he delivered it in the presence of the teaching body and the parents of the students.

My grandmother was in the audience. She smiled, wiped away a few tears, and never again asked her son to improve his ranking. Without really confronting his mother, he had literally disarmed her—in part through humor, but also by using an irrefutable argument, one with which the preacher's daughter could only agree. Better to lag behind and preserve one's moral elegance than to reach the top through boorishness!

That said, truth compels me to add that my father's line of argument was neither very rigorous nor completely honest. I happen to have all of his archives, which I don't intend to use in this narrative, for it is devoted to Botros and the people of his generation, and the other members of the family are meant to appear only as background figures. However, having read my father's school notebooks, I feel it my duty to report that he himself confessed to "spending more time in movie theaters than in classrooms" and more time by the river than in libraries, that he occasionally climbed over the school wall, and that he wrote love poems during algebra and geography class. He could probably have improved his ranking by studying more diligently; he didn't have to sabotage his classmates.

Here I am criticizing him as if, by virtue of my white hair, I had become his father and he my son. But I do so with tenderness, as he himself would have done. I was lucky to have an artistic father whose subjects of conversation were Mallarmé, Donatello, Michelangelo, and Oman Khayyám, and when my mother faulted him for not being strict with my sisters and me, he used to answer in a low voice, "We didn't have children so we could pester them."

Before concluding this digression about him, I must make two remarks. The first is that later in life he made a name for himself as a journalist, writing satirical columns for more than thirty years; they were aimed at the failings of society and of the government and were in exactly the same spirit as the letter he wrote to his mother when he was fifteen, about the old books. The second is that he also made a name for himself as a poet when he published an anthology, at twenty-nine, dedicated "to my father Botros Mokhtara Maalouf" and titled *The Beginning of Spring*. It caused a literary sensation, and several of the poems were included in the Arab literature reader I studied with. In school, when we were assigned one of my father's poems to learn by heart and the students next to me proceeded to chuckle and wink at me insistently, I had to make a great effort to conceal my pride.

But it was my grandmother who was particularly proud. She was proud of her son's early fame and, even more, of the fact that his best-known poem, which became an instant classic, had been written for her.

My father once described to me the circumstances under which he wrote it.

It was in May 1943; the French authorities had just instituted Mother's Day. A large function was organized for the occasion, and I was invited to recite a poem. I had to prepare on very short notice, but I had managed to free an evening to isolate myself and write.

I had just sat down at my desk when my friend Edward came by. He said, "Let's go to the movies, such and such a film is playing." I said, "No, not tonight, I really can't, I have to write my poem." But he wouldn't take no for an answer, and since I always found it difficult to resist such invitations, I went with him.

My eyes were on the screen, but my thoughts were elsewhere. At one point, I took my pen out of my pocket and started to write, in the dark, on the back of a pack of cigarettes. By the time we came out of the movie theater, my poem was entirely written. I didn't change a single comma. I just had to recopy it on a clean sheet of paper.

The poem is in the form of a prayer, and he constructed it around *hounnah*, an uncommon, very emphatic and very feminine rhyme in the Arabic language. The word means "they" in the feminine (a plural form of "she"). It recurs six times in the following excerpt, but can be rendered in English only by "they," "them," and "their":

> *They are our companions in the exile of the world,*
> *No paradise would be paradise without them.*
> *Lord, I requested two favors of You,*
> *To see the face of Heaven and to see their faces.*
> *It is to them that You entrusted life,*
> *You made your home inside their wombs,*
> *And you left, from among Your heartbeats,*
> *One heartbeat in their bosom . . .*

The critics in those days described my father as a fervent admirer of beauty, or a fervent admirer of woman, and in one sense, he was. But it is clear that the veneration he expressed in these verses was chiefly inspired by the matriarchal figure Nazeera had been for him and for all his siblings, at once loving and strict, fragile and indestructible, ardent and cerebral.

In fact, every year on Mother's Day it was she who received phone calls from journalists; they came to photograph her in her apartment on Jeanne d'Arc Street and interviewed her on her former life in the village. She told them about how she took over the school after her husband's death, how he had left her "with six orphans, the oldest was eleven years old, the youngest eleven months."

Sometimes her visitors said, as if she had to be consoled, "But you knew how to bring them up. Now your children tell you how grateful they are. You succeeded, you must feel you have everything you could possibly wish for . . ."

She answered that yes, of course she felt fulfilled. Actually, this attention focused on her once a year flattered her and compensated a bit for her misfortunes. But when the journalists and photographers got up to leave and she had escorted them to the door and shut it behind them, her thoughts immediately returned to the great disappointment of her life, the one incomprehensible failure that spoiled all her victories. Her thoughts returned to the one who had left, the one who had deserted her.

Not Botros, who belonged to the distant past by then, but her eldest son. He was alive, but she had no news from him; he no longer sent word, no longer wrote. A falling-out, yes, a serious falling-out, like the one that had erupted a century earlier between the priest Gerjis and his son Khalil, and later between Khalil and his son Gerji. It was a sinister family pattern, but Nazeera never thought she herself would be the victim of it one day. She thought she had done everything to make sure it wouldn't happen to her.

SIXTY-EIGHT

In Beirut, my eldest uncle had plunged himself headlong into the political fight against the French mandate. He was a man of strong convictions, capable of arguing eloquently against all sorts of opponents—just like his father, people said. There was unanimous agreement that he had a brilliant future ahead of him in this reemerging country. The entire family was behind him; they all supported him in his fight— beginning with his mother, whose apartment had become a rallying place for the students in the independence movement.

But it was 1939, the international situation was turning ugly, and my uncle's political involvement was becoming dangerous. What could be considered a legitimate national struggle in peacetime could seem treasonous in a time of war. There were rumors going around that he might be arrested, perhaps even sentenced to death. The family decided to organize his escape as quickly as possible. They arranged to get him a scholarship to an American university, and they sent him off on one of the very last ships, just before the outbreak of the Second World War. Léonore confirmed the following:

> Your uncle had a very high position in the Nationalist Party, and the French had got their hands on a document that proved he would head the organization if it went underground. They had therefore issued an arrest warrant for him. But on the document they had seized, he was referred to with a nom de guerre, and that's the name that was on the arrest warrant. By the time the authorities made the connection between his real name and his pseudonym, he had escaped . . .

Understandably, these developments didn't exactly delight my grandmother. For her, who prepared her every move years in advance, the unexpected was seldom welcome. However, she was also a realistic woman who knew how to maintain the right balance between anxiety and hope, and how to determine priorities. Her immediate prime consideration was saving her son from the possible danger he was facing.

She must also have said to herself, like so many Levantine mothers, that with all his talents, her eldest son would surely be a brilliant success in the United States, and then he could help his family much more effectively than if he remained in the old country.

My uncle left, therefore, and we had no further news from him. True, it was wartime, and the mail wasn't reliable. But after the war ended, in 1945, news came just as infrequently. He himself barely wrote, and what the family heard about him from relatives or friends who crossed the Atlantic wasn't very reassuring.

By the time I opened my eyes to the world, my American uncle had become a ghostly, fleeting figure, much more so than Gebrayel had been for the previous generation. And throughout my entire childhood I heard only worried rumors about him, and horrified whispers. After marrying and having five children, he decided to enter a convent, taking his entire brood with him. He and his two sons joined the men; his wife and his three daughters stayed with the women. They all lived in poverty, chastity, and obedience, obeying merciless rules; thus it was forbidden to let the young children know which of the "brothers" was their father and which of the "sisters" their mother. It was strictly forbidden to bring into the convent a book that deviated even slightly from the "true Catholic Faith." I dare not contemplate what Botros, man of the Enlightenment, founder of the Universal School, would have thought of these practices.

The thing that was constantly whispered in the family, as far back as I can remember, was that my uncle refused to have any contact with his relatives until they had all become as Catholic as he.

One story, among many: the year I was born, one of his brothers-in-law took advantage of the fact that he was spending time in an American university to go visit him. My uncle welcomed him and immediately launched into an impassioned statement of his beliefs. At the end of this sermon he asked his visitor, "Now that you've heard me, are you ready to become a Catholic?"

The man replied politely that he had been born into an Orthodox family and had no intention of giving up the faith of his forebears.

"In that case," said my uncle, rising, "we have nothing more to say to each other."

He handed the stunned visitor his overcoat and escorted him to the door.

I don't want to be too unfair to my uncle or make him into a caricature. His world is remote from mine, and his beliefs are the opposite of mine, but his life journey has coherence and sincerity—and is an unusual illustration of the obsessive spiritual fears that have haunted our family time and again. I am convinced that one day his story will be told by a more attentive and understanding voice than mine. As for me, I have touched on the subject only covertly in a novel, and I won't do more than touch on it again today. What I am trying to unravel is not so much the real nature of what happened over there in New England, but the real nature of what my grandmother and father heard, imagined, and felt during those long years of anxiety.

For example, I found a yellowed press clipping among Nazeera's papers; the date and name of the newspaper are gone, but it must have been cut out of a Boston daily, very likely *The Boston Globe*, in the late 1940s or early '50s.

Title, subtitle, and text, on the first page:

HARVARD STUDENTS CONVERT
Enter Monasteries to Study for the Priesthood

Following closely upon the announcement that Avery D., Harvard graduate and son of one of the country's most noted Protestant lay leaders, had entered a Jesuit novitiate to become a priest, it was learned yesterday that three more Harvard students have become converts to Catholicism and are entering monasteries to study for the priesthood. All of them are members of prominent families.

Two other Harvard students, both Catholics, have abandoned their Harvard studies to enter monasteries. All are members of the St. B. Centre of St. Paul's parish, Cambridge, which is a Catholic student centre directed by the Rev. Leonard F., S.J., noted poet and essayist, and sponsored by the Right Rev. Mgr. Augustine F. H. . . .

The converts are:

William F. M., son of Dr. Donald M. of West Cedar St., who has entered the Jesuit novitiate at Shadowbrook . . .

Walter G., son of Dr. Arthur G. of Lawrence, who has also entered the Jesuit novitiate.

George L., son of Herbert L. of Great Neck, L.I., who is entering the Benedictine monastery at Portsmouth Priory . . .

The others are Joseph J. H., son of Superior Court Judge J.L.H., who has entered the Redemptorist; and Miss Margaret M. D., daughter of Mr. and Mrs. John D., Providence, R.I., has left her studies at Radcliffe to enter the Carmelite monastery . . .

The reason my grandmother kept this article is that it tells of the birth of a religious movement that her son joined. He himself is not mentioned, but several of the people named belonged to the same movement. I imagine that in Boston at the time people must have felt they were witnessing a major event taking place, perhaps even a miracle. This is why I don't rule out the possibility that my uncle himself sent this clipping from there. The suggestion that American Protestants were converting to Catholicism en masse was not an innocuous piece of information for our family at that time.

From this—really rather localized—ferment, a conservative religious movement arose, advocating a return to the church's traditional faith and suspicious of all doctrinal "adjustments" aimed at taking into account contemporary mores. As far as I remember, my relatives never really pored over the converted uncle's theological arguments. All they knew was that his companions and he were opposed to the liberalization of the Church and that because of this they had encountered problems with the Vatican. The sentence that invariably recurred each time they were mentioned was that they were "more papist than the pope," indeed so much so that they were almost excommunicated.

Later, I did some research, which didn't contradict these impressions. My uncle and his friends venerate the Crusades, express no disapproval for the Inquisition, and have no particular sympathy for Protestants, Jews, Freemasons, or "lukewarm" Catholics. The cornerstone of their faith is that there is no salvation outside the Roman Catholic Church.

I would be incapable of explaining exactly how the religious problems in Botros's household resulted in his eldest son professing such a doctrine. I don't want to map out questionable thought processes or establish rough causalities, but when an adolescent who refused to be forced into baptism by a Catholic priest proclaims, twenty years later, that there is no salvation for people who have not been baptized in the Catholic faith and goes so far as to devote his entire life to that cause, it is inconceivable that the two facts are not linked, even if it is hard for me to say by what tortuous process.

SIXTY-NINE

Compared with the fervent American Catholics in our family, my father was bound to seem like a lukewarm Catholic. Yet he and his two younger brothers had been drawn back to the religion in which they had been baptized.

Proof of this is a document addressed to the director of the census and civil status, of which there is a copy in the archives. On it you read that the applicants "listed on the Protestant register"—we know under what circumstances—request to be included in the Greek Catholic community "by virtue of the enclosed evidence."

The latter, signed by "the Episcopal vicar of Beirut, Byblos and their dependencies," dated June 16, 1943, specifies that "in accordance with the request made by our spiritual sons . . . we are complying with their wish to be transferred from the Protestant community to our Roman Catholic community."

I heard my father mention more than once the fact

that he had gone from one denomination to another, but he never explained his reasons for doing so. I am nevertheless convinced that questions of faith had nothing to do with his taking this step. I say this without the slightest hesitation or shame. When religious communities behave like tribes, they should be treated as such.

If I tried to guess his motivations, however, I could list more than one.

He may have wanted to belong to a community that was less of a minority. Both were minority groups, but Greek Catholics numbered about six percent of the population, and Protestants one percent. In a country where important positions are all assigned on this basis, he risked being marginalized and virtually excluded.

He may also have wanted to settle an annoying administrative muddle: having been baptized in one community and registered in another must have been a headache every time he had forms to fill out.

Nor do I rule out the possibility that Uncle Theodoros insistently pressured him to take this step. By 1943 Theodoros was seventy and had moved into the apartment on Jeanne d'Arc Street so that his sister-in-law Nazeera could take care of him in his old age. Upon closer examination of the above-mentioned request, I think it may well be in Theodoros's handwriting. It may have been written by him and signed by his nephews, and then he may have taken the necessary steps at the bishopric.

My father also had another powerful reason to move away from the Protestant religion: my mother. He was very taken with her, they were beginning to discuss engagement, and it was unthinkable, inconceivable, for her ever to consider marrying a Protestant.

In her family, religion played a completely different role than in my father's. There were no mystical crises, no great theological quarrels, no rifts. No conversions, de-conversions, re-conversions, or other see-sawing of this kind. And very few clergymen. Her family was simply, completely, irreversibly Maronite. They followed the pope without argument, venerated the saints, usually went to church one Sunday a month, but four times a week if a child was sick, traveling, or preparing for exams . . . Besides, religion was chiefly the domain of women, much like cooking, sewing, gossiping, and grieving. As for the men, they worked.

My maternal grandfather, whose name was Amin, was born in a village very close to ours. As an adolescent, he had emigrated to Egypt following in the footsteps of his eldest brother. They were both civil engineers and had obtained several important building projects— bridges, roads, the draining of marshlands. Though they never amassed an enormous fortune, they had been prosperous. At the height of his career, Amin owned cotton fields and buildings in the city; like Ge- brayel in Cuba, he employed a chauffeur, a gardener, a cook, and ser- vants. (And in the end, as in Cuba, nothing remained of this wealth. By the time I was born, my grandfather had died, and the nationalist revolution had "taken back" everything he had acquired, down to the very last acre. In my family's memory, Egypt became one more lost homeland.)

When he first moved to Egypt, Amin settled in Tanta, a city on the Nile Delta. This was where he met Virginie, daughter of a judge who had left Istanbul with his family during the unrest of 1909. The young man and the young girl belonged to the same Maronite community, but their social backgrounds were quite different. He was the son of mod- est peasants, whereas she was the daughter of city notables. But he had become rich, whereas her parents had lost most of their property and status on leaving the banks of the Bosporus. Otherwise they would probably have coveted a more prestigious alliance, in accordance with the social power struggles that govern such matters.

The marriage was held in Tanta, which is where my mother was born. On the birth certificate, dated December 1921, her name is listed as Odetta Maria, but everyone always called her Odette. Shortly after her birth her parents moved to Cairo or, more precisely, to the new city of Heliopolis, built by Baron Empain in the first years of the twentieth century.

Every year, when the heat in Egypt became unbearable, my mater- nal grandparents sailed to Beirut. There they picked up their two daughters, who used to spend the winter in the boarding school of the Besançon nuns, and they all went to the cool Mountains to escape the heat. Eventually they bought a wooded hillside in Ain-el-Qabou, where they had a summer residence built in beautiful white stone. It was very near my paternal grandparents' house-school.

One of the consequences of this proximity was that the religious oddities of my father's family had always been known to my mother's parents. Known and very much looked down on. They never thought that one day their daughter would marry one of *moallem* Botros's six orphans. Unfortunate children! That their father had been an atheist could more or less be accepted, but on top of this, their mother was a Protestant! The word "Protestant," when pronounced by the Maronite members of my family, was usually accompanied by a pout or a snigger.

In short, when my father fell in love with my mother and started writing endless tender letters to her, and she began showing that she wasn't indifferent to his courtship, he and his brothers hastened to dissipate the "misunderstanding" that had hung over them ever since their father had refused to baptize them, their paternal uncle had forced a baptism on them, and their maternal uncle had taken the initiative of registering them as Protestant.

Even if these events occurred before I was born, they had an impact throughout my childhood and beyond. Though the Catholics won a sweeping victory, squabbling continued nevertheless. My mother constantly denounced the Protestant religion, perhaps out of fear that one of her children might be tempted by the demon of "the heresy." But it is true that she also used to criticize the American uncle's errors just as harshly—there too, fearing that one of us might one day be tempted to follow a similar path. She never tired of repeating a wise maxim to us, which she attributed to my father and which became a prime rule in our household: "The absence of religion is a tragedy for families, the excess of religion too!" Today I am prone to think that this holds true for all human societies.

• • •

Though in view of his marriage—which was celebrated in Cairo in 1945—my father anticipated the wishes of my mother and her family and returned, unhesitatingly, to the Catholic fold, it wasn't easy for him to give in to the other unconditional demand: the couple's children were to study in Catholic schools, with French as their principal language.

For my grandmother Nazeera and my father's side of the family, this was an aberration, incongruous, and practically a betrayal. For four generations, ever since the mid-nineteenth century, everyone in our family learned English as a second mother tongue, and everyone received an American education. The campus of the American University was an extension of our house—and vice versa. My father had studied there and later taught there; his brothers and sisters too, one after the other. This was an established, immutable, undisputed tradition.

But that was precisely the problem; my mother was wary of that tradition, where the English language, the American school, and the Protestant religion always went hand in hand. This was a "risk" she didn't want to take, and my father had to resign himself to it: their three daughters would attend the school of the Besançon nuns, like their mother, and their son would attend the school of the Jesuit Fathers, like his maternal uncles.

I can safely assume that Botros wouldn't have been too pleased about this.

SEVENTY

I was sixteen years old when my father's older brother finally got in touch with his relatives again. You can imagine the stir this event caused; it became the family's main subject of conversation. A letter arrived from America, written to my grandmother. Her son said that he was ready to welcome her if she wished to visit him, his precondition being that she first convert to Catholicism. The preacher's daughter didn't hesitate for a second. Like King Henri IV of France, who famously said that Paris was well worth a mass, she thought seeing her son was worth a mass. She discreetly became Catholic and, at age seventy, boarded a plane for the first time in her life.

I didn't find the letter written to my grandmother. It is strange that she didn't keep it. Perhaps she put it away separately somewhere and afterward it got lost. Fortunately, my uncle wrote a another letter at the same time, to his younger brother, my father, and that one I have. It is a long letter in English dated "March 27, 1965, Feast of St John of Damascus."

I remember that when you and I were little children always seen together, and also as we grew up to be bigger and bigger boys, strangers would almost take us for twins, except for the fact that you always looked a bit larger and more mature. I do not need to tell you with what overwhelming emotions I take the pen to write to the companion of all my childhood and my youth, and one who is indeed the other half of my soul. I will make only one remark, never to return to its subject any longer. I may have given you the impression of being heartless at times, and also of not appreciating the heroism of Mamma, and the way she carried the burden of the family after the untimely death of our father some forty-one years ago. How can I ever forget the time when I discovered her at three o'clock after midnight, in tears because of her worries and big responsibilities, still working with her dear hands at etamine, in spite of all the duties awaiting her on the following day, hoping to make a few pennies to meet the needs of the family. I came out of my bed and kissed her and said to her, "Don't worry, Mamma, very soon we will grow older, and we will take very good care of you," and then, noticing that her mantilla was worn, I added, "And I will buy you a new mandeel." *Well, I have never bought Mamma that* mandeel, *for I was destined, in God's inscrutable designs, to leave it to you and my other brothers and sisters to repay my mother in her old age for all the care she took of us, and with all the consolations she well deserves. I was sent far away from the family I so much loved, and for whose welfare, and the welfare of each of whose members, I have been always deeply concerned. I was destined by God's guidance to become ultimately a religious man, having consecrated my life to God through the vows of poverty, chastity, and obedience. It would seem that God has intended me to be concerned rather with the spiritual and supernatural good of our family. When I was with you, for years I had no faith whatsoever. Heaven and hell were not realities to me, and Our Lord and Our Lady meant very little. I have reasons to believe that you never entirely lost the Catholic faith, but you should have had more supernatural concern for me and the others. To borrow a phrase from a certain writer, with regard to some of the things*

I have done in my role as a kind of spiritual watchman, I say, for those who have the faith, no explanation is needed; for those who don't, no explanation is possible . . .

I don't think my father ever completely forgave his brother. On the other hand, he didn't heap reproaches on him either. Their relationship simply cooled. Though they had been unusually close, they no longer had much to say to each other. They remained courteous with each other up to the end, but their close bond had withered, it seems to me. I assume that my father answered his brother's letter, but I have no idea whether he did so with a detailed or a terse reply. What I do know is that he didn't go see him as a result of this correspondence.

Whereas I did.

This was years later, in 1978. I was living in France and working as a journalist, and I was assigned a story on the World Bank in Washington, D.C. It was my first transatlantic trip, and it was unthinkable for me not to meet the mythical uncle before returning home.

So I made a detour to Massachusetts. It was a weird sensation: I found myself face-to-face with a stranger who looked almost like my father's twin, but wore a cassock and spoke Arabic with a thick American accent. A stranger from whom many things separated me, but with whom, thanks to the miracle of family ties, an intimate conversation developed immediately.

"Your father and I were inseparable, identical-looking, yet something essential always separated us. I'm fundamentally conservative, whereas your father has always been a revolutionary."

I would have spontaneously said the opposite. My uncle was a militant, capable of sacrificing his entire life to a doctrine, whereas my father, for as long as I had known him, led a quiet existence between his home and his newspaper.

I must have looked surprised, because my uncle resumed, excitedly, "Yes, yes, believe me. That's what's always separated us. In fact, let me show you something . . ."

He took me to his room, a real monastic cell, sparsely furnished with a camp bed, a table, a chair, a few books, and nothing more.

"I was fifteen and your father fourteen when our mother said, 'I heard the call of the traveling peddler. You should both run out and buy yourselves what you need to shave.' Indeed, the down on our cheeks was beginning to look like beards; this was particularly true of your father, who was dark-haired and had always been more precocious physically. So we went, and each of us bought a brass razor. I assume that since then, your father has tried out countless different types of razors, both electric and not electric. Whereas me, I still use the same razor every morning, the razor I bought from the peddler. Look!"

He proudly brandished the yellowish razor, which didn't seem very battered after half a century of use. I was amused by his definition of conservative and revolutionary. It was true that the bathroom cabinet in my parents' house was filled with all sorts of forlorn devices, including a battery-operated razor my father had bought in China, which he probably hadn't used even once.

My uncle's disquisition continued, focused and subtly defensive.

"I wanted to maintain the noblest and oldest family tradition: sainthood. Did you know that among our ancestors there are several saints who are venerated by the Church?"

He mentioned some names that I had never heard before. In my father's house, we often praised the accomplishments of ancestors, but the ones cited were chiefly famous poets or, in a completely different vein, émigrés who had become wealthy.

"Don't ever forget that it was on our shoulders that Christianity has rested ever since the first centuries . . ."

It is odd, this propensity of my relatives to always want to locate their personal itinerary as descending from a straight line within our family. Even he, who had been gone for so long, had broken off all relations with his relatives, had done everything his father would have hated him to do, had scrapped his name to adopt a Church name, and had taken such an out-of-the-way path, even he still felt the need to explain to me that he had strayed from the common route only to better rejoin the one traced by our ancestors.

"It is that tradition that I want to pursue! The West thinks they evangelized us, whereas we actually evangelized them. Nowadays they have strayed from the real Faith, and it is our duty to bring them back to the straight and narrow. I have assigned myself the task of re-Christianizing America."

As soon as I returned to my hotel, in Boston, I tried to phone my father, but had no luck. I had to wait until I was back in Paris to talk to him, when he succeeded in reaching me. The war in Lebanon was in a critical phase, and my parents had had to flee Beirut because their neighborhood had been heavily bombed. They were in the village, in their house, temporarily in a safe haven. A clever cousin had secured them a telephone connection with France.

"I've just returned from America," I told my father eagerly. "I was able to meet my uncle."

My impressions?

"The dust hasn't settled yet . . . In any case I'm not sorry I went to see him, after all these years . . . He resembles you and doesn't resemble you . . ."

"Everyone was deceived by our physical resemblance—even us. It took time for us to realize how different we were."

"He told me the story of the razors . . ."

"What razors?"

We were cut off.

SEVENTY-ONE

When I left New England, I was certain that this would be my first and only meeting with my uncle. I couldn't predict that the day would come when it would seem to me like a mere prelude to another fateful meeting in Lebanon two years later.

At the time, I didn't know why my émigré uncle had suddenly decided to visit his native country after a whole life spent abroad. Today, from the information I gathered, I know why. My uncle was in the holy orders, he wore a cassock and had himself called "brother"—like Botros, I am tempted to say, even though it was definitely not the same "brotherhood." But he had never succeeded in being ordained, which was his dearest wish. In the United States, the Catholic hierarchy had always chosen to keep him at a distance. After much equivocation, he had been told that even if they wanted to, they couldn't possibly ordain a married man. So he thought that in his native land, in his original community, where traditions were different, he might be able to have his wish granted.

And it almost was, I was told. The Greek Catholic patriarch, pressed by my father, my uncles, and especially my cousin Nasri, had said yes, why not? But before setting the date for ordination, the patriarch realized that the future priest intended to exercise his priesthood in Massachusetts, not in Lebanon; proper procedure required requesting the consent of the archbishop of Boston. The latter made a terrible fuss, said it was like "setting the fox to mind the geese," and our patriarch felt it would be wiser to retract his offer.

It was while these negotiations were taking place that my father had his stroke, on a day of scorching heat. He had just left his office and was walking to his car when he fell. The person who was with him had heard him exclaim only a surprised "ah!" before he collapsed, unconscious. A few hours later my telephone rang in Paris. A cousin told me the news, leaving very little room for hope. "He's in a bad state, a very bad state."

I returned to my native country by the first plane and found my father in a coma. He seemed to be sleeping peacefully; he was breathing and sometimes moved a hand. It was hard to believe he was no longer alive. I begged the physicians to test his brain once again, and then a third time. It was pointless. The encephalogram was flat; he had suffered a massive hemorrhage. We had to resign ourselves.

His hospital stay lasted about ten days, and during that period there were still a few glimmers of hope—a hand that turned over, some people who came and told us they knew of patients who had came out of similar comas . . . I also remember some sinister oddballs, of the kind, I imagine, who haunt all the places of distress on the planet, wherever the minds of mortals are made vulnerable by the pressure of misfortune. A person who called himself, with a straight face, "Saint Elijah's henchman" came and fastened strips of cloth all around my father's bed and then aggressively yelled at the desolate family, "How do you expect him to recover, when none of you are praying?" In other circumstances, I might have found the scene comical; on that day, my grief was mingled only with anger and disgust.

During the long days and evenings of waiting in a state of despondency, I often found myself conversing with the prodigal uncle, as though it were natural for us to be together, side by side, in the city of

Beirut, where neither he nor I had planned to come that year. Yet I had the feeling that we had never parted and that his forty-year absence was nothing but a senseless dream that had finally been dispelled when I woke up.

It was a strange reversal: the émigré, the absent one, whom I had become accustomed to consider as virtually dead, was near me, his shoulder against mine, suddenly close, suddenly like a second father. While my other father, my real father, lay there, absent, and had emigrated far away from us forever . . .

Then came the moment that we couldn't delay, the moment when my father's heart stopped. I had gone home to rest after too many sleepless nights, when a cousin came knocking at the door. I let him in and went back to the drawing room to sit down; I didn't question him. I understood. My uncle also came by several minutes later and sat down with us. He didn't say anything either.

It was August 17, 1980. Fifty-six years, to the day, after Botros's death—and it was a Sunday as well. Then the man in the cassock and I had to confer about how to break the news to Nazeera, his mother, in the least devastating way. We agreed that I would be the one to go there and be with her, and then he would phone her.

When I arrived at her house, my grandmother clasped me in her arms for a long time, as she always did. Then, inevitably, she asked the question I dreaded most: "How is your father doing this morning?"

I had prepared an answer, coaching myself on my way over.

"I've come directly from the house. I didn't stop by the hospital . . ."

This was both the absolute truth and the most horrid lie.

A few minutes later the telephone rang. Normally I would have hurried to answer it so my grandmother would be spared the effort of getting up. On that day, I just asked if she wanted me to answer for her.

"If you could just bring the phone closer to me . . ."

I moved it closer, picked up the receiver, and handed it to her.

I couldn't hear what was being said on the other end, but I'll never forget my grandmother's response.

"Yes, I'm sitting down."

My uncle was afraid that she might be standing and might fall to the ground after hearing what he was going to tell her.

I also remember the look in her eyes as she said, "Yes, I'm sitting down." It was the look of someone condemned to death who has just seen the gallows looming in the distance. Later, when I thought about it, I realized it was probably she who had advised her children to make sure a person is sitting down before announcing devastating news. As soon as her son asked the question, she knew to expect the worst.

We cried, she and I, sitting side by side, holding hands, for a long time.

Then she said to me, "I still expected to hear that your father had regained consciousness."

"No. From the minute he collapsed, it was over."

"I still had hope," my grandmother whispered. No one had dared tell her the truth till now.

We soon lapsed into silence again, our sanctuary . . .

Written in Paris, Beirut, Havana, and Ker Mercier,
between September 2000 and December 2003

Notes and Acknowledgments

I've brought this book to a close, but I haven't completed my work on origins yet. Neither upriver—since, aside from a few lapses, I limited myself to the last one hundred and fifty years—nor downriver, since I stopped relating things in detail after the mid-1930s and brought things in an elliptical manner only to the time of my father's death.

Yet about him I have said next to nothing. I must have mentioned his first name once, told two or three stories, and recounted some snatches of our conversations. But my attachment to the memory of my relatives arose chiefly from my attachment to him. I have revered him so highly since childhood that I never considered going into any other profession but his—journalism and writing. Patiently and subtly, he initiated and shaped me, refined my rough edges, and guided me, even in my rebellions. I observed him constantly as he steered his way between passion and responsibility, naïveté and intelligence, modesty and dignity. I listened to him tirelessly. The stories he told me in my youth came back to haunt me in my mature years.

Shall I take the time one day to talk about him at greater length, and about his brothers and sisters, that generation, both serene and tormented, that was faced with the worst of wars and the most irreversible scattering? This is one of the tasks incumbent upon me if I don't want to fail in my duties of faithfulness. All the more so as I was a witness to part of these events and I presently have extensive archives at my disposal for this period, too. But at the present time, as I conclude this work, I find it hard to plan another immersion into the waters of our intimate tragedies. All this is still too recent for me. I shall wait.

I feel indebted to other ancestors as well. I shall probably never devote the same amount of attention to all those who, in a way, gave birth to me. But I cannot resign myself to letting these figures, whose life trajectories partially determined my own, remain simple strangers to me. So I still have a few more "excavations" to embark on, in Cairo, New York, Beirut, and of course Constantinople, which I've always recognized, practically by instinct, as the metropolis of our origins.

When I began my research, I resorted to a great many genealogical trees drawn by family members. I even sketched a few myself, going back twelve generations, in order to work out, for example, what the family tie was between me and the murderer of the patriarch in my novel *The Rock of Tanios*, or between me and some distant "cousins" living in Sydney, São Paulo, Córdoba, or, long ago, in Smyrna. But this exercise soon proved pointless; instead of shedding light on my pathway, it made the foliage thicker and the road darker. In dealing with an extended family that includes tens of thousands of recorded members, such trees lead nowhere. The same first names keep recurring, the faces are missing, and the dates are uncertain.

To avoid getting confused, I selected a completely different graphic representation: in the center, the descendant, surrounded by his parents; at the four points of the compass, his four grandparents; beyond

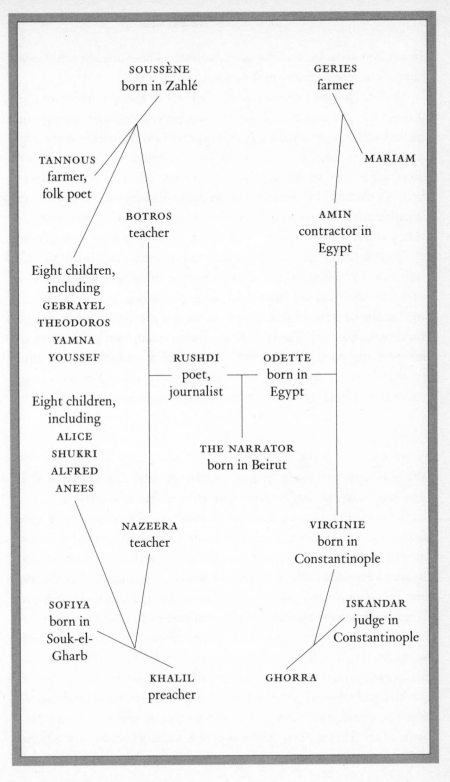

them, their parents. Instead of a tree or pyramid, my picture looks more like an encampment or road map.

I realize this is a rather egocentric vision, but it has the advantage of including all the tributaries of my origins and hence the diversity of my affiliations. Furthermore, it reverses the flow of time, which I find stimulating and helpful. We are no longer dealing with an ancestor "producing" an infinite number of descendants, but with one descendant "producing" an infinite number of ancestors: two parents, four grandparents, eight great-grandparents, then sixteen, then thirty-two . . . I calculated that thirty generations back—in other words, at the time of the Crusades—the number of ancestors reaches a billion, thereby vastly exceeding the total population of the planet. But this is a purely theoretical observation, especially among my relatives, for prior to the beginning of the twentieth century, cousins almost always intermarried. If I were to sketch the roads leading back to my distant ancestors, they would intertwine ad infinitum and end up looking like braids.

In order to reconstruct these pages in my family history, I kept several reference books at hand constantly, aside from the documents in the archives. I shall mention four that are specifically about our family.

First the book of my paternal aunt, who was my adviser and inspiration. I have already had occasion to mention how irreplaceable her contribution was; here I would just like to list the bibliographical reference for her book of reminiscences: *Memoirs of Grandma Kamal: Unique Personal Experiences and Encounters*, by Kamal Maalouf Abou-Chaar, published by World Book Publishing, Beirut, 1999.

I would also like to mention the book that has been the bible of our family history for almost a century, the book I called *The Tree*, whose Arabic title is *Dawani-l-qoutouf fi tarikh banni-l-Maalouf*; it is the work of the historian Issa Iskandar Maalouf (Imprimerie ottomane, Baabda, 1907–08). I was generously given a copy by his grandson, Fawwaz Traboulsi. I also consulted another book on several occasions; it was published in 1993 and is intended as the continuation of the previous one: *The Maalouf Family Through History.* I was given a copy by its author, Timothy Maalouf, who died, alas, a short time thereafter. His grave, incidentally, is adjacent to that of Botros, my grandfather.

Many other books kept me company during these last few years, for information or to refresh my memory: on the brigand princes, the Ottoman revolution, the Freemasons, the Levantine diaspora, or the French mandate in Lebanon. It would be tedious to list them all, but I wouldn't forgive myself if I failed to mention the one work that mentions my great-uncle Gebrayel by name, his Havana stores La Verdad, and his position among his émigré compatriots. Written by the Orientalist Rigoberto Menéndez Paredes, the book is titled *Componentes árabes en la cultura cubana* (Ediciones Boloña, Publicaciones de la Oficina del Historiador de la Ciudad, Havana, 1999).

What I have said about books is true of people as well. I asked so many questions everywhere that it would be tedious to compile a complete list of all the people who took the time to give me answers.

But I am eager to extend a few deserved words of thanks. To begin with, to those who didn't belong to our large family yet contributed to my research, through their knowledge or out of a simple desire to help. Let me mention, in alphabetical order: Mona Akl, Ahmad Beydoun, Norman Cook, Angélica and Ariel Dorfman, Jean-Claude Freydier, Peter Goldmark, Ali Hamadeh, Liliane and Roger-Xavier Lantéri, Jean Lévy, Jean Massaad, Georges Moussalli, Abdallah Naaman, Mario Rubén Sanguina, Mona and Baccar Touzani, Chadia and Ghassan Tuéni, Élie Wardini, Ruth Zauner. Nor would I like to forget Luis Domingo, Matteo, Dolores, Olguita, and María de los Angeles, who couldn't appear under their real names.

As regards my own family, the list of persons to whom I am grateful is virtually unlimited. Among the Maaloufs: Agnès, Akram, Albert, Alex, América, Ana Maria, Carl, Fahd, Fakhri, Fawzi, Héctor, Hilmi, Hind, Ibrahim, Imad, Issam, Khattar, Laurice, Leila, Leonard, Mariam, Mary, May, Mona, Nasri, Nassim, Nazmi, Odette, Peter, Ray Junior,

Roula, Rosette, Sana, Siham, Taufic, and Walid; as well as my long-standing accomplices Andrée, Ruchdi, Tarek, and Ziad. I also wish to extend a very special thank-you to Elias Eid Maalouf, without whom an essential facet of my family's history would have remained obscure.

Among the members of my family who have different last names, I would like to mention, again in alphabetical order: Sana and Iskandar Abou-Chaar; Adel, Fayzeh, and Monique Antippa; Samia Bacha; Edward Baddouh; Leila and Nicolas Bogucki; Hayat and Georges Chédid; Lonna Cosby; Marie David; Elisabeth and Angel Fernández; Antoine, Joseph, Leila, Lucy, Mirène, Nemétallah, and Sonia Ghossein; Youmna and Issa Goraieb; Nelli Hodgson Brown; Mary Kurban; Charles Nammour; Shermine Nolander; Marie and Madeleine Noujaim; Thérèse Tannous; Oumayma and Ramzi Zein; as well as Leila, Joseph, Amer, and Wadih Zoghbi. I would not like to forget Nada, Ramón, and Maeva Labbé, who were irreplaceable travel companions in Cuba. Nor should I forget Léonore, who passed away, as well as seven other people mentioned above, during the forty months it took me to write the present book.